READY, FIRE, AIM!

AN IMMIGRANT'S TALES OF ENTREPRENEURIAL TERROR

CHARLES OTA HELLER

Virginia

Praise for *Ready, Fire, Aim*
and Charles Ota Heller

"Charles Heller's incredible journey provides the basis for one of the most revealing and courageous examinations into the real 'terror' that entrepreneurs face. More importantly, this book can be an inspiration for all entrepreneurs to face their fears and overcome the odds!"

Donald F. Kuratko
Professor of Entrepreneurship, Indiana University
Author of Entrepreneurship: Theory, Process, and Practice

"Charles Heller reels the reader into 'being there' as effectively as any writer I know. He is a man of recognized success as a leader in academics, entrepreneurship, and business. And, his book provides personal experiences and insight useful to a large cross-section of professionals."

J. Phillip Samper
Former Vice Chair of Eastman Kodak,
President of Sun Microsystems Computer, CEO of Cray Research,
Managing Director of Gabriel Venture Partners

"With his gripping and inspirational life story providing the framework, Charles Heller shares a wealth of real-world lessons as a leading entrepreneur, venture capitalist, and mentor. Coming to the United States as a youth, Charlie achieved the American Dream despite obstacles and terrors he never expected in his home country. Ready, Fire, Aim! hits the mark!"

V. Burns Hargis
President of Oklahoma State University

"Ready, Fire, Aim! is an entrepreneurial adventure story. It's the story of a Holocaust survivor and escapee from Communism to whom America gave freedom and the opportunity to go as far as hard work and persistence would take him. His career has consisted not only of starting and building companies, but also of mentoring hundreds of other entrepreneurs and investing in a number of new ventures. What makes his story unusual are

extraordinary experiences not encountered by others and obstacles Charles Ota Heller had to overcome along the way. The book will serve as both inspiration and a roadmap for other entrepreneurs."

Michael D. Dingman
President and CEO, Shipston Group
Former CEO of Wheelabrator-Frye, Signal, Henley Group,
and Fisher Scientific

"A successful and dedicated entrepreneur, teacher, mentor, and gifted writer, Charles Ota Heller provides us with a pragmatic down-in-the-trenches look at what it takes to launch and grow a start-up. He played a major leadership role in building the Michael D. Dingman Center for Entrepreneurship at the University of Maryland, recognized as one of the top such centers in the country. Filled with lessons learned, the book is a must read for aspiring and practicing entrepreneurs everywhere."

Rudolph P. Lamone
Former Dean, Robert H. Smith School of Business,
University of Maryland
Professor Emeritus and Founder,
Dingman Center for Entrepreneurship

"In Ready, Fire, Aim! Charles Heller tells a remarkable, bare-knuckle story about what it takes to be an entrepreneur when the wind is not at your back. Heller's hard-won lessons will help budding entrepreneurs navigate this new world of ours — one in which change will come at a blinding pace, faster than anything we've ever known."

Mario Morino
Chairman, Morino Ventures

"I heartily recommend Ready, Fire, Aim! *to my entrepreneurship students! Charles Heller offers sage and fascinating advice about how to create, fund, and grow high-potential technology businesses."*

J. Robert Baum
Retired Chairman and CEO, Highmark Health Inc.
Professor Emeritus, Robert H. Smith School of Business,
University of Maryland

Ready, Fire, Aim! An Immigrant's Tales of Entrepreneurial Terror
© 2017 by Charles Ota Heller. All rights reserved.

This story is told from the author's experience and perspective. Some names and identifying details have been changed to protect the privacy of individuals.

Published in the United States by WriteLife Publishing
(An imprint of Boutique of Quality Books Publishing Company)
www.writelife.com

978-1-60808-181-3 (p)
978-1-60808-182-0 (e)

Library of Congress Control Number: 2017936738

Book design by Robin Krauss, www.bookformatters.com
Cover design by Marla Thompson, www.edgeofwater.com

First editor: Olivia Swenson
Second editor: Pearlie Tan

Other Books by Charles Ota Heller

Prague: My Long Journey Home (2011)

Name-droppings: Close Encounters with the Famous and Near-Famous (2013)

Table of Contents

To my loving family:
My wife Sue,
My son, David, and
My grandchildren—Sam, Sarah, and Caroline.

CHAPTER ONE

It Can Happen Here

The Gestapo came for me—again. For a fleeting moment, my mind played a trick on me when I heard heavy footsteps on the stairs. Then the door flew open.

"We're here to see the president!" one of them barked at the receptionist of our fledgling company, CADCOM.

It was precisely eleven o'clock on a cold, overcast day in early December 1969. Two men walked into my office and flashed their FBI identification cards at me. I motioned for them to sit on the guest chairs in front of my desk. Their severe expressions told me this was not a friendly visit.

"Do you wish to have your lawyer present?" asked the one named Cobb.

"No. Why would I want a lawyer? I've done nothing wrong."

"That's entirely your choice," Cobb replied as he opened a notebook and extracted a pen from his pocket.

"What is your full name?" he asked. Since I had heard his partner address him as Ty, and since the famous Ty Cobb had been a Hall of Fame baseball player, I was tempted to reply, "Babe Ruth." But I thought better of it, perhaps because the real Ty Cobb had been a son of a bitch and his G-man namesake appeared to be cut from the same cloth.

Following preliminary questions about my background, the men seemed particularly interested in the six years I had spent as a faculty member at the US Naval Academy, located just a few blocks from CADCOM's offices. Of particular significance appeared to be my application of computers to my research and teaching. After an hour or so devoted to this subject, they focused on our company— its mission, its intended customers and market, the computer-aided design software that would be our primary product, our financing, and the backgrounds of my six co-founders. Throughout the two-hour interrogation, I searched for clues as to the purpose of the questioning. Finally, when the session seemed to be coming to a close, I could no longer contain myself.

"Gentlemen, can you tell me why you're here?"

"You'll find out in due time," said Cobb. He stood up, his sidekick followed suit, and they walked out without another word.

Those bastards! I thought as I attempted to make sense of what had just taken place. *How can they just walk in here like that, try to intimidate me, and leave without an explanation? Isn't this America?!*

After composing myself, I consulted with my partners and discovered that all of them had just been accosted in much the same manner, and all at eleven o'clock. No doubt this was done so that we could not communicate with one another. While I was being questioned by Cobb and his sidekick, three other agents had entered our CADCOM offices and separately interrogated my colleagues— Fred Klappenberger, Jack Cusack, and Ed Grant. John Gebhardt, who was staying on at the Naval Academy for a year before joining us full-time, had been grabbed while crossing the street between classes. Two Academy professors, Al Adams and Dave Rogers, who were involved with us only on a part-time basis, were ambushed in their USNA offices.

As I digested this information, I began to realize that we must be in trouble, although I still failed to understand why. Better late than never, I contacted our attorney, John Ebersberger, who called the local FBI office. Not only was he unable to get any information, but the office even refused to acknowledge that the visits had taken place.

We had been waiting for the issuance of our first revenue-generating projects: two government contracts, one from the Office of Naval Research and another from the US Maritime Administration.

They were vital to our ability to get our company off the ground and to bring in desperately needed cash. In the days that followed, whenever we checked on their status, we were informed by both agencies that "someone higher up" had ordered them to hold issuance of the contracts. We were in limbo. We were being treated as if guilty of something, but we had no idea what, thereby having no way to defend or exonerate ourselves.

After a sad holiday season and several weeks of misery during which we ran out of money, our lawyer finally managed to get a piece of information. An unnamed Naval Academy faculty member had accused us of defrauding the federal government. Besides being told that the maximum penalty for this offense was a $250,000 fine and twenty-five years in jail for each principal of the company, we knew nothing more. By now, we had stopped functioning as a corporation and had become a group of guys who spent every day commiserating about their situation.

One morning in early January as I was leaving for work, Ann Cusack, the wife of Jack, our senior vice president, called my wife Sue. She said she was afraid that Jack was so depressed and frightened that he might commit suicide. I spoke with Jack and calmed him down, although my own anxiety was at its peak. I was not suicidal, but I felt paralyzed. Every day in the office proved to be an impossible chore. With the threat of prison terms and a potential shutdown of our six-month-old company hanging over our heads, it was impossible to carry on. How in the world had we defrauded the government? We were just a bunch of techies, trying to get a company off the ground. We did not even know what charges were being made against us!

In mid-January 1970, the FBI provided our attorney with a few more bits of information. Finally, we were able to piece together the problem. John Gebhardt was teaching a naval architecture course at the Naval Academy. At CADCOM, he had developed a ship design computer program, named CADSHIP, that we were attempting to sell to shipbuilders and naval architects. At the start of the fall semester, John had asked me if he could use the program in his USNA naval architecture course to teach midshipmen how to use computers in the design of ships. That seemed like a nice thing to do for the institution at which I had taught for the past six years, so I told him that I had no problem with it.

In the 1970s, complex programs ran only on very large, extremely expensive, mainframe computers. Customers who could not afford their own, "time-shared." They purchased time on vendors' machines and accessed them via telephone lines using teletype terminals. CADSHIP was running on a large mainframe based in Princeton, owned by a time-sharing company from whom both CADCOM and the Naval Academy were buying time. John simply copied our program onto the USNA account and then he and his students could access it from the classroom. The first lines of code identified the program as one belonging to "CADCOM, Inc., Annapolis, Maryland." No problem, one would think. But strange things happen when dishonest people weave their devious schemes.

Many months later, Al Adams, a CADCOM co-founder and Naval Academy professor, would discover that a fellow faculty member had been under suspicion for some unscrupulous acts; he sought to deflect attention from himself by telling the bureau that we had stolen government-owned software and used it as a backbone of our business offerings. As proof, he pointed to the fact that the first line of a program stored on USNA's slice of the computer's memory contained CADCOM's name. Furthermore, he claimed that we had used terminals owned by the US government to develop software for our business purposes, on a Navy account and on Navy property and time. No wonder we were being investigated!

Once we knew what the charges were, it was easy to submit a report that explained what had actually taken place. This proved insufficient to satisfy the bureau's "guilty until proven innocent" philosophy. We expected to be exonerated quickly, but instead continued to wait as our customers still held back on signing our contracts. Dead broke, we were close to liquidating the company.

As a last-gasp measure, I drove to Washington in early March in an attempt to convince the Office of Naval Research to sign our contract and release our advance payment. Our customer, Ben Friedman, was sympathetic but powerless until he was given the go-ahead from "higher up."

I pounded the steering wheel in anger as I drove through a snowstorm up Independence Avenue on my way back to Annapolis. Washington-area drivers are notorious for their inability to drive in snow, and the traffic mess only added to my frustration. Suddenly, a faint outline of the Capitol dome appeared on my left through the curtain of snow. My fury peaked as I stared at this symbol of freedom.

I didn't survive the Nazis and escape from the Communists so that I would be subjected to arbitrary punishment by faceless bureaucrats in America! What kind of shit is that?

I was out of control when I stopped for a red light near the Rayburn House Office Building. Then I regained my composure as an idea came to me.

I'll go to see my congressman. What do I have to lose at this point?

A few minutes later, I walked into the office of Congressman Rogers C.B. Morton, who represented our first congressional district of Maryland. I was ushered into the office of the congressman's administrative aide, William Mills. Bill listened to my story and, when I vented my frustration at being treated in a way that reminded me of the Gestapo, he inquired about my family's history. I gave him a condensed version and he listened patiently. The passive expression he wore that was reserved for constituent requests disappeared when I told him about my father's service with the Allies during the war.

"Your father fought with Patton?" His face lit up. "So did I! That makes your dad and me brothers. Don't worry. We'll help you."

I sat there, my mouth open, as he stormed out the door. He returned a few minutes later and instructed me to follow him. We walked into the office of Congressman Morton, head of the Republican National Committee. After a brief introduction, Mills asked me to tell Morton about my company's problem. The congressman listened attentively and asked a few questions. Finally, he buzzed his secretary.

"Get me the head Navy JAG guy," he ordered. In less than two minutes, the judge advocate general was on the phone. Congressman Morton told him my story.

"I have the CEO of the company in my office right now," he said at the end of the brief conversation. "I'm going to tell him that this thing will be resolved no later than tomorrow. Thank you." He hung up, looked at me, and smiled.

"Go home and get a good night's sleep," he said. "I'll be in touch tomorrow."

I was so happy as I walked out of the building that I had to fight the urge to lie down on the white sidewalk and make snow angels. Yet, as I drove home, skepticism began to creep into my mind. This situation had been going on for so long, and we had been treated so shabbily by our government—could I really believe that it would be solved with one phone call?

The following morning, I walked into my office and found a pink phone message slip from my secretary in the middle of my desk. It read, "Bill Mills called and said you can pick up your Navy contract this afternoon."

I drove back to DC, signed the contract to design a modular submarine, and CADCOM was on its way. Although a staunch Democrat, I voted for Rog Morton when he ran again for Congress, after which he was named secretary of the interior by President Nixon and secretary of commerce by President Ford. When Bill Mills, also a Republican, ran for Rog's congressional seat, I voted for him as well.

The intervention of a Washington powerbroker notwithstanding, the FBI refused to exonerate us. Despite the pleadings of our attorney, the bureau would not issue a letter stating that we had been innocent of any wrongdoing. The case was simply dropped. To them, it seemed that harassing innocent American citizens was just business as usual.

To me, it was much more than that. During the twenty years I had lived in America, I had given little thought to the fear and powerlessness I had experienced as a child hiding from the Gestapo who wished to ship me off to a death camp and escaping

Czechoslovakia's Communist police state. Shortly after setting foot on American soil, my father instructed me to forget everything that had happened to me on the other side of the Atlantic. But now, the FBI episode brought back long-suppressed memories.

CHAPTER TWO

Hidden Child

I was born Ota Karel Heller on January 25, 1936, in Prague, Czechoslovakia, three years before our nation was occupied by German troops. My entrepreneurial genes were bequeathed to me by Gustav Neumann, my maternal great-grandfather, whom I called *Dědeček* (Czech for grandpa). Unbeknownst to me, I also inherited from him the legacy of Abraham, Isaac, and Jacob. Dědeček and his two sons were Jews. One of his sons, Artur, became my grandfather when he had a child with a Christian woman whom he did not marry. That child, my mother Ilona, became a devout Roman Catholic. She married a handsome young man who came to work in Dědeček's clothing factory after graduating from business school. This man, my father, Rudolph Heller, was Jewish too. I was baptized at the Church of St. Vitus across the road from our family's home in the small town of Kojetice, a few kilometers north of Prague.

The four Jewish men in our household—my great-grandfather, grandfather, great uncle, and father—were secular Czech patriots; they never attended synagogue, nor did they speak Hebrew or Yiddish. As a church-going Catholic boy, I had no idea what a Jew was, much less that I was three-quarters Jewish. Our entire family celebrated Christmas, Easter, and All Saints Day, just like all my friends in Kojetice. Except for the fact that we were wealthier, I was unaware that we were different from our neighbors.

Soon after the Nazis came, my relatives—those in our household as well as my paternal grandmother, uncles, aunts, and cousins who lived in nearby towns—began to disappear. In 1940, my father escaped from Czechoslovakia in order to join the British army and fight against the Germans. Eventually, our family was reduced to three—Dědeček, Mother, and me. We were expelled from our home, and the Germans took over our family's clothing factory. Farmer neighbors took us in. Mother, who had been surrounded by servants all her life and had attended the finest schools, became a farmhand, spending six days a week in the fields, while Dědeček and I helped with chores. When it came time for me to enter school, Mother informed me tearfully that it would be impossible "because your father is fighting against the Germans."

This lie became the party line each time I wondered why we were being deprived of decent food, why we could not go to movies or soccer games, and why I had to stay within the confines of the farm and could not play with other children. The fact that Papa was shooting Germans became a point of pride to which I clung through pain and loneliness.

Eighty-two-year-old Dědeček, with whom I spent most of my time, became my best friend. He entertained me with stories of his world travels and prophesied that I would someday be a famous explorer who would eventually settle down in order to build a great enterprise. I absorbed his every word and managed to convince myself that someday the Germans would be driven out and life would be good again.

The most devastating moment of my young life came when Dědeček was taken from us. Wearing a gray, three-piece suit with a strange yellow star sewn on his lapel, my great grandfather stood in the kitchen one morning with an old suitcase at his side. When I asked where he was going, he told me that he would be away for only a short time. I failed to understand why Mother and our friends wept when we bade him goodbye at the train station. At the end of the war, we discovered that he had been transported to the Terezín concentration camp. After several months in the only such camp in the Czech lands, he was taken on another transport, this time to the Treblinka death camp in Poland, where he was murdered immediately upon arrival.

Two years after Dědeček's departure, Mother received orders to report to a slave labor camp for Christian wives of Jewish men. I was perplexed by her near hysteria as she boarded a train at the Kojetice station.

"I am leaving you my most prized possession," she cried out to our farmer friends, Vladimír and Marie Tůma. "Please take care of him and hide him."

I only discovered why I needed to be hidden many years later. One of the Nazis' many definitions of a Jew was anyone with three Jewish grandparents. Thus, this devout little Catholic boy was a Jew—and the Germans wanted to deport me to a death camp. Although this was kept from me, I was keenly aware that something bad would happen if the Nazis found me. I was frightened each time Mrs. Tůma hid me in a closet when the Gestapo or their Czech collaborators came looking for me.

In the meantime, Papa had made his way south to Yugoslavia, where he was arrested as a British spy. He escaped from prison with the help of a Serbian partisan, and the Resistance transported him clandestinely to Palestine, where he became one of the first volunteers in the new Czechoslovak division of the British army.

He fought against the Germans and Italians in the desert of North Africa. Eventually, his unit ended up in England in time for the D-Day invasion of continental Europe. He fought in the Battle of the Bulge and, at its conclusion, was assigned to General George Patton's Third Army, which was preparing to liberate Czechoslovakia. Sadly, that would not be the case. General Eisenhower made a pact with a Soviet field marshal that it would be the Red Army that would swoop down from Berlin and free us of our oppressors. Patton's troops got no further than the westernmost Czech city, Plzeň (Pilsen).

By the first week of May 1945, the war was nearly over and the Germans were on the run. Discarding weapons, they headed west out of Czechoslovakia in order to be captured unarmed by civilized Americans or Brits rather than the brutal Red Army. I found a loaded pistol and, with two village boys egging me on as we hid in the bushes, I stood up, took aim, and fired on an escaping Nazi loading furniture onto a truck. He crumpled to the ground.

I took off running and hid behind a building, terrified that the Germans would find and kill me. No one came. After months of hiding like an animal, I felt liberated. I was nine years old, and I had helped my father defeat the Nazis!

Mother escaped from the labor camp after the German guards decided to drown their sorrow in booze. She came home just as Prague was being liberated by the Red Army on May 9, 1945. Two days later, Patton ordered a group of Czech soldiers to proceed to Prague. My father was in the group. Just as Mother and I had no idea whether or not he was alive, he knew nothing of our fate. Now, he was a mere ten miles away from us.

Upon reaching Prague, Papa borrowed a motorcycle from a Czech civilian. As he neared Kojetice, many of the people who were outside celebrating their newly found freedom recognized him, and the telephone wires began to buzz with the news that Rudy Heller had made it through the war and was now heading home, dressed in an American uniform!

When we heard that Papa was headed in our direction, Mother and I took off running to meet him. I heard the sound of the motorcycle seconds before Papa roared around a curve. He screeched to a halt, the bike flying away onto its side, and ran to meet us. I tackled him and held on to his leg as tightly as I could while he and Mother hugged and kissed. I was not about to let go—ever again. To this day, I can recall the feel of those beautiful, scratchy, woolen uniform trousers. My war-hero father, my courageous mother, and I had been reunited after more than five years!

At least twenty-five members of our Heller and Neumann family failed to survive the Holocaust. My parents and I were the sole survivors. Months later, we would learn that the Nazis had murdered six million Jews in the death camps.

Despite the devastating losses, my parents began to piece our lives back together. In less than three years, my father rebuilt the clothing factory into the largest of its kind in Central Europe. I started school for the first time, in the third grade. I was ecstatic because I could play with friends, and I displayed special skills as an athlete, devoting much of my time to soccer, hockey, tennis, and skiing. Although I thought nothing of it at the time, there were early signs of my future as an entrepreneur. I became the official captain or unofficial leader of every team, and I practiced harder and longer than the other kids. Whenever there was a need to take charge of a situation, I stepped up.

Tragically, Dwight Eisenhower's agreement to allow the Soviets to liberate us from the Germans in 1945 provided an opening for Communists to infiltrate the post-war government of Czechoslovakia. Slowly but surely over the next two years, Communist thugs took control of most branches of government and rendered our democratic President Beneš ineffective.

Our family's happy peacetime interlude ended in February 1948 with the Reds' total takeover. Our factory was nationalized and Papa—a "bourgeois capitalist" who had fought with the western forces during the war—officially became an enemy of the state, which meant that he was subject to imprisonment or possibly death. Once again, he was forced to go into exile. This time, he took us with him. The sole survivors in our once large family would not be separated again.

Carrying only a few possessions in order to avoid suspicion, we traveled by car, bus, and train to a farm on the Czech-German border. At midnight, the well-compensated farmer took us to the edge of a forest and pointed west.

"Walk a few kilometers in that direction and, if you're lucky and the border guards don't shoot you, you'll run into American soldiers. Good luck."

It was dark and scary in the woods. We avoided footpaths in order not to be detected. I carried a bundle of blankets that contained valuable jewelry. Mother toted one valise and Papa lugged two suitcases, one in front and the other in the back, connected by a strap over his shoulder. I kept tripping over roots, stumbling and falling, all the time frightened that the noise would give us away. I was exhausted when, after three hours, we reached the edge of the forest. Out of the darkness appeared two men in uniform

Oh, my God! I thought. *They've caught us. Now they'll take my parents away from me, just like the Germans.*

My father did not appear to be worried as he began to speak to the soldiers in a strange language. They were Americans. We had made it to the US zone of Germany.

We spent the next fifteen months in three different refugee camps, awaiting visas that would gain us admission to the United States as political refugees. The accommodations varied from terrible to tolerable. Neighboring Germans made no secret of their hatred for the inferior Slavs living in the camps, and there was never enough food or sufficient calories to sustain a growing boy. My saving grace was in the occasional CARE package from America. I fell madly in love with a delicacy that came in a blue, rectangular container with rounded edges. It was called Spam.

Finally, in May 1949, we waved goodbye to Europe from a Liberty ship departing from Bremerhaven. After six days in the angry Atlantic, we spotted the Statue of Liberty in the morning mist. I was thirteen years old, and I knew this was a sacred moment in our lives, the beginning of a new adventure. I was excited. But then I began to shiver, not from the chill morning air, but from fright. Other than our sponsors, the Eisner family on Long Island, I knew no one in America. I worried about school. Since I had spent the war in hiding and fifteen months in refugee camps, my formal education consisted of two weeks of third grade, full years in the fourth and fifth grades, and a half-year in the sixth. On top of that, I spoke only two words of English: "Sank you." Yet Papa told me that, in the fall, I would be starting eighth grade. How on earth was I going to survive an American eighth grade?

Then he added to my anxiety.

"Do you remember how I taught you to swim after the war?"

Papa asked as the New York City skyline came into view. "We waded into the river and then I threw you into the middle. You had two choices: to sink and drown or to figure out how to swim back to me. You learned fast. Life in America is going to be a lot like that. You're going to be thrown into the river and will have to swim in order to survive.

"America is the land of opportunity. But we're immigrants, starting from nothing. There'll be a lot of hurdles in the way, and there'll be no one around to help you. Here is what I want from you: I want you to forget everything that happened to you on the other side of the Atlantic. I want you to devote all your energies to becoming one hundred percent American and to gaining the respect of Americans. You'll start by learning to speak fluent English; a year from now, I want you to speak without an accent. When you open your mouth, I want people to think that you're a native."

One did not argue with a European father of that era. One simply saluted smartly and said "yes, sir." I did not salute, but I did say "yes, sir"—in Czech, of course.

CHAPTER THREE

Learning to Swim

The summer of 1949 was a whirlwind of changes and discoveries. My name was Americanized: Ota Karel Heller became Charles Ota Heller. I began learning American sports from Steve Eisner, the younger son of our sponsors. I discovered television.

My acculturation was not easy. I spent the first months learning about the strange habits of the natives. Traditional Czech food, which I loved and had dreamed about in the refugee camps, was replaced by stringy, tasteless turkey, undercooked and bloody steaks, and something called sweet potatoes. *Can anyone really eat a potato that is sweet?* I wondered.

Spam was nowhere to be found. And how strangely Americans ate! Quite properly, they held the knife in the right hand and the fork in the left while they cut their meat. But then they performed a maneuver that I found incomprehensible. After cutting a piece of meat, they placed the knife on the side of the plate, moved the fork into their right hand, stabbed the cut piece, and put it in their mouths. To cut the next piece of meat, they switched the fork back into the left hand, picked up the knife with the right, and repeated the drill. Why didn't they just keep the knife in the right hand and the fork in the left like normal people?

It took me a while to learn to say "fine" when Americans greeted me with "how are you?" even when I felt lousy. Then there were the primitive American weights and measures. Europeans grow up with the metric system, where the logic of multiples of ten applies. A meter consists of a hundred centimeters, a kilometer is a thousand meters, and there are a thousand grams in a kilogram. Suddenly, I had to work with inches and feet that were based on the length of the tip of some English king's thumb. Was the king's foot really equal to exactly twelve times the tip of his thumb?

In Czechoslovakia, women's last names had feminine endings, generally attaching the suffix "ová" to the man's name. For example, while my father and I were named "Heller," my mother was "Hellerová." It came as a shock to me that American women had "masculine" names. My very feminine mother had become "Ilona Heller."

The fact that Americans did not think that *real* football—or "soccer," as they called it—was the most beautiful, graceful sport came as a terrible disappointment. And, later that first year, I discovered that the natives did not consider Christmas Eve the holiest of all days, as it was by Czechs. Americans did not celebrate the holiday until the next day, when presents were delivered by a funny-looking, fat old man named Santa Claus rather than by Baby Jesus.

Perhaps most shocking to me was the amount of waste I noticed in the homes of my new friends, no matter how rich or poor their parents were. Uneaten food was thrown away in large quantities; paper tissues, rather than reusable cloth handkerchiefs, were used to wipe noses; broken toys and household items were thrown away and replaced by new ones rather than repaired. In our home, we continued to practice frugal European ways: we generated very little waste and lights were turned off each time we left a room. Of course, much of this was dictated by our state of poverty in those early months.

In September 1949, I entered the eighth grade at Alexander Hamilton School in Morristown, New Jersey. I was embraced by my teacher, Miss Agnes Leonard, as well as my classmates, and I thrived. I did well in the classroom and began to excel at newly learned American sports. When I entered Morristown High School the following year, I spoke English without a trace of an accent. So far, I had managed to swim.

My parents purchased a home in Morris Township, about two

miles north of Morristown. Papa worked in nearby Dover as a pattern-cutter for McGregor Sportswear. Mother became a cleaning lady at a girls' boarding school. Neither earned much money, yet they were able to save enough to make a 50 percent down payment and take out a five-year mortgage on the balance. Papa, who had been a successful entrepreneur in Europe, had an aversion to owing money to anyone, and he was not going to borrow a penny more than he had to.

Our neighbors, who lived in a house considerably larger than ours, became our family's close friends, despite the economic chasm between us. Jack Geils was vice president of the storied communications think tank, Bell Telephone Laboratories. His wife, Lynne, was a pert lady with a memorable laugh. Their only child, John W. Geils Jr., whom we called Jay, would one day become the leader of the internationally famous rock group, The J. Geils Band.

In less than a year, Papa rose through the ranks at McGregor and became a foreman in the cutting department. His salary more than doubled. Mother quit her cleaning job and took a better-paying position as a seamstress for brassiere manufacturer Maidenform. We had a car—a cream-colored 1949 Studebaker Champion—that my parents bought with cash. We were beginning to live the American Dream.

I enjoyed high school. Although I was more interested in sports than academics, I did well. I made many friends, the most important of whom was a gorgeous brunette named Susan Elizabeth Holsten. Sue and I decided to "go steady" near the end of my junior year.

I played baseball and tennis and ran track, but my passion was basketball. Although a lack of rapport with the coach prevented me from distinguishing myself on the high school team, I made my mark—and caught the eyes of several college coaches—playing in various New Jersey leagues against high-level competition. I received scholarship offers from Rutgers University and two smaller midwestern schools, but I was obsessed with playing for Henry P. Iba, the legendary coach of Oklahoma A&M College (today, Oklahoma

State University). Despite good words put in on my behalf by a Boston Celtics player and an OSU professor—a Czech family friend named Jan Tuma—Mr. Iba did not offer me a scholarship. But he agreed to allow me to walk on to the team in an attempt to earn a free ride (to be, in today's jargon, a "preferred walk-on").

I walked on and earned a partial scholarship. However, I never realized my dream of becoming a collegiate star and had to settle for being primarily a practice player with occasional seats near the end of the bench. I majored in civil engineering with a concentration in the analysis and design of structures such as bridges, buildings, and towers, following in the footsteps of Professor Tuma.

Sue was one year behind me in high school, and when I went off to college, our romance withered a bit. A year later, she entered Trenton State College (today, the College of New Jersey). Despondent over the thought of once again being fifteen hundred miles away from her, I made a last-minute decision not to return to OSU. Without informing anyone, I drove to the Rutgers University campus, located less than an hour from Trenton State, and registered for the fall semester. My parents were livid. When I also tried to change my major to journalism, my father put his foot down.

"Do you remember what I told you about never giving up?" he shouted. "Obviously engineering is tough, and you're looking for an easy way out. It's not going to happen! You're not giving up just because something is hard!"

In retaliation, I joined a partying fraternity and only bought a single textbook for the one course that interested me, city planning. Predictably, I flunked the majority of my classes. My father still would not be moved.

A couple of weeks into the spring semester, I thought back on Papa's words to me about hard work, never quitting, and gaining respect.

What the hell are you trying to do? I asked myself. *Papa is not about to change his mind, and you're doing nothing but ruining your life. Have some self-respect and get your ass out of the sling. Start working!*

The same day, I went to the university book store and purchased all my required texts. I moved out of the frat house and hit the books. I saw Sue on weekends, but I studied hard through the week. My grades began to climb, and I finished the semester with a low B average. Pretty good for a guy who had flunked nearly everything the previous term!

In the middle of a year-end softball game between faculty and students, the dean of engineering summoned me to his office. I was all smiles when I entered his inner sanctum, thinking that he wanted to give me the "Comeback Student of the Year" award. Instead, Dean Easton informed me that I had dug such a deep hole with my nonperformance during the fall semester that I failed to meet the standards for "academic progress toward graduation." I was expelled.

I walked out of the dean's office in a daze. I had disappointed my parents and Sue. Just as importantly, I had failed myself. My initial reaction was to escape. I would drive down to Florida, get a job, and disappear from sight. No one would be able to find me, and I would not have to explain my defeat.

That plan fell apart two exits down the New Jersey Turnpike. As my head began to clear, I thought about my parents: what they had been through during the war, how Mother protected me from the Nazis, our escape from the Communists, and Papa's hopes for me in America. I had to go home, face the music, and accept the consequences. I turned my car around. It was not obvious at the time, but this became one of my life's defining moments.

When I arrived home, I anticipated the worst. I expected Mother to cry and Papa to fly into a rage. Instead, I was met with love, kindness, and understanding.

"Listen to me," Papa said. "We beat the Germans, and we beat the Communists. We'll beat this together, too." With that, he called Professor Jan Tuma at Oklahoma State University. What happened next was nothing short of miraculous. OSU not only took me back, but Jan Tuma somehow managed to convince the registrar to obliterate my failing grades and transfer only my As, Bs, and Cs. In the end, I ended up losing one semester. Emboldened, I wrote a letter to Coach Iba. Incredibly, he restored my half scholarship, although he warned me that I would be primarily a practice player (in today's basketball lingo, a member of the scout team). Sue was as understanding as my parents. We agreed that, although we would be a half continent apart again, we would consider ourselves "unofficially engaged." We would date others if we wished, but, if our love endured, we would get married as soon as both of us received our degrees.

Back at OSU, I still enjoyed drinking beer with my friends, pulling sophomoric pranks, and—above all—competing in varsity and intramural sports. However, I was obsessed with showing my gratitude to my parents, to Professor Tuma, to Mr. Iba, and to the school I came to love for the faith it had exhibited in me. While I refused to become one dimensional, I was committed to excel in my studies. Perhaps this marked the beginning of my life as an entrepreneur. I had used basketball as a means to get into college. Now, realizing that I would not be able to make sports a career, I jumped at the next best opportunity: to make it as an engineer.

I studied long into the night. I became story editor and later managing editor of the *Oklahoma State Engineer* magazine and, together with my roommate Don Gafford and several of my Acacia fraternity brothers, built it into the number one ranked student engineering publication in the nation. Jim Cobb, a Korean War veteran a bit older and wiser than I and married, became my close friend. Considerably more mature than my other buddies, he whipped me into shape each time I slacked off. We took the same classes, studied together, and both received our bachelor's degrees in civil engineering in January 1959. Much to my—and my parents'—amazement, the civil engineering faculty proclaimed me "Outstanding Graduate."

Jim and I stayed on to study for our master's degrees, teaming up to do research in structural analysis under the tutelage of Professor Tuma. In June 1959, immediately after Sue graduated from Trenton State College and halfway through my master's program, we were married. Following the wedding reception in New Jersey, we headed for OSU with our meager belongings packed into a small U-Haul trailer hitched to our 1953 Studebaker.

I completed my MS requirements in January 1960. Sue and I traded in the Studebaker on a brand new, baby-blue, 1960 Volkswagen Bug. We packed it with all our worldly possessions, said goodbye to OSU and our friends, and—like the Okies of the Dust Bowl years—set out for California to seek our fortune.

CHAPTER FOUR

Race to Space

The last part of my college career at OSU coincided with the start of the space race, which began when the Soviet Union launched the first satellite, *Sputnik*, in 1957. A year later, the United States answered by launching its first orbiter, *Explorer I*. During my senior year, the USSR shocked the world by crashing the *Luna 2* probe onto the moon's surface. The race was on.

I was drawn toward the excitement, glamour—and money—of space. During the fall of 1959, I interviewed with two aerospace companies, Boeing in Wichita, Kansas, and McDonnell Corporation in St. Louis. Because I wanted to see California at someone else's expense, I also accepted a trip to interview for a non-aerospace job with Kaiser Steel in Fontana. The job did not interest me and sweltering, inland Fontana was hardly the Southern California I had long admired from magazine photos and movies.

I extended my stay and spent a couple of days with my OSU fraternity brother, Bob Larkin, and his wife Peggy, who lived in Long Beach. They gave me a tour of the California I had read and dreamed about—Laguna Beach, Malibu, Pacific Palisades, Palos Verdes, Muscle Beach. I was in love, particularly with Santa Monica and her stately palms, beautiful people, and sparkling white beaches. This is where I wanted to live, and I was sure that Sue would agree. But I needed a job—although not one with Kaiser Steel in Fontana. Bob was working for Douglas Aircraft Company in Long Beach, doing structural analysis of airplanes. When I informed him that I wanted to get involved in the space program, he told me about Douglas's

Missiles and Space Division located in, of all places, Santa Monica.

Bob and I thumbed through his Douglas phone directory and came up with the name of Adrain O'Neal, the guy in charge of all structural analysis on the space side. When I returned to Stillwater, I told Sue about my discovery, and she became as enthusiastic as I about trying to get to Santa Monica. I wrote a letter to O'Neal, enclosed my resume, and requested a job interview. I was incredulous when, instead of an invitation to come out for a look-see, I received a job offer in the mail. At $660 per month, it was less money than I had been offered by Boeing, but I accepted without hesitation or negotiation.

When I completed my master's at the end of January 1960, we packed our meager belongings into our VW bug and headed west. We celebrated the start of our new life by sightseeing in New Mexico and Arizona, stopping at the Grand Canyon, the Meteor Crater, and Indian cave dwellings, never straying far from Route 66.

Eventually, we arrived at the western terminus of the famous highway, where it dead-ended at the most beautiful street in the world, Ocean Avenue in Santa Monica. The next morning, we set out in search of an apartment to rent. We drove north on Ocean Avenue, along palisades that towered above endless beaches. Beyond, the blue Pacific stretched westward to the horizon. We looked at one another. Neither one of us needed to say what each was thinking: *If this isn't paradise on earth, I don't know what is.*

A few minutes later, we turned east onto San Vicente Boulevard, a wide street with a grass median and a combination of new apartment houses and stately, old mansions on both sides. A couple of hundred yards up from Ocean Avenue, on the right side, we spotted a "For Rent" sign in front of an older, two-story, tan-colored stucco house surrounded by immaculate flowerbeds resplendent with red blossoms. There, we found our new home: a fully furnished, one-bedroom apartment, for $125 per month, on the ground floor. The rent included all utilities and the use of a carport in the back. We were thrilled. Most of what little money we had, we put up as our advance rent payment and moved in. Being down to our last few dollars would be no problem because I would start work the next day, and I knew from Bob Larkin that every Friday was payday at Douglas.

The next morning, after arriving at the company which was located adjacent to Santa Monica's municipal airport, I was put through the normal drill of a first-day employee. I filled out a variety of forms, applied for a security clearance, and had my photo taken.

"No smiles, no profiles," instructed the crabby woman who took pictures for the company badge.

Late in the morning, I submitted my completed paperwork to the personnel department, anxious to meet my boss and co-workers.

"I see that you're a naturalized citizen," said the woman behind the desk.

"Yes, I am."

"May I see your naturalization papers, please?"

I explained to her that my naturalization certificate was in a safe deposit box in a New Jersey bank, and that no one had told me I would need it at Douglas. I asked if I could begin work while the certificate was en route to me from my parents.

"Absolutely not," she hissed. "You can't work in the space program without at least a temporary confidential security clearance, and we can't give it to you until we have a copy of your naturalization certificate on file."

I was devastated because we were broke. There was no FedEx or UPS, and fax machines had not been invented. My parents would need to air-mail the paper to me—a delay of four or five days. In this era before credit cards (for which we would not have qualified, anyway), Sue and I had $20 to our name.

The thrill of having arrived in paradise was on hold as the waiting began. In the meantime, we ate bread and little Vienna sausages out of a can and got ourselves invited to a couple of dinners by the Larkins. It took a week for my papers to travel from the East Coast to the West and, finally, I began work as an aerospace engineer.

At Douglas, I discovered why I was offered a job so quickly and without an interview. In 1960, advanced technical degrees were rare, and the company was trying to make itself more competitive by hiring as many engineers with Master's degrees as it could find. In the Strength (structural analysis) Section to which I was assigned, I was one of only two people out of nearly a hundred with an advanced degree. The other was the section chief, Adrain O'Neal, a graduate of Mississippi State University. Yet, despite my glorified academic standing, my initial work consisted of checking the calculations of others. Whenever I found an error, I marked it with a red circle. A correct calculation received a red dot above the result. So much for the glamour of designing spaceships. The only daily excitement was a lunchtime game of hearts.

One day while eating breakfast prior to leaving home for work, I spotted an article on the second page of the *Los Angeles Times*. "Wernher von Braun to Visit Southland," read the headline. Reading further, I discovered that he would be visiting several of the area's aerospace companies. Douglas would be one of them.

"May I have your attention?" O'Neal called out as soon as we settled in at our desks. "We're in for a special treat today. Around eleven o'clock this morning, the great Dr. Wernher von Braun will visit our section. When he comes, I want all of you to stand and applaud and then come to the front of the room, where he will address us."

I looked around and saw smiles on the faces of my colleagues. Clearly, they felt honored to have been selected for a meeting with the world-renowned rocket scientist. I buried my head in my work, pretending to analyze the stresses in the engine section of the Thor Delta rocket. Instead, I closed my eyes and flashed back to my life as a child hiding from our German occupiers during World War II. I imagined five hundred German V-2 rockets raining terror upon the citizens of London, while their chief architect, von Braun, sat in his office in Peenemunde, Germany, surrounded by thousands of slaves working around the clock to complete the construction of fifteen hundred ballistic missiles designed to bring England to her knees.

Now, this man and his German team of technicians were on our side, running the American space program out of Huntsville, Alabama.

I wanted to stand on top of my desk and shout these facts to my fellow engineers. But I knew it would be futile. In my few years in the United States, I had discovered that, shockingly, Americans, except for those who had personally fought so valiantly to liberate Europe, felt a strange kinship toward Germans. They seemed to hate the Japanese, their other major enemy in the war, but they appeared to have forgiven Germany, a nation that had killed millions of innocent people, as well as thousands of American GIs.

I decided on a personal silent protest.

At exactly 11 a.m., a group of a dozen dignitaries, including CEO Donald Douglas Jr. and some local politicians, appeared at the front of our bullpen. From the vantage point of my desk, some hundred feet away, I saw that the center of everyone's attention was a tall, distinguished-looking man with graying hair matching the color of his suit. Like an army company when a general enters, the Strength Section of the Douglas Missiles and Space Systems Division came to attention. Then they applauded. All but one "soldier."

Pretending not to have noticed the commotion, I wrote nonsensical numbers and words on the quadrille pad in front of me. While my colleagues gathered around von Braun and the visiting party, I pulled a brown bag out of the drawer of my desk and extracted a sandwich. As the leader of America's space program gave my fellow engineers a pep talk in his German-accented English, I made a show of munching on a very European sandwich, hard salami and Swiss cheese with mustard on rye bread. From the corner of my eye, I saw heads turning toward me, just as I had hoped. On a couple of occasions, I thought that von Braun spotted me over the heads of his audience.

After about twenty minutes, our visitors left and my colleagues returned to their respective desks. No one said a word to me, but my best friend, Don Griffin, smiled at me before he sat down in the row in front of me, indicating that he understood. Then, as I had expected, my boss approached.

"Charlie, can I talk to you a minute?"

"Sure," I replied and followed him out into the hallway.

"What the hell was that all about?" O'Neal asked. "Don't you realize that you just insulted the greatest rocket scientist in the world?"

"Adrain, do you know anything about my background?"

"Yeah, I heard."

"Well, then, I hope you understand that I just insulted a goddamned Nazi murderer. I hope I didn't cause you and Douglas any hardship, but I'll be damned if I'm going to stand and applaud a bastard who killed or maimed nearly ten thousand Brits."

With that, I walked back to my desk and finished my lunch.

When we first arrived in California, Sue had difficulties finding a teaching job. Consequently, she became a teller at the Santa Monica branch of the Bank of America. While it was only an interim stop for her, she enjoyed the notoriety that came with it. The beautiful brunette became the most popular teller in the bank. When I came to pick her up each Friday evening, I marveled at the long line of customers— some of them familiar-looking movie stars—at her window, while other tellers had hardly anyone waiting.

"What are you giving away?" I would joke, and she would only shrug and smile.

Within a year, Sue was finally able to enter her chosen profession. She was assigned a second grade at the Madrona School in Torrance, a town about an hour's drive down the coast from our home.

For me, the initial exhilaration of working in the space program at the height of the race with the Soviet Union wore off quickly. It was exciting to tell family and friends that I was part of the small team that designed the aft four feet—the engine section—of the Delta rocket, which over the years would boost more craft into outer space than any other missile. And I was proud to tell them that I had been in charge of the design and manufacture of the canister that contained the *Echo* balloon, a communications satellite still orbiting the earth. But in reality, the work was routine and boring. I was looking for a greater challenge. After some cajoling, I managed to convince my bosses that I could make a more meaningful contribution elsewhere in the company. My timing was good.

Under the management of a superb leader named Ray Zaller, a small structures research group was being formed. At the outset, it consisted of its director, Howard Levy, and me. I was energized as Howard and I began to apply pioneering computer techniques to the analysis and design of aerospace structures. I was learning a great deal but often found that my knowledge was inadequate to tackle the complexities of the problems. Now, after months of boredom and simpleton engineering, I was in over my head. For the first time, I began to think about returning to school.

I expressed this to my father when he and Mother visited us in 1961, but I told him that Sue and I could not afford the luxury of returning to academia. Late that year, Papa spoke with family friend and Bell Labs VP, Jack Geils, about it. When we came east for the Christmas holidays, Jack asked if I would be interested in coming back to work at the Labs. I told him Sue and I had no interest in moving to New Jersey and, if I were going to change jobs, I would also want to start working on a PhD. That seemed to be the end of that.

I had an appointment as a part-time lecturer at UCLA, where I was teaching a course in space structures. I found teaching exciting and satisfying and began to toy with the idea of going into academia full-time. I interviewed at Sacramento State College (today, California State University, Sacramento) and was offered a position as assistant professor. I was intrigued but knew this would not help me toward getting the next degree.

Jack Geils to the rescue. I received a letter from Bell Labs and, without so much as an interview, I was offered a choice of three jobs: two in New Jersey—at Murray Hill or Holmdel—and a third at a field laboratory in Baltimore, Maryland. All of them would be part of a special program wherein I would be allowed to attend classes toward a doctorate up to three half-days per week. Sue and I eliminated Murray Hill and Holmdel because the only university with an appropriate curriculum for me would be Columbia. There was no way I was going to commute to New York, a city of which I was not particularly fond.

Baltimore sounded interesting, and the University of Maryland had a doctoral program that suited me. Sue agreed to resign her teaching position in Torrance at the end of the school year and to seek one in Baltimore. Sight unseen, I accepted the job there. With some sadness, we said goodbye to our friends and to the Southern California we had learned to love and headed east in our blue VW Beetle.

CHAPTER FIVE

Land of Pleasant Living

"Holy Christ! What have we done?"

I pulled over to the curb on a wide street lined on both sides with identical two-story houses that seemed to extend to the horizon. After nearly three years of living in paradise, we had entered a place that could have been called "Hell" rather than "Baltimore." There were no palm trees, no movie-star mansions, no gaily colored buildings, no cheerful flowers or shrubbery. Even on this sunny June day, the predominant color was gray.

Sue perused the map we had examined back on the West Coast. It showed lots of water—just like Southern California. "Let's keep going until we get to the ocean," she suggested after minutes of silence. "I'm sure things will look a lot better."

We found Pratt Street, parked the car, and set out in search of that blue stuff on the map. We spotted it, surrounded by ugly brown warehouses. Like the rest of the city, the water was gray, except for the multicolored flotsam bobbing near the seawall: papers, rotten fruit, old tires, and dead fish with their white bellies exposed to the stinking air. When we caught sight of a rat balancing itself on a dock line while attempting to board a ship tied up alongside one of the warehouses, we ran like hell.

Our next task was to check out the elementary school at which Sue had accepted a teaching job for the fall, sight unseen from our perch in sunny California. When we pulled up in front of the two-story brick building in a blighted area called Westport, Sue gasped.

"God!" she whispered as she stared at the broken windows and the filthy words sprayed on the walls.

"You're not going to teach here," I said without hesitation.

"Thank you," she replied and kissed me lightly on the cheek. I could feel her tears on my skin. I stepped on the accelerator and got out of the area as quickly as possible.

The following day, it was time to check out my new place of work. We got on the newly opened Baltimore Beltway and headed southeast. After driving through the Harbor Tunnel, we exited the freeway and entered Dundalk. The blue-collar town within a city was nothing like Westport, but it was not Santa Monica, either. "Charming" was not the adjective that popped into my mind. We passed the Lever Brothers soap factory and drove by a large General Motors truck manufacturing plant. Following the disappointment of our first day at the Baltimore waterfront, I did not expect sandy beaches and volleyball courts where we had seen blue water on our map. Nevertheless, I was overwhelmed by what we did see.

As we turned right onto Broening Highway, there, spread out in front of us, was the biggest factory I had ever seen. Beyond the large building with a Western Electric sign, what seemed like hundreds of smaller buildings were scattered in every direction. Someplace in there would be the Bell Labs field laboratory and my future office. Through a fence topped by barbed wire, I could see huge coils of cable stacked among the structures. Workers were scurrying around on bicycles and on foot, dodging fork-lift trucks, each seeming to be going in a different direction. Across the street, a huge parking lot filled to capacity seemed to spread toward infinity. It, too, was surrounded by a fence befitting a federal penitentiary. I noticed that the two electrically controlled gates were locked in the middle of the workday, as if to keep the prisoner-workers from escaping. From the car window, I imagined a scene inside the factory walls reminiscent of those about which I had read in books about pre-Industrial Revolution sweatshops.

"So, this is why I earned two engineering degrees and am about to start work on my third one," I said to Sue. "To work in a goddamn prison!"

I was trapped. Unlike Sue and her school, I could not say "no, thanks" to Bell Labs and go find another job. Mother Bell, as parent company AT&T was known, had paid our moving expenses and I had signed a letter agreeing to take the job. The company had also prepaid my tuition at the University of Maryland for the fall semester. As I had done many times previously, I remembered my father's edict to suck it up.

The Bell Labs field laboratory was devoted solely to the design and operation of the transatlantic telephone cable, manufactured by Western Electric. To my surprise, the work I was assigned proved challenging at first. I performed the structural design of the cable connections to repeaters, analyzed stresses in the complex multi-material structure of the cable, and assisted in the design of the ship-mounted cable-laying equipment. While not as glamorous, the actual engineering and mathematics associated with the ocean cable were nearly as complicated as those of missiles and spacecraft.

In September 1962, I started coursework toward my PhD at the University of Maryland in College Park, located in the Washington suburbs. When I had selected Maryland from three thousand miles away, I had not realized that—unlike most urban universities—it failed to cater to part-time students like me. It was extremely difficult to design class schedules to dovetail with my work-allowed three afternoons per week, but I managed.

Subsequent to the completion of my second semester at the University of Maryland in May 1963, I was able to sit back and contemplate my life and our future. Sue was teaching second grade at Woodlawn Elementary School near our home, we had made new friends, and we were happy with our social life. I enjoyed the benefits that came with working at Bell Labs—getting time off to attend school and playing basketball and softball in industrial leagues—but I no longer enjoyed my work. After the first few months, it had become monotonous and boring. On the heels of having been a player, albeit a small one, in America's glamorous space program, I found it difficult to get excited about designing the inner conductor of the transoceanic telephone cable. I had a sense of guilt because I was not doing anything creative. Perhaps I was arrogant, but I thought that I had been put on this earth to make an impact—and making sure that a cable would not break on the bottom of the ocean did not meet that standard. Most of all, my experiences at Douglas and Mother Bell convinced me that being a tiny pawn in *any* large company was not what I wanted to do with my life. There had to be a better way!

While I was in this contemplative mode, fate interfered once again. The Labs hired a fellow who had just gotten out of the Navy. His last assignment had been at the Naval Academy, where he had been an engineering instructor. When I quizzed him about it, he told me that a major change was in the works at the Academy—"a transformation from a trade school to an honest-to-God university," he said. I had loved teaching as a graduate assistant at Oklahoma State and as a lecturer at UCLA, so I was intrigued.

Like most Europeans, my parents held teachers in high esteem. I knew they would be overjoyed if their son became a college professor. I would earn their respect, as well as that of my fellow Americans. Moreover, my hero, President John F. Kennedy, had issued a challenge to young people to join his government in order to establish a New Frontier. Many had heeded the charismatic president's call, and I had been wondering if there was a place where I could fit in. Now, I saw an opportunity to combine an act of patriotism with doing something I enjoyed and that would bring me the respect I yearned.

My ex-Navy friend called the Naval Academy and set up an appointment for me with the head of the Engineering Department. I drove the thirty-five miles to Annapolis and, after meeting with the chair of engineering, Navy Captain Wayne Hoof, and taking a tour of the academic and athletic facilities, I was sold. I received an offer to join the faculty as an assistant professor for $8,500 a year, some 30 percent less than I was making at Bell Labs. Sue and I visited

Annapolis and immediately fell in love with the historic town on the Severn River. I accepted the job without negotiation.

The Academy was one year away from transitioning to a majors program. My agreement with administration was that, once we changed, I would be part of the small initial nucleus of the new Aerospace Engineering Committee. For the first year, though, while all midshipmen still took the standard core curriculum, I would be part of the Third-Class Committee. At the service academies, first-year students are known as fourth-classmen, second-year students are third-classmen, and so on. Thus, our committee taught the engineering courses taken by all sophomores: Statics and Dynamics, Strength of Materials, and Engineering Materials.

Before the academic year began, I made certain that the committee chair, Professor Jack Smith, knew that while I was strong in the other two courses, I had never even taken a course in engineering materials, other than one metallurgy class at OSU, which I had barely passed and which had been the cause of my departure from the basketball program.

"Please don't ask me to teach it," I begged Smith.

"No problem," he said. "You'll teach Statics in the fall and Strength in the spring. You'll have three sections of each."

It did not take me long to discover why many people outside the Academy, as well as some of the faculty, used the derisive term "trade school" when referring to the old academic program. In that first year, there were no majors or elective courses. All midshipmen were in a single core curriculum. Moreover, the faculty, which was half civilian and half military, had essentially no freedom to innovate in the classroom. All sections of a course were taught from a single, standardized syllabus. In engineering, the four committees held weekly meetings at which professors were told exactly what they would teach during the week that followed. My fellow rookie profs and I joked that we could walk down the hall of a classroom building and, if the doors were open, we could hear a continuous lecture without missing a beat.

I tolerated this environment only because I knew that better days were coming. The Navy had made the momentous decision to transform the United States Naval Academy into a military service university. The magic date for this earth-shaking transition would be September 1964, one year after my arrival in Annapolis. Quite a few civilian professors were hired at the same time, and many others would come the following summer in preparation for the "new USNA."

In the meantime, I gritted my teeth, held my nose, and went along with the old system. At the same time, there was a side of the Academy that I embraced with enthusiasm. The athletic facilities were fantastic—and faculty members were encouraged to use them. I played tennis and basketball during breaks and on weekends, and I learned to play squash. I became a volunteer coach with the plebe (freshman) soccer and basketball teams. Although I continued coursework toward my doctorate at the University of Maryland, I had lots of free time. Preparation for lectures was easy and grading homework and tests was not time-consuming in that first year. I knew that all this would change the following fall, so I immersed myself in sports while I could.

Many of the faculty members, both civilian and military, were young, and we had a great deal in common. We visited one another's homes for dinner and partied at the Officers' Club. Initial conversations with new friends everywhere always seemed to include the question, "Where are you from, originally?" Whereas our new friends would reply "New York" or "Chicago" or "Texas," and Sue would tell them "New Jersey," I became an instant curiosity when I responded with "Czechoslovakia." Invariably, the next inquiry would be about World War II, and I would answer with my standard party-line: "After the Nazis came, my father escaped and joined the British army. Because they knew that he was fighting against them, the Germans put my mother in a slave labor camp, and I was hidden out on a farm." Each retelling over the years reinforced the story. By repeating it as an automaton, I came to believe that we were mistreated by the

Germans solely because of my father's service in the Allied forces and I blocked the real reason—that the majority of my family was Jewish—from my mind.

Sometimes I would add drama: "We lost fifteen members of our family in the war." (It would be many years later before I would discover that the actual number was at least twenty-five.) I would get a perverse kick out of my audience's horrified looks. But the tone of my voice made it obvious that I had no interest in discussing how or why. With marriage, job, friends, sports, and studies, I was completely immersed in the present, and I had no interest in thinking about, or discussing, my ethnicity or any other part of a past that my father had ordered me to forget.

CHAPTER SIX

It's a Boy!

The biggest event for the entire family arrived just as I was starting at the Naval Academy—Sue announced that she was pregnant! Since she and I were only children, both sets of parents were ecstatic about the prospect of their first grandchild. With the baby due in April 1964, we decided that Sue would continue to teach at Woodlawn Elementary in the Baltimore suburbs until Christmas, at which time we would move to Annapolis. The city did not offer many choices back then, but we found an unfurnished unit at the Admiral Farragut apartments off Spa Road.

On November 22, 1963, I gave my last lecture of the day at the Academy and prepared to drive to College Park to attend an afternoon class. But first I had promised Sue that I would stop at the new apartment to measure windows so that she could purchase curtains. I climbed the stairs to the rental office in order to borrow a key. When I opened the door, I found two women staring at a small black-and-white TV screen and crying.

"What happened?" I inquired.

"The president's been shot." It took me a long moment to realize that she was talking about President Kennedy.

"Is he dead?"

"No, they're trying to save his life."

My memory of what followed is vague. I think I went through the motions of measuring the windows in our future apartment, and I must have wondered if the University of Maryland had cancelled classes. I know that I got in my car and began driving on Route 50 in the direction of College Park, hanging onto every word of a radio announcer coming from Parkland Hospital in Dallas. A few minutes after 2:30, as I approached the ramp onto the Washington Beltway, the announcement came:

"The president of the United States, John Fitzgerald Kennedy, is dead."

"No!" I screamed as tears made it impossible for me to drive any further. I pulled onto the shoulder, laid my head on the steering wheel, and cried while the radio played funeral music. Jack Kennedy was my hero, and his challenge—"Ask not what your country can do for you. Ask what you can do for your country"—had been a major motivator for my coming to the Naval Academy to prepare midshipmen to serve our nation. As I sat there on the side of the road, cars whizzing by, memories of my past life came rushing at me.

This is the way they do things in Europe, I thought. *When they're unhappy with their governments, they murder the leaders. This is America. How can it happen here?* For this immigrant, this cataclysmic event represented the beginning of a loss of innocence.

After some time, I continued toward the university, although I must have realized that even if my class were held, I would have no interest in the lecture. In a daze, I walked into the deserted engineering building and trudged down a long corridor toward the classroom. There, in the doorway, stood three of my classmates, talking quietly about the assassination. One of them, a fellow Naval Academy faculty member named Gerry Schlimm, was speaking as I walked up.

"It couldn't have happened to a better guy," I heard him say.

Incredulous, I looked up at his face to make certain that I had heard him correctly. His smirk told me that I had. Schlimm was three or four inches taller than I, but I managed to catch him square in the jaw as I smashed my fist into his laughing face. Then I walked away. Somehow, I managed to drive home to Baltimore to find Sue sobbing as she watched JFK's casket being loaded onto Air Force One for the flight to Washington. The sight of the grief-stricken Jackie, coat smeared with blood, left us speechless as we sat holding hands and wondering how we—and our nation—could get through this.

Lyndon Johnson took over as president and our collective wound began to heal. But the pain remained. Unbeknownst to any of us, we were moving from the innocence of the fifties to a new era of turmoil. Fortunately for Sue and me, the expected arrival of our baby helped to take our minds off the country's tumult. We moved into our Annapolis apartment a few days after Christmas. We did not have to worry about preparing for the baby's arrival because my parents went on a buying spree each time they visited. The baby's room was fully furnished long before the April due date.

As we approached the start of the spring semester, my boss, Jack Smith, entered our bullpen office in Isherwood Hall.

"Charlie, I have a problem," he said. "I know you're slated to teach Strength of Materials in the spring, but I've lost a faculty member and I need someone to teach three sections of Engineering Materials."

I stopped breathing. "Jack, I told you that I've never even *taken* a course in engineering materials. How can I possibly *teach* it?"

"You're going to do the best you can," he replied. "You're a smart guy. I know you can do it. I just don't have any other choice. Besides, you're the junior member of the Third-Class Committee."

I had expected the spring of 1964 to be challenging. Now I wondered if I was up to the challenge. Sue and I would be caring for a baby. I would still be commuting to the University of Maryland and studying for my doctorate. I would be spending time as a volunteer coach of the plebe basketball team. I would be looking for consulting work to make up for the fact that Sue would not be receiving income from teaching. Now, I would also have to study harder than the midshipmen in order to teach a subject about which I knew next to nothing.

When the spring semester began, I discovered that my concerns about Engineering Materials were justified. I managed to stay one lesson ahead of my students, all the time working diligently to keep my ignorance a secret from them.

Early in the morning on Thursday, April 9, 1964, Sue woke me up.

"It's time to go," she said calmly.

I dressed quickly, and we drove to Anne Arundel General Hospital in downtown Annapolis. I smoked an entire pack of Kent cigarettes as I walked laps around the hospital grounds, regularly popping back into the waiting room to check on the progress of Sue's labor.

"It's a boy!" a nurse finally informed me after four agonizing hours. When I was allowed to see Sue, she was asleep and the baby had been taken into a room full of tiny cribs. I was only allowed to see my son through the nursery window and, with his body and most of his head covered by a little white blanket, I could only see his eyes and nose. But I knew that he had to be a beautiful baby—because he was *our* baby!

The doctor informed me that it had been a difficult delivery. The baby had turned and they had to use forceps to extract him. The physician said that, in the process, Sue had suffered some minor injuries that would have to heal before she could go home. He told me that there was nothing to worry about; the baby was fine and Sue would have to stay in the hospital only a few days.

I went home and called Sue's parents to tell them all was well. Then I called my parents to inform them that we had a son named David Arthur Heller, the middle name in honor of Mother's father, Artur Neumann, the man I had called *Děda* before the Germans murdered him during his attempted escape through Yugoslavia. Mother cried and Papa was ecstatic. I went out, bought a box of cigars, and distributed them among my fellow faculty members in Isherwood Hall. I spent the evening with Sue in her hospital room and went out to the nursery window, but I was not able to see David. His little crib was in the back and there was no one on the other side of the window whom I could ask to bring him close for me to see.

The following morning before my class, I stopped at the hospital. I looked in on Sue and then walked over to the baby-viewing window.

A nurse wheeled David up close. His color was different from the pinkish white of the other babies. His skin had a grayish-blue tinge. I waved for the nurse to come out and expressed my concern to her.

"Are you a first-time father?" she asked.

"Yes, I am."

"This is typical. Most first-time dads find something to worry about. There's nothing different about your baby. Trust me."

I was skeptical, but I believed her. I drove to the Academy and taught my three classes of Engineering Materials. While sitting at my desk, an image of little David, looking unlike the other babies, kept popping up in front of my eyes. An unseen force drew me back to the hospital. I drove there and rushed to the nursery window. There was David, in the front row now, surrounded by pinkish white babies. He was blue! I knew he looked different! I stormed the nurses' station and raised hell.

"Don't dismiss me as an idiot!" I yelled. "Somebody please come with me and explain why my son looks different from all the other babies!"

A nurse looked in the window with me, and this time, my concerns were not shrugged off as those of a confused first-time father. Immediately, she called the pediatrician on duty. He examined David and came out into the hall.

"Something is definitely wrong. He was bleeding a bit from his scalp where the forceps had cut him, and the bleeding has not stopped since he was born. There may have been some internal bleeding, too. That would explain his color. I need to make a call to consult with someone." He left me, shaken and wondering what was coming next, standing in the hallway. After a few minutes, he emerged.

"We need a laboratory evaluation of his blood," he said. "We don't have the capability here, and the best people in this field are at the National Institutes of Health in Bethesda. I'm going to take a blood sample now and arrange to have it delivered to the NIH."

Along with the nurse, he stepped inside the nursery and I watched through the window as he inserted a huge needle into David's tiny arm. When he finished, he and the nurse disappeared. Another few minutes—which seemed like hours—went by as I waited anxiously. Finally, the doctor came out, holding open a small box. Inside were two test tubes half-filled with David's blood. The third vial, I was told, contained a sample of Sue's blood.

"We have a regular shuttle service between here and the National Institutes of Health. The shuttle is at NIH now and won't be leaving here again till late afternoon. We may be looking at a critical situation here, and I don't think it's a good idea to wait. If you want to shortcut this, you can drive the blood samples to the NIH yourself."

I did not have time to think about the bizarre nature of his request and told the doctor that I would leave immediately. He gave me directions, and I was on my way. I had a Triumph TR-3, and I used my experience as a race driver (I had raced sports cars in college) to set a record of sorts that afternoon, traversing fifty miles of Washington area's crowded roads in the middle of a workday in forty-five minutes. Miraculously, I managed to avoid the police. An NIH researcher was waiting for me, and he also took a sample of my blood. Now, the NIH had test tubes with blood samples from all three of us.

A doctor came to the waiting room to ask me a few questions about my family's history. I was astonished by his persistent questioning about any possibility of royal European blood in the Heller or Neumann families. When I insisted that this was unlikely, he explained. There was a possibility that David had hemophilia, a disease common among royals and brought about by intermarriage within the families. He departed, and I sat in the waiting room for nearly an hour, feeling helpless as strangers made life and death decisions about our baby. Finally, the physician emerged.

"Your son is not a hemophiliac. But there is an antibody in his blood that is killing off the platelets," he said. "Platelets are tiny coin-shaped particles that cause clotting. He must be bleeding internally and, without platelets, there's nothing to stop the blood flow. The only way to fix this is with a complete transfusion of blood. This is an emergency, and we need to get him to Johns Hopkins. I've already called Hopkins, and I'll call over to Anne Arundel to arrange to get him there right away."

I thanked the man and ran back to my car. I intended to drive straight to Baltimore in order to be at Johns Hopkins when David arrived. But then I changed my mind. Considering how the situation had been handled at Anne Arundel General Hospital, I no longer trusted the people there. Their arrogance and seeming indifference made it imperative for me to stay in control of the crisis. Of course, there were no cell phones then, so I had to tackle it in person. I had to go back to Annapolis to make sure our baby's transport to Hopkins was being handled properly and expediently. Less than an hour later, I arrived just as David was being loaded into an Eastport Fire Department ambulance. Again, I hopped into my car. I practically glued my front bumper to the rear end of the station wagon as it sped north to Baltimore.

By the time I parked my car and filled out a few forms at Johns Hopkins, David was already in the operating room. The next two hours were excruciating. No one had told me so, but I had a feeling that the little guy's life was hanging in balance on the other side of the stark walls of the waiting room. He was not quite two days old, and already I loved him dearly; I longed to be there holding him while the doctors worked to save his life. I thought about the fact that this little boy was the realization of the dreams of two sets of grandparents, each pair of whom had had only one child and thus counted on Sue and me to give them a grandchild. I thought about my own dreams for our son: to be an outstanding student, a sports star, a famous scientist, and perhaps even a future president of our country. Now, I just prayed that he would live. After two hours that seemed like two lifetimes, two men wearing white smocks—one thin, dark-skinned, with jet-black hair, and the other slightly shorter, heavier, and with brown hair—came into the room.

"I'm Dr. Katz," said the shorter one, "and this is Dr. Rodriguez. Your little boy is out of danger now. We made two complete blood exchanges, a last resort in critical cases like this, and they worked. We don't know the cause of his condition or what was killing the platelets, but it is gone now. The only remaining question is how much internal bleeding there was. It's unlikely, but he may have had some bleeding into his brain. Only time will tell if there is brain damage."

I was relieved but horrified. David was taken into the children's wing of the hospital, and I was allowed to go in. When I bent down to kiss my son for the first time, I noticed that half his head had been shaved and looked lumpy and slightly lopsided. He may have appeared peculiar to a casual observer, but he was beautiful in my eyes, even with tubes and hoses attached to his little body.

Now it was time to return to Annapolis and recount the day's events to Sue. I was under the impression that she was lying in the hospital, unaware of what had taken place. Much to my surprise, she already knew and had spent a terrifying afternoon waiting for news of David.

"I knew about NIH when they came to draw my blood," she said. "I never saw David until they told me they were taking him to Hopkins. I insisted on seeing him before he left Anne Arundel. When they brought him to me, he was unresponsive and very gray-blue."

I gave her the good news about the outcome of the procedure and about my harrowing drives to and from NIH and then from Annapolis to Baltimore.

On the way back, I had decided to give her only the good news and to withhold the fact that there existed the possibility of brain damage. That could wait until she came home. I was totally exhausted when I left her hospital room and, after calling both sets of David's grandparents, I crashed on our living room sofa.

For the next week, each day consisted of two visits with Sue at Anne Arundel, teaching my classes, a visit to Hopkins to see David, and, on two of the days, also attending classes at the University of Maryland. Being one lesson ahead of my midshipmen now shrank to being even with them. Each night, I studied only enough to get through the next class.

The Naval Academy had a requirement that every faculty member's teaching must be observed and evaluated once each semester. During the second week of my crazy merry-go-round, Jack Smith informed me that he would be coming to my class to observe me. The man was aware of the conditions of my wife and son and the fact that he had forced me to teach a subject about which I knew little. He must have known that I was an emotional train wreck. Yet, he chose that time to evaluate my performance. *Nice guy,* I thought. *He must really like me!* Miraculously, I got through the evaluation and whatever he wrote in his little book did not affect my standing at the Academy.

Sue came home after two weeks in the hospital, and I finally informed her of the potential aftereffects of David's near-death experience. I told her that I had learned from Dr. Katz that David's disease was called Neonatal Thrombocytopenic Purpura, that the cause was unknown to the medical community, and that the chance of total recovery was around 75 percent. Dr. Katz also told me that the fact that David's scalp had been cut during delivery had turned out to be a stroke of luck. If the doctors and nurses in Annapolis had not seen that his cut was still bleeding after more than twenty-four hours, they may not have agreed with me that something was wrong; this outcome would have been disastrous.

After several more days of recuperation from her injury, Sue began to accompany me on visits to the children's wing of Johns Hopkins. Every day brought better news. David was getting stronger and, so far at least, did not exhibit any signs of brain damage. The key indicator, we were told by those wonderful doctors who had saved his life, was the fact that he was "active." We and the hospital staff were ecstatic each time he kicked his legs, punched the air with his tiny fists, and screamed.

At the end of the first week of May, the big day finally arrived. David came home after a three-week stay at Hopkins. My parents drove down from New Jersey and were there to welcome us when we brought home the little guy with the big lump on his partially shaved head. After the angst of the past month, Sue and I were ready to start a new life as parents.

One year later, we were back at Johns Hopkins. This time, the patient was Sue. The incompetence or carelessness of the physicians at the Annapolis hospital not only nearly cost our baby his life, but now we discovered that they had done heretofore undetected damage to Sue's bladder. Once again, it was Johns Hopkins to the rescue. They repaired Sue's bladder in the summer of 1965 and, after nearly two weeks of recovery, she came home to take care of David.

There would be some serious consequences of David's trauma. He was a late bloomer in many functions—talking, reading, writing, physical coordination—and doctors and school psychologists kept up their guessing game called "diagnosis." They described his difficulties as "perceptual handicaps" or "minimal brain dysfunction" or "dyslexia." Any and all these scared the hell out of us. This went on for the first seven years of his life until Mother's closest friend, Dr. Jane Emele, read an article in a medical journal describing many of David's symptoms. The article stated that, in many children, the symptoms were indicators of vision problems and went on to discuss an emerging field called "developmental optometry" and its foremost expert, Dr. Morton Davis. As luck would have it, Dr. Davis was based in Maryland.

We took David to see him, and tests revealed that our seven-year-old son lacked many of the visual, motor, and language-development skills required to complete the visual-verbal matching necessary for learning. David had absolutely no depth perception, no bifocal vision (his eyes could not focus on a single close-up point), and vision in his left eye was suppressed. No wonder the poor kid struggled with learning! And now I understood how difficult it was for him to read, write, or catch a baseball.

Dr. Davis, a decorated World War II veteran, became an important part of our lives. He put David on a strict therapy schedule consisting primarily of eye-muscle training exercises. Our son exhibited immediate improvement. Sue and I took turns driving him to Davis's office in Columbia, about twenty miles away, twice a week for the next five years. At the end of this time, Dr. Davis declared him cured, and David's quality of life, and ours, improved dramatically.

CHAPTER SEVEN

Anchors Aweigh!

I was sitting in my Naval Academy office one day in June 1964 when the phone rang.

"There's a man here to see you. He says he's from the US government."

As I walked to the front office to meet him, I thought, *He's from the US government? We're at the US Naval Academy. We're all from the US government. What the hell is this about?*

The man introduced himself and asked if we could go for a walk. We exited Isherwood Hall and turned left toward the Severn River. It was a warm summer afternoon, and the day could not have been more serene. Newly arrived midshipmen were running laps around the soccer field while, out on the river, other plebes were learning to sail downwind in Knockabouts under blue and gold spinnakers.

"I'm with the Central Intelligence Agency," the man said after some time. Immediately, I began to search my memory for something I might have done to bring the CIA down on me. Nothing came to mind.

"We've checked your background very carefully," he continued. "We're putting together teams of young men with ideal physical, intellectual, and language skills to send back into their native Communist countries. We consider you one of the top candidates to parachute into Czechoslovakia."

"Parachute into Czechoslovakia? What would I do there?" I asked, astonished.

"You'd go in with a few other Czechoslovak-Americans to start a resistance movement. I can't tell you any more right now. Are you interested?"

My immediate reaction was an emphatic "No!"—perhaps even a "Hell, no!" Yet I hesitated before responding. I looked at the river, the sailboats, the playing fields. *I have a great thing going here. I have a wife, I have a son, and soon I'll have a doctorate. Why the hell should I do something so crazy?* Still, I vacillated.

"I can't give you an immediate answer to something so life-altering," I said. "I'll have to give it a lot of thought and talk it over with my wife."

"No!" he exclaimed. "You can take some time to think it over, but you can't say a word to your wife or anybody else. This is top secret information."

"Okay, I'll keep it to myself. But I need a week to think about it," I said as we turned back toward the engineering building.

He gave me his card which, sure enough, identified his organization as "US Government" and contained his phone number. As we parted, I asked when this mission would begin and how long it would last. He told me that I would find out "in due time."

I went home that evening and looked at my baby son and my beautiful wife. How could I leave them and risk never coming back? I thought about my job: Would I still have it when I returned, if I returned? And what of my doctoral studies—could I afford to interrupt my education? My parents had ordered me to forget the past and only to look forward. How would they react once they found out that I would be returning to the place from which we had escaped at great risk?

There were many reasons to reject the CIA's inquiry. But this was the time of the Vietnam War. Almost weekly I received devastating news of my former students, now Naval aviators or Marine Corps officers, being killed, wounded, or captured. I grieved for them and had a sense of guilt standing in front of my classes, talking about atoms and molecules, knowing that in a few months, this information would be useless to these young men. They would be fighting the enemy, and I would be safe in my classroom, facing another group of bright-eyed midshipmen who would soon be trying to stay alive in Southeast Asia. I opposed the war, and I disagreed vehemently with the so-called "domino theory" used to justify it. But I appreciated and honored the young people who were sent to fight. I felt remorseful about the fact that they were performing a patriotic act while I was doing nothing of importance for my country. I thought about my father and his heroic military career.

At the same time, I recalled the words of the man whom I had so admired, President John F. Kennedy:

"Ask not what your country can do for you. Ask what you can do for your country."

This was *my* country, and I had to answer its call and join its fight against Communist oppression. I called the CIA man and told him that I would volunteer for the mission, whatever it might be. I was invited to come to the Old Post Office building in Washington, DC.

I entered an office suite that had the trappings of an apartment; it was furnished with second-hand sofas, chairs, and tables from the Salvation Army. I sat on a sofa with broken springs while three men interrogated me for an hour about my life, family, political beliefs, friends, and future plans. Apparently satisfied with my answers, one of the men dropped a stack of newspapers on the coffee table in front of me. On top was an Italian paper, *Il Tempo*.

"Please read it out loud," he said.

"I don't know Italian," I replied.

"That's okay. Just start reading as best you can."

I began reading the lead article, doing my best to pronounce the words in the same manner as the parents of my many first-generation Italian friends in New Jersey. After a few minutes, I was told to stop. The men looked at each other.

"Are you sure you don't know Italian?" one of them asked.

When I assured him that I did not, he picked up the next newspaper from the top of the pile, the French daily, *Le Figaro*.

"Begin, please," he requested.

I did, with a similar result. I had taken two years of French in high school, and I occasionally entertained my friends in French-accented English, which they found comical. The intelligence guys were blown away by the fact that, although I did not know what I was reading, I sounded like a Frenchman, only minutes after I had sounded like an Italian. I glanced over to the pile and saw a copy of the Russian daily, *Pravda*.

"Do you know Russian?" one of my hosts asked.

"I took a year of it in Czechoslovakia when it wasn't an elective. I learned the Cyrillic alphabet, but I don't remember much else, although a lot of the words are similar to Czech."

Again I read, this time more slowly, as I converted the Russian letters before pronouncing each word. I passed the test and, finally, they handed me the Prague paper of the Communist Party, *Rudé Právo*. This time, I not only read flawlessly, but I was able to translate the article.

"That's terrific," said my original CIA contact. "You're a fine linguist, and that's important to the mission. Thanks for coming. We'll be in touch again shortly."

I walked out of the building confused and conflicted, wondering what this had been about, why I had not been told anything more about the operation, and what would happen next. I began to have doubts when I heard nothing for a month. Finally, I received a phone call and was asked to come to another Washington, DC, address. This one turned out to be that of a multistory apartment building off Connecticut Avenue. I took the elevator to the third floor and rang the bell. When the door opened, I was taken aback by the fact that the room, which appeared to be the living room, was devoid of furniture. There were just four bare white walls and a wooden floor. I was led to a rear bedroom, and my first impression was that I had blundered into a dentist's office.

A closer examination of the white, lacquered machine in front of me revealed that this was not a dentist's drill with its associated contraptions. I had never seen a polygraph machine, but I suspected that I was about to be subjected to a different kind of drilling. Soon, a guy in a white frock—looking every bit like a periodontist—came in, sat me down, and strapped me in. He informed me that he would be conducting a lie-detector test. First, he asked me a number of basic questions: my name, address, date of birth, Mother's maiden name. Then came a series of questions similar to those I had been asked at my previous session, including the names of friends and acquaintances in Czechoslovakia. Finally, he hit me with very personal queries. Did I enjoy sex? When did I first have sex? Did I ever have a desire to have sex with a man?

I was not accustomed to discussing such subjects with perfect strangers, and I was embarrassed to do it now. I hesitated before responding to each inquiry. The dentist/interrogator repeated the procedure three times, asking the same questions. I was concerned that he thought I was lying. When he finished, he took off my straps, thanked me for my cooperation, and told me I would be hearing from the CIA soon.

I returned to Annapolis and went about my daily routine, all the time wondering when I would be leaving for paratrooper training and what lies I would have to tell Sue and my superiors at USNA. Although I had no clue as to what was coming next, I assumed that the natural next step in weeding out people would be to eliminate those who would be unwilling or unable to jump out of an airplane. I was anxious, wondering if I would have the courage.

I waited—and waited. I let six weeks go by before I called the phone number on the card given to me by the man from the US government.

"The number you have called has been disconnected," said the recorded voice at the other end.

Finally, on October 5, 1964, I received a two-paragraph letter on plain paper, with no letterhead and no return address, that read: "We regret to inform you that, due to budgetary cuts, the program for which you were scheduled has now been cancelled." The writer who identified himself as "Special Activities Coordinator" thanked me and promised to get in touch "should these cuts be restored."

A few years later, not having heard back from my government friends, I felt it was safe to tell Sue of my experience. She stared at me in disbelief.

"You would have left us and jumped back into Czechoslovakia?"

"Well, I hadn't committed," I reassured her. "I only agreed to go through the process. I wanted to find out what it was about, and probably I wouldn't have gone."

But I knew differently. I had to admit to myself that, having read a few spy novels and seen some espionage TV shows, I was attracted to the adventure and perceived glory. The entrepreneur in me would never let me outgrow my overwhelming desire to do things that were risky and a bit out of the ordinary. Moreover, I felt an almost uncontrollable desire to prove myself a patriotic American. Another chance to do so arrived a year later.

The mid-sixties were not only years of great turmoil in America, they were also the apogee of the space race between the United States and the Soviet Union. My fascination with our space program continued, despite the disillusionment I had experienced at Douglas. Although the courses I taught at the Naval Academy dealt primarily with the structural analysis and design of airplanes, I managed to include a considerable amount of material on spacecraft design, as a means of vicarious participation. I had a year-long consulting stint with Lockheed Electronics at NASA Goddard, but the work was only indirectly related to sending astronauts into space. As a result, I was deliriously happy when, in early 1965, I received a letter from the National Academy of Sciences (NAS), encouraging me to become part of NASA's fledgling scientist-astronaut program.

During the early stages of the space race, the NAS had put pressure on the space agency to bring astronauts trained in science and engineering into the program in order to generate more returns from space missions. The scientist-astronaut program was born as a reaction to the Soviets' launch of *Voshkod 1*, its three-man crew promoted as the first "scientific passengers in space." The United States had to respond. Despite the fact that my acceptance into the program would have meant leaving the Naval Academy, displacing my family, and interrupting my PhD studies, I could not resist. How could I? My great grandfather had predicted that someday I would be a famous explorer. There was no greater challenge than exploring outer space. Once again, the inner entrepreneur and risk-taker seeking to gain respect won out over the sensible, responsible family man.

I submitted my application, and then passed a physical examination and a series of tests, including a harrowing ride in a centrifuge. Then, along with the other candidates I had met, I was amazed when NASA informed those of us who had made it through the first round that all scientist-astronauts would have to train and qualify as jet pilots. After swallowing hard, I decided that I was up to the task.

However, I was not prepared for the next setback. Several weeks later, I received a letter from NASA stating that, due to size limitations of the *Gemini* spacecraft, astronauts more than six feet tall were being terminated from the program. For a moment, I considered cutting an inch off the bottoms of my feet to qualify. My "career" as an astronaut was over before my first orbit.

The aerospace engineering faculty at the Naval Academy became a close-knit group of friends. We were referred to simply as "Aero." All of us were young, and all of us were new. Dick Mathieu and Bernard "Bud" Carson, both with doctorates from Penn State, arrived soon after me. Dave Rogers came from Rensselaer Polytechnic Institute with a sterling pedigree as an aerodynamicist. Andy Pouring taught propulsion courses. All of them were civilians. Naval officers, all of them aviators, generally stayed with us for two years before returning to the fleet. My closest friend among the Navy men was Commander Norm Deam, a flyer from Michigan.

We became known among other faculty as "the party group." Nearly every weekend, we gathered at one another's homes with our wives for cocktails, conversation, and singing—lots of singing. Bud Carson led the music sessions on his guitar and, after a few drinks, performed his amazingly accurate imitation of Louis Armstrong, complete with Satchmo's famous brow-wiping white handkerchief.

In the early days of Aero, I was the only civilian professor without a doctorate. This put added pressure on me to complete my studies. Besides peer pressure, there was the matter of attaining associate professor rank, gaining tenure, and earning more money. Accordingly, I began a routine that would become a way of life for many years to come: the hundred-hour workweek. In addition to teaching two flight structures courses, I was the faculty representative to the student chapter of the American Institute of Aeronautics and Astronautics. I supervised the research projects of several midshipmen, the most significant of which was one in the field of photoelasticity by a student named Bill Peters. Most rewarding, besides teaching, was my job as an adviser to a number of mids. Several became my friends, particularly those whom I assisted in receiving Guggenheim Fellowships to do graduate work at Columbia University after leaving USNA. One of them, Edward "Ted" Lewis, joined the Marine Corps. He served honorably in Vietnam, became a White House aide, was named deputy secretary of veterans' affairs, and eventually retired as a full colonel. We remain friends to this day.

To supplement my meager income, I took on consulting assignments, which included designing skis for the Head Ski Company, analyzing submarine structures for the Navy, and working on the far-out concept of a 50-knot sailboat for the Hydrodynamic Development Corporation.

My struggles with the University of Maryland's antipathy toward working students continued. I was running out of courses I could take toward my degree because most were scheduled during my workday. I had met several fellow faculty members at the Academy who had run into the same problem and had solved it by transferring to The Catholic University of America, located in Washington, DC, which catered to part-time students and offered most graduate courses in the late afternoon or evening. I visited CUA, met the man who would become my advisor, Dr. Michael Soteriades, and decided to make the move. It proved to be one of my better decisions.

CUA was perfect for me. The classes were small and the professors—some full-time and others adjuncts doing practical work by day—were both knowledgeable and approachable. I thrived in the environment, completed my coursework in January 1967, and passed my comprehensive exams.

In those days, nearly all US universities required PhD candidates in all disciplines to pass tests in one or two foreign languages. At CUA, one had to be able to translate several foreign-language pages of a text in the student's chosen field. I visited the dean's office in order to sign up for a language test, expecting to spend the next few months boning up on one of the "major" languages that had been the only ones approved at the University of Maryland: French, German, or Russian. I had already flunked the Russian test once at Maryland, but I was prepared to try it once again.

"You need one foreign language," said the lady behind the desk. "Which one do you want to be tested in?"

"What are my choices?" I asked, believing that I knew the answer.

"Any language other than English," she replied.

"*Any* language?" I inquired, incredulously.

"Yes."

"Okay," I said, expecting a laugh or a rejection. "Czech."

"How do you spell that?"

"C-Z-E-C-H." She entered it on the form.

Having just shortened my doctoral program by several months, I was elated. I returned a couple of weeks later in order to schedule my translation exam.

"We had a terrible time locating a faculty member who could

test you," said the dean's assistant, "but we found one. His name is Professor Connelly. He teaches mathematics, and he studied at Charles University in Prague in the 1930s."

The following week, carrying several Czech-language texts on structures and physics given to me by my parents' friend, Frank Cífka, I knocked on Professor Connelly's office door. I was greeted by a short man in his sixties with a cherubic Irish face and twinkling eyes.

"I've been looking forward to this," he greeted me. "I haven't tried to speak Czech in more than thirty years."

He thumbed through the books I placed in front of him. Then he surprised me.

"I'll tell you what," he said. "We're going to reverse the process of this oral exam. I'm going to see if I can translate and you're going to tell me whether I'm right or wrong."

With that, he began to read out loud in Czech, with a heavy accent and much difficulty with Czech letters such as "ř" and "ch" (yes, "ch" is a single letter in the Czech alphabet). Then he translated. After only having spoken English at home from the day we arrived in America, I was a bit rusty in my native language. But I was able to gently correct his mispronunciations and erroneous translations. Professor Connelly was enjoying himself, and I was having so much fun that I forgot I was the one being examined. This went on for two hours before Professor Connelly leaned back in his chair.

"This has been fun," he said. "It brought back so many memories for me. I loved Prague. Needless to say, you pass. And I thank you."

The foreign language requirement out of the way, I could concentrate on completing my dissertation, the subject of which arose from my consulting work for the Navy in which I had attempted to analyze the structural behavior of very complex reinforced aluminum plates used as decking in submarines. By now, I was eligible for sabbatical leave from the Naval Academy—either a full year at half pay or a half-year at full pay. I chose the latter because I could not afford a cut in salary. Then CUA's engineering dean made things even sweeter.

"I have discretionary funds," Dean Marlowe told me. "I'm going to use some of them to give you the Dean's Scholarship, which means a free ride for the next six months while you finish your thesis."

With this financial support from both Catholic University and the Naval Academy, I was able to devote all my time to writing, and I submitted the manuscript of "Behavior of Quadrilateral Orthotropic Plates" to Dr. Soteriades in April 1968. After a few edits, I was ready to defend my thesis before a committee of faculty members. But first, I was instructed to stop in the dean's office to fill out some forms.

"Which degree would you like, doctor of engineering or doctor of philosophy in engineering?" asked Dean Marlowe's assistant.

I was surprised by the fact that I had a choice, but responded without hesitation.

"Doctor of philosophy. I want a PhD."

"The D. Eng. degree is conferred by the College of Engineering, but the PhD is granted by the College of Arts and Sciences," she explained. "This is a mere technicality, with one exception. For your dissertation defense, your committee will have to have at least one member of the College of Arts and Sciences faculty."

This did not bother me in the least. On the contrary, I figured that such a person or persons would know nothing about the subject matter and would be incapable of participating in the grilling.

On the appointed day, I entered a classroom occupied by seven faculty members who stood between me and a doctorate. Six, including my advisor, were from engineering. The seventh was the arts and sciences representative, a professor of psychology.

The early questions were softballs, and I began to relax. Even as the degree of difficulty increased, I found it easy to respond either verbally or with equations on the chalkboard. For three hours, the psychologist sat in silence with my dissertation closed in front of him. I thought I was home free. Suddenly, the quiet man came to life.

"What do you mean by 'behavior'?" he nearly shouted, referring to the first word of my title. "These plates you're discussing can't 'behave.' They're inanimate!"

What the hell's with this guy? I wondered. *How do I respond to such a dumb-ass question?*

"'Behavior' is a term commonly used in our field to describe the response of various structures—beams, plates, shells—to loads," I finally stuttered.

The psychologist became more animated as he embarked on a long discourse, explaining why only living things could "behave."

Again, I attempted to argue my case and again, he parried with the same theme. Finally, Mike Soteriades came to my rescue. He explained that, while the psychologist might have been technically correct, the term "behavior" had been used by engineering researchers for many years and as such, had appeared in journals and academic texts. Thus it was perfectly suitable to be used in the title of my dissertation.

"However," Soteriades continued, "since you object, we'll replace it with something that is acceptable to you. Charlie, why don't you change your title to 'Bending of Quadrilateral, Orthotropic Plates'?"

What could I say at such a critical moment? "Sure, that's fine," I mumbled. The episode completely broke my concentration, shattered my confidence, put me on the defensive, and took me off my game. The final hour was a calamity. I was in a trance and recall only the fact that I failed to answer correctly most of the questions that followed.

When the ordeal ended, I shook the hands of all committee members, thanked them, and hightailed it out of the room, convinced I had failed the exam. My advisor caught up with me near the door out of the building.

"I'm really sorry, Dr. Soteriades," I blabbered. "I don't know what happened to me. My mind just seemed to shut down in there."

He patted my shoulder and, without a word, walked back toward the classroom where the seven men would decide my fate.

I drove home in a fog. When Sue returned from teaching her kindergarten class at the Naval Academy Primary School, I apologized to her for the fact that all her sacrifices had been for naught. I would join the ranks of hundreds of losers known as ABTs (All But the Thesis). Then the phone rang.

"Congratulations, Dr. Heller," said Dr. Soteriades matter-of-factly. "Well, you're not formally a doctor yet. That will come when they hand you your diploma. But you've earned it."

For the second time that day, I was in shock. Sue and I celebrated. My parents were ecstatic.

On a beautiful, sunny June day soon after, following a commencement speech by Senator Edward Brooke, and after all the other degrees had been handed out, the University's president announced, "And now The Catholic University of America will award the highest of all honors: the doctoral degree."

Sue, dressed in a bright yellow dress, held four-year-old David and stood alongside my parents and hers as I walked to the podium where I received my diploma inside a leather portfolio. Walking off the platform, I felt the strain of the past few years dissipating. Until that moment, I had been under enormous pressure—to take another step toward the elusive American Dream of success, to overcome another obstacle faced by immigrants, and to gain the prestige and respect that I craved. I had encountered many instances during which I wondered if I had reached my limit. At such times, my father's words of wisdom, imprinted on me when we arrived in America, rang in my ears: "Don't ever let anyone tell you that you're not capable of doing something. Put your head down, and go do it! And, no matter what you do, don't ever give up." I had done it. I had made my parents proud!

We arrived back at our house in Severna Park and everyone toasted me with champagne.

"Charlie, I didn't realize that your diploma would be written in Latin," said my mother, as my diploma made the rounds of our family.

I had been so overwhelmed by the day's events and my new status as "Dr. Heller" that I had not even looked at it. Mother held it open for me.

"That's a mistake," I said. "I was given a choice of having the diploma written in Latin or English. I told them I wanted it in English. I'll have it changed."

The following week, I drove to Washington and walked into CUA's Office of the Registrar.

"Good morning," I said to the lady behind the counter. "I received my doctorate last week, but a mistake was made with my diploma. When I filled out the form, I had requested that the diploma be in English, but it's in Latin." I handed her the certificate. She examined it and laughed.

"It *is* in English," she said.

I took the paper from her and began to read, "*Catholica Universitas Americae. A leone P.P. XIII literis apostolicis*—that's English?"

"Read your name," she replied.

"Charles Ota Heller."

"See, it's in English!"

"My name?" I asked, incredulously.

"Yes. All our diplomas are written in the language of the Church— Latin. But graduates have a choice of having their names written in either Latin or English. You chose English, and that's what you got."

Both of us laughed. As far as I was concerned, they could have written it in Swahili. *Dr.* Heller had his diploma. The Naval Academy promoted me to associate professor and made me the youngest faculty member with tenure in its history. I was thirty-two years old—and eager to take on the world.

CHAPTER EIGHT

Bite of the Entrepreneurial Bug

Like most immigrants, I came to America frightened. In high school, football coach Bill Flynn had called me an "immigrant freak" for kicking field goals soccer-style, instead of booting from straight ahead like "real Americans." I felt as though he had pissed in my soup. But I had already met many of my new countrymen who were not Flynns. They were willing to give me every opportunity to go wherever my talent and ambition would take me. That zeal would bring me a great deal of satisfaction, success, and—most importantly—respect. But it would also cause me to experience many moments of entrepreneurial terror and a crisis that would nearly break apart our family.

At the Naval Academy, I was an assistant professor at a very young age, only a couple of years older than some of my students. Before reaching my thirtieth birthday, I had been named "Outstanding Teacher" by the midshipmen. Now at thirty-two, I had my doctorate; I was an associate professor with tenure that guaranteed me a lifetime job in academia. But I wanted more.

I was at the forefront of a technology revolution as a researcher at the Academy and with my PhD dissertation work. We called it "interactive computing"—the use of time-shared computers for real-time communication between man and machine. This was a quantum leap over traditional "batch computing" of that period, wherein the user wrote a program, punched hundreds of so-called "IBM cards" (each representing one line of code) and submitted a boxful to be run on a huge mainframe machine to a central computing center. The following day, the center provided the user with a print-out listing his or her programming errors. In a complex program, there might be twenty to thirty mistakes.

After correcting the errors and punching new cards, the coder submitted a revised program. In the days that followed, the drill was repeated, until one had a running program. By contrast, *interactive* computing allowed us to perform such runs and corrections almost in real time. Sitting at a terminal connected to a large mainframe computer at some remote location via a telephone line, we communicated with the machine at the speed of electrons flowing across a copper conductor in the cable. Called "time-sharing," this technology constituted a change that would soon revolutionize engineering, science, and even manufacturing. With the Naval Academy as one of the world's largest users of time-sharing, I was lucky to be in the right place at the right time.

To use a computer in the early days, one had to write the program that would perform the task at hand—no "apps" created by someone else. In the technology world, we used a programming language called FORTRAN; accountants and bankers programmed in COBOL. Both were difficult to learn. It was no wonder that it often took days to hone a running program.

I was using the new interactive computing in my consulting work to design skis, sailboats, submarine decks, and antenna dishes. This put me on the cutting edge of technology. At the same time, this outside work supplemented my professor's salary and gave me a tantalizing taste of being in business for myself. I negotiated fees, scopes of work, and deadlines with my clients. I performed work according to the terms and conditions of my contracts. I got paid. This led me to think that starting and building a company would be a natural—and simple—next step.

When my boss, aerospace engineering chairman Dick Mathieu, approached me, I thought my dream of becoming part of something big was about to come true.

"Do you know Pat McBride?" he asked.

"I know he runs the computing center here at the Academy, but I don't know him."

"Well, Pat has a great idea," said Dick. "It has to do with applying interactive computing to education. He's thinking of forming a company and would like to have a few of us who've been involved with this technology join him."

Several of us met and heard McBride (not his real name) describe his idea for a company that would build software with content for a variety of elementary and high school courses. Lectures, supplementary materials, and tests would reside on a large computer. Schools would purchase terminals with which they would access this content via phone lines. Each student would work individually and at his or her own pace. This would revolutionize education, McBride said, because the brightest students would be able to advance quickly, while the laggards would still have the opportunity to learn without holding back the remainder of the class.

This was a groundbreaking concept in 1968. We were impressed. Despite the fact that none of us knew a thing about starting a business, we decided to form a company. We called it Bay Tech Associates and we elected McBride the CEO. The remaining six co-founders became vice presidents. We pooled our money—just enough to rent office space on West Street in Annapolis, pay time-sharing charges, and hire a small support staff. We purchased a few used two-drawer filing cabinets and some chairs. We went to a nearby lumber yard and bought a stack of cheap doors. We nailed the doors together in order to partition off several offices. Inside each cubicle, we placed a door across two filing cabinets to make a desk. We were ready for business.

We began to develop computer-based course content and informed school districts of our concept. Everyone seemed to love it. But we had no clue about packaging our software as a product, pricing it, promoting it, and selling it. We had a company top-heavy with guys who considered themselves equal partners/owners. Each of us had a different opinion about strategy and, due to our lack of knowledge and experience, none of us knew what he was talking about. It was a clear case of the blind leading the blind. We had an intriguing new product, but no one was willing to pay for it. Bay Tech was going nowhere.

At the same time, I was experiencing a personal crisis. With doctorate in hand, promotion to associate professor, and the honor of being the youngest tenured professor in the history of the Academy, I was full of myself. After years of balancing job, studies, consulting, and family obligations, I decided that it was time to kick back and enjoy the fruits of my labors. Conveniently, I forgot that Sue had shared the struggles with me and had supported me all the way. I wanted to be free of responsibilities, have fun at playing hot-shot entrepreneur, and bask in my newfound glory.

When our CEO turned out to be a practitioner of what would be called sexual harassment today, his victims—our female employees—sought me out to air their grievances. My ego stroked, I attempted to intercede on their behalf, thus creating a rift between McBride and me.

As their self-designated protector, I began to hang out with the single members of our staff—having drinks after work and sometimes meeting on weekends. I envied their freedom and carefree lifestyles. I began to wonder if I wanted to continue with the responsibilities of husband, father, and homeowner. Our marriage began to fall apart. Out of desperation, Sue consulted with my father and our family friend, Dr. Jane Emele. Afraid that Mother would have a nervous breakdown, no one informed her of the crisis.

Papa summoned me home to New Jersey. When he realized that he would be unable to convince me of the error of my ways, he extracted a promise from me: I agreed to undergo counseling sessions with Dr. Edward Panzer, a Polish immigrant, practicing psychiatrist, and a close friend of my parents.

I made three Saturday trips to Highland Park, New Jersey, to visit with Dr. Panzer. He was unable to convince me that I should curtail my foolish thoughts and actions. After each of the first two sessions, I jumped in my car and headed south, all the time planning to party with my new friends the following week. The third session was no different. After a couple of hours, it was coming to a close.

"What about David?" the psychiatrist asked suddenly.

"Oh, he's very young. He won't miss me," I replied.

Dr. Panzer hesitated, and then rolled his chair so close to mine that our faces were only inches apart.

"Yes, but will you miss him?" he asked.

I stared at his face and then at the ceiling. I contemplated the answer, but I did not have one. After a few minutes of deathly silence, I stood up, thanked Dr. Panzer, and left the office. By the time I passed Exit 6 on the New Jersey Turnpike, I was crying so uncontrollably that I had to pull over to the shoulder.

Yes, I would miss him terribly—and I'd miss Sue just as much, I admitted to myself. I resolved to apologize to Sue and promise to be a good husband and father once again. I spent the remainder of the weekend at home alone, waiting for Sue and David to return from Lady Lake, Florida, where they were visiting her parents.

After they returned on Monday, I read a bedtime story to David and then asked Sue to sit with me in the living room. I apologized for my actions of the past few weeks, explained that I knew that I had been wrong and promised to do all the right things in the future. I hoped that she would embrace and kiss me and tell me that everything was fine. Instead, she stood up and looked down at me.

"I'm glad you've come around," she said sternly. "But I don't trust you now. You'll have to earn that trust again." With that, she walked out of the room.

I spent the next few months earning my way back into her good graces. Eventually, we resumed our loving relationship. But it took time.

Once I removed the blinders, I also realized that I had been acting unprofessionally. I was a co-founder and vice president of Bay Tech. As such, I had an obligation to my partners to devote all my energies toward making the company successful. Instead, I had acted like an immature jerk, cavorting with our employees instead of leading them. With a clear head, I made a vow to myself: I would always treat my employees with respect and dignity. However, I would not "go native"—not be "one of them." In order to lead them, and maintain their respect, I would always keep a degree of separation between us.

In the meantime, Bay Tech continued to flounder. Then we got lucky. A group of executives from nearby Westinghouse had formed a company called Oceans General. They were intrigued by our technology (if not our business acumen). They acquired Bay Tech for a bargain-basement price. For once, all the principals agreed unanimously: It was time to bail out. We may not have achieved the goals we had set for ourselves at the onset, but I knew that I would build on the experience as I set out to chase entrepreneurial success.

CHAPTER NINE

Ready, Fire, Aim!

At first, I was disheartened by the Bay Tech experience and considered it a failure. I did not realize that most entrepreneurs lose money on their first venture, whereas I had actually come out a few hundred dollars ahead. More importantly, I had absorbed some valuable lessons.

First, I learned that a successful high-tech company must be market- and customer-driven, not technology-driven. In other words, having a beautiful, sophisticated, or even revolutionary product or service means nothing if there is no real need for it in the marketplace.

Second, I discovered that a company cannot be run by a committee, as Bay Tech had been. It may have partners, shareholders, and co-founders, but there must be only one leader. As writer and humorist Lewis Grizzard once said, "Life is like a dog sled team. If you ain't the lead dog, the scenery never changes." I wanted to be the lead dog.

Third, I learned that an entrepreneurial team in a start-up must be a compatible group of people with divergent skills. We had started Bay Tech with seven technology guys. None of us knew a thing about taking a product from the lab to the market, no one understood sales, and we had no clue about accounting or finance. We were too naive to realize it at the time, but this was a recipe for disaster. Of the seven co-founders, only one left his job to pursue Bay Tech business on a full-time basis. The rest of us continued to teach at the Naval Academy and to draw our paychecks every other Friday.

My fourth lesson was that there is a huge difference between the risk-averse person with a safety net and the entrepreneur who goes all-in—one for whom failure would be a personal disaster. The entrepreneur with "skin in the game" works harder, with more desperation, than the person who has a fallback position. For me, next time would be total immersion. I was not aware of it at the time, but being all-in would mean experiencing periods of entrepreneurial terror. *Will I be able make payroll? Will the bank repossess my house that I had pledged as loan collateral? Will the IRS shut us down because we failed to make a payment?*

Fifth, I learned the hard way to stick to something I knew. I was a good engineer, I was something of an expert at applying the most modern computer techniques to the design of products, and I knew a great deal about sports. I may have succeeded as an entrepreneur in any one of these fields. However, although I was a college professor, I knew very little about computer-aided education, as we had called our innovation at Bay Tech.

Having come from large companies and academia, I had entered the new world of entrepreneurship spoiled by the luxury of time. In both environments, there had been plenty of opportunity to delay decisions while meticulously researching every detail and holding endless discussions with colleagues. My sixth lesson was that this kind of procrastination led to death in the fast-paced world of young growth companies. Right or wrong, every issue required a quick decision. Often, it had to be "ready, fire, aim!" Successful entrepreneurs had to be right many more times than they were wrong.

Finally, I started on the road to understanding how to motivate and incentivize an entrepreneurial team. Members of the team have to be treated with respect—like colleagues rather than employees. I also came to the conclusion that people have to work for something more than a paycheck. I decided that everyone in the company—from the lowest-level clerk to a member of management—should be a co-owner. I would accomplish this by providing all team members with stock options. This would become a principle by which I would stand throughout my career, sometimes to the chagrin of shareholders and investment bankers.

Only a few months after we sold Bay Tech, I saw an opportunity to exploit interactive computing as a more efficient, accurate, and economical method to design objects such as automobiles, airplanes, ships, and buildings. Fortunately, I had six like-minded friends and colleagues.

In August 1969, we launched CADCOM (an acronym for Computer-Aided Design COMpany). I resigned from the Naval Academy and, without a salary, spent the next eight weeks seeking seed capital. Never having raised money before, I relied on networking and asked friends who had business ties for introductions to people with capital. The brother of one my co-founders introduced me to a few wealthy Florida angel investors who were ready to bet $300,000 (about two million in today's dollars) on an inexperienced team with a good idea.

Then the stock market crashed, and the investors and their money disappeared. As CEO, I managed to save the company by selling a controlling interest to a Florida firm called Ocean Measurements, Inc. (OMI). Co-founders Jack Cusack, Fred Klappenberger, and Ed Grant joined me on a full-time basis; John Gebhardt decided to keep his Naval Academy professorship for twelve months until we got the business off the ground; Al Adams and Dave Rogers, both USNA professors, chose to stay in academia and to work with us part-time.

I became a star student in the school of hard knocks, learning by first screwing up and then trying to do it correctly the second time. Accounting, marketing, sales, financial forecasting, shareholder relationships—I had not studied these disciplines as an engineering student. Now I wished I had. My fellow founders were able to fill only some of the voids. John Gebhardt had a doctorate in naval architecture and a background in academia. Fred Klappenberger had been a technician when we worked together at Bell Labs; he had recently completed his night-school degree and was a whiz in computer science, but he had no business background. Fred and John were in their late twenties, and I was thirty-three. Ed Grant had sales experience in the automobile industry. The gray hair in our founder group was provided by Jack Cusack, who was ten years my senior. Jack had spent most of his professional career in Washington as a program manager for the US Navy. As such, he understood the arcane world of government contracting, but he was no more savvy in the ways of "real-world" business than the rest of us.

It was a good thing we did not know the extent of our deficiencies, so they did not get in the way. Every day became an adventure, and we attacked problems with real passion and a belief in our ultimate success.

While the initial investment by Ocean Measurements was a lifeline, we found the relationship with our parent company con-fining. OMI was cash-starved and stood in the way of some of the innovative work we wished to undertake. We wanted to be our own bosses. It was our good fortune that OMI's other subsidiaries got into financial trouble while CADCOM, though not yet profitable, was the only member of the corporate family generating significant revenues.

I was named to the OMI board of directors and was invited to my first board meeting, held at a swanky resort in Palm Beach, Florida. I was in awe of the luminaries with whom I shared a conference table—the president of Mobil Oil, the heir to the Greyhound Bus fortune, and the CEO of a utility company, among others. But my first OMI board meeting turned out to be my last.

After the first day's meetings, all the directors went to their rooms to change into swim trunks and then we met our wives for drinks by the large hotel pool. I downed my Mai-Tai and pulled Sue into the pool with me, anxious to tell her about my day of hobnobbing with the titans of business. I began to regale her with my story when someone tapped me on the shoulder.

"Charlie, can I talk to you for a few minutes?" asked Bill Jeffries, the chairman of the board.

"Of course," I replied and asked Sue to wait for me to return.

Bill walked to the side of the pool, and I followed. I had expected to hear more of the same kudos I had heard about my company's performance throughout the day. But the serious look on Bill's face foretold something else.

"I'm afraid I have some bad news," he said. I wanted to stick my head under water so that I would not have to hear what was coming next. "As you've heard, our other companies are losing money at an alarming clip. We need cash to keep OMI going. And you guys, CADCOM, are the only viable entity we have. We need to sell you."

I was perplexed. *Is this good news or bad news?* I wondered. *On the one hand, we'll be getting rid of our masters who are holding us back from doing what we want. On the other hand, how do we know that the company that buys OMI's piece of us will be any better?*

"Do you have a buyer, Bill?" I asked after I recovered from my initial bewilderment.

"No. We decided to leave it in your hands. That way, you guys can find the partner you'll be happy with."

Wow! This could be a hell of a deal.

"Thanks for your confidence, Bill," I said out loud.

"At tomorrow's meeting, we'll come up with some general parameters for the sale," he said before he pushed off the wall and swam toward his wife.

The next day, the OMI board gave me a simple set of instructions. "We'd like to get a half million dollars for CADCOM—all cash and as quickly as possible."

"We'll try," I promised. *Is that all these guys think we're worth? This will be a piece of cake!*

On the flight home, I made a list of potential buyers, most of them computer hardware companies to whom we could add our software expertise as well as some software giants that could use our expertise in computer-aided design in order to expand their markets. The next day, my enthusiastic partners added several names to the list.

That was the easy part. Next came the arduous process of writing a business plan. Putting on paper a strategic plan and financial projections was not an easy task for a greenhorn entrepreneur. It was something I would do several hundred times in my future life, but this one—the first—was time-consuming and overwhelming. I consulted a couple of entrepreneurship books and relied on the advice of a couple of friends. A month later, we had a document and were ready to show it to potential buyers who, we were certain, were out there waiting for a fabulous deal: a majority stake in an up-and-coming outfit with revolutionary technology.

What followed was phase two of the entrepreneurship learning process: Nothing ever turns out the way one expects, and everything takes five times as long as one anticipates. I would have opportunities to verify this many times throughout my career, but at this point, it was something new and unexpected. I made calls that were never returned. I wrote letters and received no responses. I passed the word to a few friends, and they made inquiries on our behalf. When five of these turned into positive leads, I learned the value of networking. Although we got as far as negotiations with three of the companies, my partners and I concluded each time that we would not be happy with any of them.

One stands out in my mind. Bradford was a large services company in New York City, one that handled stock transfer transactions for hundreds of publicly listed firms. I was informed that its CEO, a man named Saul, was intrigued by our software expertise and that he wanted to explore a merger. I was aware of Bradford's reputation as a market leader, and I was anxious to pursue the possibility. At the same time, I was concerned because I had been warned that the CEO could be gruff and obnoxious. I planned my strategy for dealing with him as I rode the train to New York.

The opulence of Bradford's lobby made it clear that I was in the big time. I felt intimidated as I rode the elevator to the executive floor. But Saul's secretary greeted me with a smile, and I regained my nerve as I sat in her office sipping a cup of black coffee. Finally, a buzzer informed her that it was time to lead me into her boss's office. She opened the door and ushered me in.

"This is Dr. Heller, here to see you, sir," she said and exited. Saul did not look up from scribbling something on a yellow legal pad. I sat down and still could not see his face. Only his short, black, gray-speckled hair showed as he continued to write. I stared at him, waiting for a word of welcome. Beyond him, I could see the Empire State Building and a portion of the New York skyline. I did not dare look away for too long as I waited for the great man to acknowledge me. Five minutes, which seemed like five hours, went by. Still nothing. At this point, my nervousness began to turn to anger, and I decided to walk out. I stood up, made for the door, and finally his head moved.

"What the fuck do you want?" he growled.

I was struck dumb. It took me a while to gain my composure and to explain who I was and why I was there. The conversation that followed, which was quite civil, revealed that Saul had known who I was and why I was in his office all along and that this was his method for gaining the upper hand in a negotiation.

After several visits back and forth between New York and Annapolis, we received an offer from Bradford. But the sour taste of the experience of that first meeting never left me. My partners and I decided that if Saul treated us this way when he was wooing us, he would treat us even more harshly once his firm became majority owner of CADCOM. We declined the offer.

Now, we were out of merger candidates. The good news for us was that, since I had been designated by the OMI board to have sole decision-making power over any acquisition, we were in control. We could reject anyone we did not like—and we had. Our attorney, a gentleman named Fred Israel with an office in Washington, advised us to do a private placement of stock representing a 52 percent piece of the company, the proportion owned by OMI. We learned that this meant determining a price of our stock and then selling shares to friends and family. We set out to do this and, in three months, raised enough money to make OMI an offer. The total was a hundred thousand less than the parent company had wanted, and a lot less than we thought we were worth, but OMI had little choice. They accepted. With the assistance of our friends and family, we now owned our company.

The final chapter of our flight to freedom was played out in a suitable venue. Fred Israel's conference room on Washington's 17th Street was being used by one of his partners on the day of the closing of our deal with OMI. But Fred had a client in the same building, and they allowed us to use their meeting room. The client was Ringling Brothers, and their room was modeled after a circus tent—complete with striped, slanted tent poles and miniature trapezes. The setting was appropriate for a group of guys who had clowned their way through their first year in business and their first major financial transaction. But we were free and in control of our destiny.

The money we raised from our new shareholders paid off OMI, but it did not provide us with operating capital. We were generating sales, but not enough to cover our expenses. In order to generate much-needed cash, we branched out from our core CAD software business and performed engineering services in structural analysis, pollution abatement, and naval architecture. We brought in Joe Reynolds, who started as a one-man band that provided loss and accident analysis to insurance companies and law firms. Eventually, he would build the business into a profitable forensic engineering division of CADCOM. (A few years later, it would become a standalone, major public company called FTI Consulting.)

I brought in my closest friend from our days in California, Don Griffin, to be head of engineering and to provide adult supervision to a growing, young, and sometimes undisciplined professional staff. Don, his wife Sue and their children settled in Round Bay, only a couple of miles north of our home in Rugby Hall. Our families resumed their friendship, and we spent a great deal of time together. The Griffins became Uncle Don and Aunt Sue to our son David, and we became Uncle Charlie and Aunt Sue to Clayton, Lenore, and Melissa.

Prior to starting CADCOM, I had a naive vision of the life of a CEO of a high-tech company. I pictured myself sitting with my feet on my desk, dreaming up new, innovative products and services that would disrupt the way things worked and improve people's lives. It came as a shock to discover that running a growing start-up was much more mundane and hectic. I found out that a growing company devours cash, and we were always short of it. For that reason, I spent more than half my time searching for funding.

We received two loans, totaling $750,000 (about five million in today's dollars), from Maryland National Bank. The loans were guaranteed by the Small Business Administration and by second mortgages on the homes of the four principals of CADCOM: Jack Cusack, John Gebhardt, Fred Klappenberger, and me. Over time, we paid off the loans, although we discovered how bureaucratic and ridiculous the SBA (by its charter a friend of small business) could be. After we paid the loan down to $90,000, we requested to have one of our principals released from the personal guarantee. After all, the combined value of our four homes was at least ten times the amount we owed. Our partner was getting divorced and the house was part of the settlement. The government agency refused.

The search for funding continued. We sold more stock privately, we aborted an Initial Public Offering when the stock market tanked, and we brought in some venture capital.

Understanding that we needed to fill some holes in our collective knowledge, and to expand our network of contacts, we put together a strong board of outside directors. The first to join was Jack Geils, who had been my mentor for many years and who had been promoted from vice president of Bell Labs to vice president of the parent company, AT&T. Bryson Goss, a financial planner, had a wide network of high-net-worth individuals who constituted a pool of potential investors in CADCOM. He and his wife Linda were Sue's and my good friends; we played golf and took skiing vacations together. He was next to go on the board. Knut Aarsand was a former investment banker and a serial entrepreneur; he brought to us knowledge of the financial markets and contacts with potential customers. Jeff Crum, inventor of a wire-drawing system used by steel companies throughout the world, made a substantial investment in CADCOM. Taking advantage of an IRS tax shelter, Jeff purchased a computer that he leased to us for use by a small subscription-fulfillment company we acquired.

The board was rounded out by two CADCOM insiders: Jack Cusack and me. I was double-hatted as CEO and board chairman.

My closest friend at the Naval Academy had been Bernard "Bud" Carson, a fellow professor of aerospace engineering. Despite my urging, Bud had no interest in leaving academia and joining our company. However, he came around often and got to know several of our engineers and software developers. Bud became my eyes and ears. He enjoyed having a drink or two at the end of the work day and often joined some of our employees at their favorite Annapolis watering holes.

"The guys in the trenches are wondering what you do all day," he informed me one day. "I tried to explain to them that the guy at the top does a lot of things that are not visible to the staff and that he takes a lot of risks. But they're skeptical. You need to have a talk with them."

This exchange was a wake-up call for me, one that led to the inception of monthly all-hands company meetings. At these sessions, my management team and I brought everyone up-to-date on the state of the company—the good, the bad, and the ugly—and we answered all questions. The feedback we received was very positive, attitudes changed almost immediately, and all of us felt very much part of the same team. Yet, there was more work to be done.

"Your backroom guys are a bunch of Communists," Bud Carson said to me a few weeks later. "They think you guys who run the company are obsessed with profitability. They don't understand why."

It was time to innovate. At the next all-hands meeting, I gave a perfunctory lesson on cash flow. Seeing how bored my audience was while staring at monthly columns of collections from sales and investments, offset by expenditures for rent, travel, marketing materials, and other seeming trivial items, I found a way to get their attention.

"Take a look at the biggest number of dollars going out each month," I said. "It's listed under the line item 'wages and salaries.'

When the number of dollars we spend is bigger than the number of dollars we collect, guess what we have to do?"

Silence.

"Yeah," I continued. "We either cut salaries or we lay off people. Guys and gals, that's how a market economy works. If we can't make a profit, we won't have a company. We'll all be out of work."

Everyone understood—even the "Communists." Following that session, we developed an informal orientation program, during which our chief financial officer taught every new employee the rudiments of accounting: how to read a profit and loss statement, a balance sheet, and—most importantly—a cash flow report. I would continue the practice of regular all-hands meetings and finance orientations throughout my career as head of companies and organizations.

The experience also taught me a lesson about maintaining frequent personal communications with our team members. I became a practitioner of "walking the ship": rather than staying isolated in my office on "executive row," I made certain to take time at least once a week to pop in on people in their offices and talk about everything from their current projects to last night's ballgame to their families.

One of my dreams was to be in business someday with David, our only child. By now, he was twelve years old and a computer whiz. Very few kids his age had ever seen a computer, much less had one of their own. David was the proud owner of one of the early Apple models and spent night after night in our basement, staring at the tiny green monitor as he wrote programs. When he began to work for CADCOM after school and in the summer, I was concerned that the "Communists" in the back room would resent his presence and accuse me of nepotism. Instead, I was ecstatic by their reports of David's positive contributions to our development efforts.

CADCOM continued to grow. While sales climbed steadily, some months we showed a small profit, and other months we lost money. Our reputation as a technology innovator far outstripped our actual size. With nearly two hundred staff members (including part-timers), we became one of the largest employers in the Annapolis area. But we needed something radical to jump-start our quest to be a big-time player. That "something" came seemingly out of nowhere.

CHAPTER TEN

Focus-Pocus

In early 1972, CADCOM was nearly three years old, and we were battling to make a profit. There were times when making payroll was a struggle and, while our employees never missed a paycheck, we co-founders sometimes had to forego monetary compensation. Instead of real money, the amounts owed us found their way into the company's books as "deferred salary." This is an accounting term for a technique used by highly compensated executives who wish to delay payment until future years for tax reasons. In our case, "deferred salary" meant simply, "we can't afford to pay ourselves— yet."

Our financial difficulties stemmed from the fact that we were trying to introduce a revolutionary technology into a market with a huge amount of inertia. It is a long-standing fact that people are comfortable with that which they have or what they are doing and are reluctant to change. Geoffrey Moore, a Silicon Valley marketing strategist, would write a book about this phenomenon and call it "the chasm." Those companies that managed to cross their customers' chasm of inertia became successful; those firms that never got past the few brave early-adapters failed. The great majority of high-tech start-ups fall into the latter category—and never emerge.

Without understanding this "chasm theory," we knew that we had to find another way to generate more cash while continuing to push the computer-aided design revolution out to the world. The low-hanging fruit for us were federal government contracts. We took on several computer-related tasks for NASA, but most of our work was for the Department of Defense. Jack Cusack had worked for the Navy for many years before joining us, and we rode his contacts to a variety of assignments. Because of John Gebhardt's expertise as a naval architect, the majority of the work pertained to ship design, and this allowed us to build a small, high-level team in this field.

The Vietnam War was raging. The Navy was running small patrol boats up and down that country's rivers, engaging the Viet Cong who located their enclaves on or near river banks. These riverine patrol boats had a high mortality rate. (They would become famous years later when John Kerry, skipper of one of these boats, would run for president of the United States.) Many were hit and either sunk or damaged beyond repair. The Navy found it difficult and expensive to continually replace them. They decided on a solution: build them in Vietnam, with native materials. A Navy representative came to Annapolis in order to engage us in a discussion of candidate materials.

"Let's start with this," he said. "There is no fiberglass, steel, or aluminum in Vietnam. What are the alternatives?"

We looked at each other, all thinking the same thing: *These are the common boat- and shipbuilding materials. What else is there?* Then John Gebhardt, who could always be counted on to come up with the most innovative idea, spoke up.

"How about concrete?" he asked. "There are people building ferro-cement boats in all parts of the world."

"Yeah, but 'ferro' in ferro-cement refers to steel reinforcing," said the Navy guy. "Concrete has great compressive strength but no tensile strength. The steel supplies that. You've got to have both in a boat hull."

Again, we looked at each other, puzzled. And again, John's brain was operating on all cylinders.

"This may sound crazy, but I'll tell you about a material native to Vietnam. Don't they have a lot of bamboo?" he asked. The Navy man nodded, and John continued: "I bet that bamboo has good tensile properties and we could use it as reinforcing rods in the cement."

"That's an intriguing idea," said our visitor. "But I see a problem with using concrete. It's just too heavy. They may be okay once on the water, but the sailors and Marines often have to carry them a long way through the jungle to the rivers. And once in the water, these boats have to move fast. They can't be heavy."

Until then, I and the others in the room had been mere spectators. Now, I could see John looking at me as if to say, *Okay, you're the structural engineer. What's your solution?* The truth was that, while I had three degrees in civil and structural engineering, I had only analyzed and designed spacecraft and airplanes. And we did not make those out of concrete. I was out of my league. However, I had to say something. We needed the business.

"There are ways to make concrete lighter," I said. "Can you give us a couple of weeks to research this, and we'll get back to you?"

"You guys have come up with the best idea I've heard so far," the Navy man replied. "Check it out and we'll get together again."

After the departure of our potential customer, Jack Cusack spoke up for the first time. His seemingly innocent comment would, for the next three years, create more buzz than CADCOM had experienced in its brief history and, at the same time, lead us down a hundred blind alleys.

"I know an Englishman who has a company called Fillite, which is peddling a material to the Navy that he claims has some amazing properties," Jack told us. "He says it has incredible resistance to pressure and weighs practically nothing. I think he calls these things cenospheres, and he's trying to get the Navy to use them as buoyancy material in submarines. I wonder if we might be able to mix this stuff with cement to make concrete lighter."

Never one to pass up a chance to try something new, John Gebhardt picked up on the idea and ran with it. Jack ordered a batch of cenospheres from Fillite, and the detached garage behind John and Judy Gebhardt's house on Conduit Street in Annapolis became a laboratory of sorts. John used orange-juice cans as molds for cylinders that we sent to a lab for compression testing. Experimenting with a variety of mixtures, we determined that we could achieve the same compressive strength as traditional concrete with a thirty percent weight saving. Moreover, the surface of the material could be made smoother than concrete, and the stuff was easily workable and could even be cut with a saw.

I was well aware of the fact that the worst sin a small high-tech company could commit was to lose its focus. We were a software company. What the hell were we doing even discussing lightweight concrete? Yet the prospect of bringing a revolutionary material to the world was so exciting—and potentially so lucrative—that we had to pursue it. We decided to brand the material with a piece of our company name and called it Cadcrete. We trademarked the name and filed a patent application.

In the meantime, Congress voted to end the war in Vietnam. So much for the Navy's interest in building better riverine patrol boats. This did not deter us one bit. When we informed our board of our invention of a new, game-changing material, the directors went gonzo. During past board meetings, they sat passively as we gave progress reports about our mainstream business: software. They seldom commented or offered suggestions. Now they came to life.

Jack Geils, who was vice president of AT&T, informed us that its subsidiary, Western Electric, had lost a major supplier of wooden telephone poles. Maybe poles could be built of Cadcrete? Bryson Goss introduced us to Don Hood, CFO of McLean Construction Company, which agreed to make a prototype pole. Another director brought in Wise Chemical Company, which wanted to form a joint venture to line concrete pipes with Cadcrete in order to help meet Environmental Protection Agency standards. Yet another director connected us with a shipbuilding company that took an interest in manufacturing fireproof Cadcrete bulkheads that would replace panels containing recently outlawed asbestos.

Suddenly our small company, whose core competency remained computer-aided design software, was stretched to its limits. Our financial situation had not changed, so we did not have the funding necessary to pursue a major research and development effort. Experts informed me that to bring a new material to market in the 1970s, one needed at least a million dollars. Since we were about a million dollars short of that requirement, we attempted to enter into cooperative ventures with two materials giants, Johns Manville and Certain-Teed. Both turned us down because they viewed Cadcrete as a potential competitor to their own materials. So we continued our own poor people's R&D effort.

At the same time, we began to look at the economics of cenospheres. They are the buoyant component of fly ash, a residue generated by the combustion of coal. In coal-burning power plants, fly ash is captured by electrostatic precipitators or other kinds of filters. These filters are continuously washed with water that flows into holding ponds. The heavy parts of fly ash, such as carbon and iron, drop to the bottom, while the surface of the ponds is covered with a white material— the only buoyant components of fly ash. These are cenospheres: tiny hollow spheres made of glass and containing nitrogen gas. It is this gas that provides them with great compressive strength and very low density (about 0.5 grams per cubic centimeter). Our problem was that Fillite was the only supplier of these precious little spheres. They purchased them in the UK, wet from the pond, and could ship them to us in containers at $48 per ton, with one-quarter of that ton being water. This was simply uneconomical for the large-volume opportunities we were investigating. We would have to find our own sources of supply.

Consequently, Jack Cusack and I visited American Electric Power Company in Charleston, West Virginia, and the Tennessee Valley Authority, both producers of thousands of tons of cenospheres that sat on the surfaces of their holding ponds, unused. They were more than willing to part with a material they considered a pollutant, at no cost to us. All we had to do was take it away. So, now this young software company that knew little about bringing a new building material to market also had to confront the fact that it knew even less about harvesting, drying, shipping, and storing the basic stuff it needed to make Cadcrete. We decided that we would be able to outsource the supply part of the cycle to others. On we marched.

Of the opportunities presented to us, the most lucrative was that of the telephone poles. Western Electric (an arm of AT&T) installed 300,000 to 500,000 poles each year. In August 1973, we made a presentation to the president of Western and his management team. We stressed Cadcrete's light weight, long life, strength-to-weight ratio, and resistance to rot. Playing devil's advocate, the Western Electric team questioned costs and pointed out issues they would have with having to make changes in erection, handling and climbing equipment, as well as the hardware at the top of a pole. Despite that, Jack Geils informed us that we should expect a $50,000 contract for building a single prototype. We were encouraged because, if AT&T was impressed by the prototype, millions of dollars would follow.

We became even more excited when Bryson Goss called to say that he had spoken with an energy company in Pennsylvania, GPU Service Corporation, and they, too, seemed very keen on Cadcrete poles. They were purchasing 40,000 wooden poles per year from a Mexican supplier who was going out of business.

Unfortunately, the phone pole opportunities vanished almost as quickly as they had appeared. Western Electric's contract for a prototype never materialized because its engineers became concerned about "long-term durability problems from loads imposed during transportation." Almost at the same time, GPU found new suppliers for wooden poles in Finland and Russia.

But other options continued to fly at us from all sides. There were bus shelters in Rochester, New York, boats in Maryland, prefab buildings in New Jersey, swimming pools in Delaware, refrigerated buildings in Virginia, pipes for the Trans-Alaska pipeline—and even coffins. USAID called and asked if we could build a prototype boat for Bangladeshi fishermen. At one point, we were asked whether Cadcrete sheds, if erected in national parks, would stand up to bear attacks. As in all cases, our answer was, "Oh, yes. Sure."

We spent weeks, even months, following up on leads. A company named Ferro-Boat in nearby Deale manufactured a sailing dinghy from Cadcrete, based on a design by John Gebhardt. We called her *Crete*, and she was featured in a national boating magazine.

While all this was happening, I was desperately trying to find funding for CADCOM. I met with bankers, angel investors, and venture capitalists. I went to Wall Street, where Jack Geils introduced me to the managing partner of a boutique investment banking firm called Hay, Failes & Company. While I described CADCOM's software business to him, the banker nearly went to sleep. When I told him about Cadcrete, he jumped out of his chair and shouted, "Let's take this puppy public!"

He told me that the potential of a new, lightweight material made with a pollutant aggregate was a story that would resonate with Wall Street. It would let us raise several million dollars from the public markets. When I boarded the LaGuardia-Washington National shuttle, I was on cloud nine. Our financial worries would soon be over, and we could concentrate on building the company. But then, as I stood at the bar in the rear of the *Constellation*, sipping a vodka tonic while flying over the farms of South Jersey, reality began to settle over me.

How in the hell am I going to handle this? I wondered. *Not only will I have to manage CADCOM's main line of business and the development and marketing for Cadcrete, but I'll have to devote the majority of my time to preparing for an IPO. A hundred hours a week in the office won't be nearly enough.*

Somehow, I managed to juggle all the balls at once, with great assistance from my fellow co-founders. Fred Klappenberger ran the software effort, John Gebhardt continued the Cadcrete development, while Jack Cusack and I prepared the massive documentation required to take the company public. All of us participated in marketing and sales because we had fired our VP of Sales after he failed to bring in significant business after nearly two years on the job.

As all this was going on, the country was slipping into a recession.

Not only was this affecting our sales efforts, but I began to worry about our IPO. When the stock market tanks, one of the first victims is the initial public offering market. Our underwriters assured me that stocks would remain strong despite the state of the economy, so we marched on. After spending thousands of dollars in attorney and accountant fees, we filed with the Securities and Exchange Commission. Two weeks later, we received a comment letter containing fourteen items to which we were asked to respond. We were nearly finished with our reply to the SEC when our underwriters' prediction proved to be wide of the mark—very wide! The stock market crashed. We did not bother to complete our response and, instead, notified the SEC that we were withdrawing our IPO.

I was forced to return to our former potential sources of funding. But with a lousy equity market, it was no time to attract either angel investors or venture capitalists. I turned back to our friends at Maryland National Bank, who had previously provided us with a loan of $400,000, guaranteed by the Small Business Administration and collateralized, severally and jointly, by second mortgages on the homes of us four co-founders. Once again, we were bailed out by MNB, this time with $350,000, and again with our personal guarantees.

When I told my non-entrepreneur friends that I was on the hook for $750,000, they were stunned. They were happy receiving their regular paychecks from their employers, did not work one-hundred-hour weeks, and took no risks on behalf of their companies or agencies. How could I possibly sleep at night, and why did I place my family at risk? They did not understand the entrepreneurial mind and the determination to succeed. I did not try to explain a phenomenon my partners and I called "entrepreneurial terror:" losing a great deal of sleep while worrying about meeting next week's payroll and about closing the next deal in order to keep the company alive.

The typhoon of Cadcrete opportunities continued to blow at us from every direction. Jack Geils of AT&T and Ed Nolan of Farinon Electric, both personal investors in CADCOM, kept bringing new opportunities in the communications field. Sandia Corporation inquired about building parabolic antennas from Cadcrete. A Saudi Arabian firm asked about building 400,000 dwellings in the desert. Mountain Bell wanted to erect equipment shelters in remote areas. Mobil Oil called to find out if we could supply Cadcrete for oilfield applications. The opportunities made our heads spin.

But there was one major problem. Everyone requested pricing data and a detailed list of Cadcrete properties: compressive strength, density, shear strength, water absorption, freeze-thaw resistance. These would be reasonable requests if we were developing the material in the traditional way—with certified laboratories conducting a major testing program for a variety of formulations of Cadcrete. They would be logical if we had a group of experts who could track the economics of the entire supply chain of cenospheres. Instead, and unbeknownst to the outside world, we were still making samples in John's garage using orange juice cans as molds while flailing around unsuccessfully trying to find a way to purchase huge quantities of the little white spheres cheaply. We had no idea about the economics, and we had incomplete information about the material's properties.

For me, the tipping point arrived one evening when I came home after another long day at the office.

"You know those little Cadcrete cylinders we've been pulling in and out of the freezer?" asked Sue before I had a chance to put down my briefcase.

"Of course," I answered. We had been conducting a poor-man's freeze-thaw test by having the samples undergo alternating cycles of three days in the freezer and three days at room temperature while noting the number of the cycles in a notebook.

"Well, you're not going to like what's happened," Sue said.

She led me into the kitchen where, on the counter, she had placed five cylinders she had removed from the freezer. Three of them had deep, 45-degree cracks.

"The damn things are cracking after only five freeze-thaw cycles, and this is with no loads on them!" I exclaimed. "How in the hell can we recommend this stuff to anybody who'd use it someplace where there's a big temperature variation?"

The next day, I gathered our management team. We discussed this and all the other issues we were facing. Nearly three years after we had begun this journey, we made a wise decision. We had received a patent on Cadcrete, and now we would try to sell it to someone who had the knowledge and deep pockets to bring the material to the market.

Unfortunately, the world had moved on. Some companies were beginning to use fly ash and other additives to make lightweight concrete, and, while potential users of Cadcrete were as excited as ever, materials manufacturers were not. Johns Manville, Certain Teed, 3M, and Wise Chemical—among others—had lost interest. It was time to give it up.

On October 4, 1976, I received a call from an executive at AT&T who inquired about the possibility of making insulated Cadcrete panels for small telephone equipment buildings.

"I'm sorry," I told him. "We're out of the materials business. We're exclusively a software and computer services company."

Thus ended the saga of Cadcrete—with one postscript: John Gebhardt kept *Crete*, the Cadcrete dinghy, on a beach on Spa Creek in Annapolis. One night, someone stole *Crete*. All that was left of our effort to become a producer of a material that would revolutionize the world were a few broken cylinders that had been molded in orange-juice cans.

Our management team—and perhaps even our board of directors—had learned a lesson, one I should have remembered from the Bay Tech blunder: Stick to your core business and avoid undertakings you do not understand. We had allowed ourselves to be suckered by the promise of huge sales and profits, but we had neither the capital nor the knowledge to execute a plan. We were a software company; what in the world were we thinking when we decided to bring a revolutionary building material to the market?

CHAPTER ELEVEN

Decision Time

Most young technology companies have a common problem: a shortage of funds. When they have trouble selling their products or services, there is insufficient cash to cover expenses. When they gain acceptance in the marketplace, there is a need for rapid growth. This growth is fueled by cash, of which there is seldom enough.

A retail store or a restaurant can survive by maintaining the status quo. For an entrepreneurial high-tech company, however, holding things constant leads to certain death. To survive in a highly competitive environment, we must grow at a rate considerably faster than the market and substantially faster than our competition. Moreover, the most important assets of a technology company are its employees. These exceptional people need to learn, grow, and take on increasing responsibilities, and they must be fairly compensated. These needs can be satisfied only by a growing company, one that offers new and expanding challenges to its people—and good pay.

At CADCOM, we financed both the down times and periods of rapid growth with bank loans guaranteed by the US Small Business Administration and co-guaranteed by the personal assets of the four founders. Nearly nine years into our venture, the technology we had helped to pioneer—computer-aided design—finally had crossed the chasm and was being adopted by industry. We had been a leading player at the outset of CAD, but now we were just a small niche player, sucking the tailwinds of firms such as Auto-trol, Computervision, and Intergraph. We needed a large infusion of capital to compete with these guys.

The Initial Public Offering (IPO) market was not available to us because the now-recovered Wall Street insisted on greater sales and profitability than those we were posting. Venture capital had retreated and was being doled out only to sure-fire deals. We were too risky for the VCs, and angel investors did not have sufficiently deep pockets to satisfy our needs. Without discussing it with my partners, I began to formulate a new strategy.

In the past, we had been pursued by several companies who wished to acquire, or merge with, us. Now, with CAD systems having been accepted by the markets, with our sales up, and with small but positive profitability, I posited that we should be an attractive acquisition candidate for someone. Over time, I convinced myself that this was our best course. This, despite the fact that I had carefully studied a book titled *Welcome to Our Conglomerate, You're Fired!* At the same time, I knew that my partners had been opposed to overtures from companies such as Syscon, Operations Research, Inc., Nesco, and Universal Analytics in the past because they had not liked either the people or the proposed deals.

All of us, myself included, were reluctant to give up control of our destiny and the freedom of running the company our own way. But this time, things were different—at least for me. My dream had been to build a large company that would maintain its entrepreneurial culture. Reluctantly, I concluded that we simply could not get there on our own. Now I had to convince my co-founders to go along with me.

In February 1978, we convened a two-day off-site meeting to discuss the company's future. Deliberately, I set no agenda, required no preparation, and announced that no minutes would be kept. I asked my three partners to come without preconceptions, without concerns for the everyday problems we faced in the office, and with open minds. We would not construct SWOT (Strengths/Weaknesses/Opportunities/Threats) charts or take notes. We would speak freely and without inhibitions. This would be an informal, bare-our-souls session during which we would formulate a vision for the future of

CADCOM, an entity that was more than a business to all of us. We had poured our hearts and souls, our energies and brainpower, as well as our material possessions into our baby. Now we had to face reality and consider all possible alternatives as we faced an uncertain future.

Jack, John, Fred, and I walked the beaches in Ocean City, Maryland, for two days. The weather was pleasant for midwinter, the breaking waves proving a soothing background refrain. An occasional gust of wind kicked sand into our faces, causing us to pause, wipe our eyes, and clear our minds.

After hours of back and forth about where we had been, where we wanted to be, and the options for getting there, we reached a unanimous conclusion: We needed to find a partner, a larger company with greater resources. That company would not only need to possess the funding and contractual vehicles that we needed desperately, but it also had to be one that would not change our corporate culture of collaboration, mutual respect, and having fun. Such was the broad-based goal we established. Next would come the hard part: I would have to go out and find that partner.

CHAPTER TWELVE

Welcome to Our Conglomerate

A couple of months after our decision to find a merger partner, our plans nearly changed. Earlier that year, we had bid on a large—multimillion, multiyear—contract for a variety of engineering and computer services for the David Taylor Naval Ship Research & Development Center (DTNSRDC). The contract was set aside for a small business. Since we lacked some of the specified requirements, we brought in a large firm, Operations Research, Inc. (ORI), as a subcontractor to fill those voids. We thought we had a decent chance to win the contract on the basis of our previous work for DTNSRDC, but we were well aware that the competition was stiff.

When the Navy called to inform us that we had won, we were overjoyed. A huge weight was lifted from my shoulders: *Our financial problems are over! We don't need to get acquired by anyone! We're ready to build CADCOM into a major player!* We celebrated in the office and out—but not for long.

While we were gearing up to start work as soon as the contract would be signed, we were informed that one of the losing bidders had filed a protest against the award. The protester was ManTech International Corporation, a Maryland firm that was developing a reputation as a formidable player in the government technical services sector, and one that was quickly growing out of the "small business" categories (some based on the number of employees, others on sales) for various types of work, as specified by the feds.

ManTech's chairman, George Pedersen, was known for his expertise in strategizing to win government contracts and for using the rules to his full advantage. Following the award of the DTNSRDC contract to CADCOM, Pedersen requested a copy of our proposal, read it, and found a fatal semantic glitch. It consisted of the use of one word that nearly sank our company—"partner." In the proposal, we had made the mistake of calling ORI a partner, rather than a subcontractor. Pedersen filed a protest stating that since CADCOM and ORI were partners, adding together the sales of the two firms placed us in the "large business" category and thus made us ineligible for a contract set aside for small businesses. Despite our argument that the wording was an unintentional error and that the proposal was structured such that we were the prime contractor and ORI the subcontractor, the Navy bought George Pedersen's story. We were disqualified. ManTech International, which had come in second in the scoring, was awarded the lucrative, multimillion-dollar multiyear contract.

My management team and I were devastated. It was back to the original plan: Find a larger company with greater resources and merge with it. As luck would have it, a couple of weeks after we lost the contract that would have propelled CADCOM to new heights, I received a surprise phone call.

"Hello, Charlie," said the friendly voice of my enemy, George Pedersen. "We need to talk. You guys know DTNSRDC inside and out, and you have the skills we need to perform most of the tasks in the contract. We don't. We'd like to figure out a way to get you involved."

Swallowing my pride and submerging my anger over the injustice of the contract award reversal, I agreed to meet. After all, we needed the sales.

I walked into our lunch meeting the next day with a chip on my shoulder. I did not have to like the guy with whom I was dealing. This would be strictly business. Then came my second surprise: I liked the red-headed man from the moment we shook hands. He was affable and courteous as he apologized for the protest. He explained that his firm protested all procurements it lost whenever they believed that something was improper and could be used to reverse the decision. They had been surprised to discover a flaw in our proposal.

As we sipped our cocktails, I discovered that George Pedersen was a self-made man in the tradition of great American entrepreneurs. The son of Norwegian immigrants, he had been orphaned at an early age and raised by his aunt and uncle on Staten Island. He completed one year of college before dropping out due to a lack of money and going to work. In 1968, he and a partner, Franc Wertheimer, started a company to provide technical services to the Department of Defense. Eventually, ManTech of New Jersey became ManTech International and moved its headquarters to the Washington, DC, metropolitan area.

Just under six feet tall, George dressed impeccably in three-piece designer suits and wore a gold watch and Gucci shoes. Although he ran a ten-million-dollar company, he had the aura of a Fortune 500 CEO as he navigated the Washington Beltway in his Cadillac in search of new business. George and I were the same age, pursued similar interests and ambitions, and had the same type-A personalities. We found immediate rapport.

When our discussion turned back to business, George hit me with another surprise. Rather than offering to subcontract bits and pieces of the large Navy job to us, he made a more radical proposal.

"We should merge our companies," he said. "We're looking to broaden our technical base and to expand into some commercial markets. I know that you guys have a great technical team and excellent management, but you could use government contractual vehicles and the resources of a bigger company like ManTech. One plus one would equal three."

I downed my drink before asking a few probing questions about how such a merger would work. Although it became obvious that "merger" was a polite term for "acquisition," I was intrigued.

Because our companies seemed to dovetail perfectly and the two leading players got along well, I came away from our three-hour lunch buoyed by the prospect. I promised to get back to George after speaking with my partners.

That evening, I presented the proposition to Jack Cusack, John Gebhardt, and Fred Klappenberger. All were still stung by the protest that blew away our future as an independent company. Following a number of cynical and caustic comments, we thought back to the strategy we had devised on the wind-driven beaches of Ocean City: We needed a larger partner. *Why not ManTech?* we asked ourselves. I was tasked with negotiating a deal with George Pedersen.

We managed to work through the details of the merger in six weeks. CADCOM would become a semi-autonomous division of ManTech International and our shareholders would receive cash for their stock according to an earn-out formula based on future sales. With no obstacles in the way, we scheduled the formal closing of the deal for a Thursday afternoon in late August 1978 in the office of ManTech's Washington lawyer.

From the outset, the meeting had felt like a sheer formality with the two parties' lawyers exchanging papers and George Pedersen, Franc Wertheimer, and I signing them. Seated on opposite sides of the long, gleaming conference table, we exchanged pleasantries while drinking coffee and munching on cookies. After months of sleepless nights and stressful days, I was relaxed and happy now that CADCOM had a clear future and I would be relieved of the never-ending task of chasing after money. I even had high hopes of getting away from the meeting early enough to miss the rush-hour traffic out of Washington in order to make a six o'clock skippers' meeting at the Annapolis Yacht Club. I paid little attention to the lawyers' conversation as I thought ahead to the weekend and the national championship regatta that would begin the next morning on the Chesapeake Bay. We would face tough, world-class competition for our Catalina 27 sailboat, *Serene*.

The meeting was almost over when the lawyers reached the final stage of the process: the certification of financial statements. I listened halfheartedly, but heard CADCOM's attorney, Barry Berman, say something about contingent liabilities. George Pedersen's scream penetrated the cool air of the conference room.

"Contingent liabilities! What contingent liabilities?" he shouted from across the table and threw down the cookie he had been chewing. The cookie exploded and its shrapnel scattered across the documents. The redheaded man's ears and cheeks turned the color of his hair and the stare of his blue eyes seemed to penetrate the up-to-now calm exterior of Berman, who was sitting by my side.

Barry tried to explain that we knew of no such problems and that using the word "contingent" simply allowed for the possibility of a currently unknown issue to be dealt with after the closing.

Suddenly, I saw a different George Pedersen from the affable guy I had come to know and like. His face resembled an overripe tomato about to split. He pushed back his chair with such ferocity that it smashed into the wall behind him. He grabbed the papers in front of him and shoved them into his briefcase.

"Franc, let's get the hell out of here. This deal is dead!"

With that, the two ManTech partners headed out the door, followed by their lawyer, Mike Golden. Berman and I stared at each other in total disbelief. Finally, Barry broke the silence.

"They're bluffing," he said. "Let's go home and sit back until we hear from them."

As an outside party, our lawyer could afford to be blasé about what had just transpired. But I had a company to save and run. I drove back to Annapolis in a daze. Suddenly, the weight of the world was back on my shoulders. What would my partners say? How would I explain this to our outside shareholders? We had been preparing our employees for life after the merger for weeks. What would they think? How would we survive going it alone, since we had suspended all other fundraising efforts?

I missed the skippers' meeting and, over the weekend, sailed the *Yachting Magazine* National Offshore One-Design Regatta in a funk. As skipper of the Catalina Yachts' "factory boat," I did not do well by my sponsor. We finished somewhere in the middle of the pack.

The entire time, I stewed over one question: Was George Pedersen bluffing? When I did not hear from him for a week, I was convinced that his blowup had been no charade. Then, the first week of October, I received a call from Franc Wertheimer. Playing the role of the "good cop," he suggested that we "start from the beginning." We did and proceeded to negotiate the deal all over again. This time, we closed. The terms were a bit more skewed in ManTech's favor than the first time. It was January 1979.

Had George Pedersen been bluffing so that he could drive a better deal? He would never admit that to me, even after we became close friends and business partners. But by then, I had been on George's side in many negotiations—and I knew the answer.

———◆———

The sale of CADCOM to ManTech was structured as an "earn-out." The amount to be paid CADCOM shareholders (in cash) was dependent upon our sales over the next two years. There were two formulas for converting annual sales to the pay-out: one for sales from federal government contracts and another for our more profitable commercial business. The latter came primarily from our forensic engineering division, which performed loss and accident analysis for insurance companies, utilities, and law firms.

CADCOM became a division of ManTech, and I was its executive director. The integration went relatively smoothly. In order to do business with agencies of the federal government, a company needs contractual vehicles. Obtaining such contracts is a tedious, time-consuming process involving strategic pricing to beat out the competitors, adjusting to numerous changes in the requests for proposals by the customer, and withstanding protests after awards. Prior to our merger, we had many government customers—Navy, Coast Guard, Maritime Administration, NASA, Bureau of Standards (today, NIST)—who were anxious to take advantage of our offerings in computer-aided design, software development, and various areas of engineering. However, while the feds were sometimes able to award us contracts on a sole-source basis, we failed to win enough of the competitive ones because larger firms offered lower prices. Too often, our potential customers were unable to engage us, despite the fact that they preferred our technical expertise.

ManTech came to our rescue. George Pedersen was a master at responding to the needs of the feds and winning large "omnibus" contracts and versatile basic ordering agreements. Now, these were available to us and the government side of our business thrived. Under a Department of Transportation contract, we developed the CADSHIP workstation—a computer with graphics capability into which we built a program to evaluate ships whose owners were applying for US Coast Guard certification. This opened up a world-wide market to commercial shippers who desired to fly the American flag.

We wrote software for NASA's robotics effort and assisted the space agency in the development of the most massive structural analysis (finite element) program of all time, NASTRAN. Our engineering staff assisted the Navy in its ship pollution abatement projects, and it provided support to a team developing new materials for ship construction.

Back in 1969, when we started CADCOM, our promotional materials announced to the world that we were in the business of "transferring technology" from advanced to more mundane industries. Without realizing it at the time, we had invented a term— "technology transfer"—that would become prominent for years. Following the ManTech merger and the availability of the parent firm's contracts, we began working with the newly named Navy Technology Transfer Office, with operations in Washington, DC, and China Lake, California. We searched for inventions that originated in Navy laboratories and made recommendations about those we deemed to have commercial applications. Our most distinguished writing guru, Arlene Swerdloff, developed and edited the Navy's *Tech Transfer* newsletter, a publication that described and publicized these promising intellectual properties.

Arlene, a native of Baltimore, had previously worked for Senator Howard Metzenbaum on the Hill and thus was knowledgeable about the workings of Washington. However, that experience did not prepare her for dealing with our Navy customer. A quirky guy named Perry drove Arlene (and me) mad with his off-the-wall ideas, ever-changing requests, and an attitude that civil servants are superior human beings to the rest of us. I was grateful to Arlene for having the patience to indulge the man. He shredded the adage that "the customer is always right." But we needed the sales, so we pretended that he was.

We opened offices in Norfolk, Virginia, and Panama City, Florida, both of which provided engineering support to nearby Navy offices. We took over from another ManTech division the management of a large office in Lexington Park, Maryland, near the Naval Air Station Patuxent River.

In the summer of 1980, ManTech acquired a Raytheon business unit that performed intelligence work for the US Army. I found a kindred spirit in Dick Pomroy, the head of this organization that, like CADCOM, became a division of ManTech. Over the next couple of years, Dick and I, along with Les Wright, president of a ManTech subsidiary called TMC, met regularly for lunch to discuss one another's issues and problems and to provide each other with suggestions and moral support.

The first three years of coexistence went relatively smoothly. There were a few clashes of culture, and ManTech's top management was not always happy with our progress. Some months our sales were up, other months they were down. But the overall trajectory was ascending, so everyone was satisfied. When George Pedersen called me one day in June 1982 and asked me to join him and Franc Wertheimer for lunch, I expected a routine "state-of-the-company" discussion, similar to many such meetings we had held previously.

"Interest rates are killing us," said George, after we ordered glasses of Pinot Noir. "The prime rate is 22.5 percent!"

"I know," I replied. I was well aware that, unlike our old CADCOM where we used a combination of equity and debt, ManTech relied entirely on bank loans to finance its growth.

"The profit we're allowed to make on government contracts just doesn't cut it in this climate. Borrowing at these interest rates and working for the feds, it's almost impossible to be profitable." I wondered where the conversation was headed.

George took a sip of his wine before continuing. "We need to get the company into more profitable markets. We don't want to get out of the government business—that's our bread and butter. But we have to change the mix and be in more commercial markets."

"Right now, the only nongovernment business we have in the whole company comes from your forensic engineering group," Franc added. "We need more."

"We must have some pockets of innovative stuff in the company," said Pedersen. "The trick is finding it, deciding what has commercial merit, and then figuring out how to get it to market and make a profit on it."

I sipped my wine and looked from George to Franc, expecting to hear a plan of action now that the problem had been presented. I did not have to wait long.

"Franc and I have decided to put you in charge of this effort," said George. "We're going to ask you to start searching throughout ManTech and hopefully find a few pearls that we can exploit. We can make new divisions out of them. We can make them into separate companies and fund them with venture capital. We can even sell them to other companies. Whatever might be appropriate and help make us more profitable."

"How do I do this and run CADCOM?" I asked. "I wouldn't want to do a half-assed job of both."

"No, you'll have to devote all your time to the new job," said Franc. "Someone else will run CADCOM."

"Do you see that as a permanent situation or would we put in an interim head of CADCOM?"

"Permanent," Franc replied. "We'll make you vice president for corporate development of ManTech and move you to the Rockville office."

Oh, my God! I thought. *I'm going to have to commute from Annapolis to Rockville!* I had gotten comfortable with a ten-minute drive to work; spending two hours a day on the Washington Beltway had little appeal.

"You're going to spend a lot of your time traveling," George said, reading my mind. "So, it really doesn't matter that much where your office is located. But if you're not going to be running CADCOM, you really should clear out of there so that your replacement can have free reign. And you and I are going to spend a lot of time together, strategizing. So it will be best to have our offices close together."

George smiled and gripped my arm. "Listen, this is a hell of an opportunity for you and for ManTech. We're going to make it worth your while. You're the best guy in the company for this job, you're gonna do great, and we're gonna have a lot of fun doing it together."

My resistance melted. I had been running CADCOM for thirteen years, I had engineered a merger that assured its future and provided security for its employees, and things were going pretty well. It was time for a new challenge. Besides, I liked and respected George, and I was intrigued by the idea of working closely with him. What the hell! The daily commute would not be so bad.

"I'm in," I told George and Franc. "Do you have someone in mind to take over CADCOM?"

"No," said Franc. "That's your call. I think I know who your pick will be, but take a few days to think about it and then give us your recommendation."

When I came home that evening and told Sue, I was surprised by her reaction. I had expected some pushback, but she said simply,

"That sounds like a nice opportunity for you. I think you need a change. And I don't think David and I will see less of you than we do now. You never get home before eight in the evening anyway, so that should stay the same. You'll just have to get up a little earlier."

The following day, back in my CADCOM office, I began to contemplate the idea of giving up the reins. After so many years, it would be difficult. And who should succeed me? Naturally, it would have to be one of my fellow co-founders: Jack Cusack, John Gebhardt, or Fred Klappenberger. We had been through a lot together, we had risked everything to get the company off the ground, we were a good team, and we were close friends.

Yet I was conflicted. On a page in my journal, I wrote down the prerequisites I felt were needed to lead the organization: leadership, maturity, management expertise, financial knowhow, technology smarts, lots of energy, and the ability to work with peers who ran other ManTech divisions and subsidiaries. Each of my partners had excellent credentials and met nearly all the requirements. But no one met them all. I closed my office door, pulled out my brown-bag lunch, and, as I chewed on a salami and cheese sandwich, I made my decision.

"Do you and Franc have some time this afternoon to talk about my successor?" I asked George Pedersen on the phone.

"Sure, come on over anytime."

The three of us sat down in George's office. Jaye Free, the company's executive administrator, served us coffee.

"So, do you think Jack Cusack will do a good job?" asked Franc, smiling because he was certain that he had predicted my choice.

"Well, yes, Franc. He'll do a great job—doing what he has been doing."

The two ManTech principals looked at one another, and then at me.

"Actually," I said, "the person I believe will be best at running CADCOM is Don Griffin."

George jumped up, grinned, and shook my hand. "We agree with you completely. We just didn't think you'd ever pick anyone but one of your co-founders. Don's a great choice. We've been very impressed by his work, his management style, and his attitude. Done deal! Let's announce the changes right away."

Making the decision had been relatively easy compared to the task of announcing it to my partners, particularly Jack Cusack, who—ten years my senior—had always been the wise mentor to our younger team members and a confidante to me. First, I broke the news to Don Griffin. After expressing surprise, and then delight, he began to worry.

"Everybody knows we're best friends. My kids walk in here and call you Uncle Charlie. You brought me here from California after you guys took all the financial risks. How is this going to go down with Jack, John, and Fred?"

"Don, I won't deny that you're my best friend," I said. "But please believe me when I tell you that my decision had absolutely nothing to do with our friendship. You're just simply the best person for the job. I may have to take some shit, but I have to do what's best for CADCOM. And I'm doing it."

Despite Don's fears and my apprehension, the meeting with my three co-founders went smoothly. If any of them resented my selection, they did not show it. All of them expressed their respect for Don and confidence in his ability to lead the organization. I knew they were being good team players and probably felt some bitterness toward me. But I appreciated their cooperation. I announced the changes to our entire CADCOM team and concluded with: "I'm not going anywhere. We're still part of the same company." But I knew that I really was going somewhere—and that things would be different. While I presented the change as a positive move for everyone, I felt a great deal of sadness as I gave up "my baby."

Over the weekend, with the help of Sue and David, I packed up everything I had gathered over thirteen years as CADCOM's head and moved most of the boxes to a room on "executive row" at ManTech's headquarters in Rockville. Out of my element and preparing to go into uncharted waters, I faced the future with some trepidation.

CHAPTER THIRTEEN

Entrepreneur Once More

$\mathbf{M}$anTech's operating philosophy was to open offices next door to its customers, wherever they might be. Although the majority of our people were in the Washington, DC, area, there were outposts scattered throughout the country, most of them "outside the fences" of government facilities such as Wright-Patterson Air Force Base in Dayton, Ohio, and the Naval Shipyard in Norfolk, Virginia. I hit the ground running, visiting many of the locations and interrogating managers, engineers, and computer scientists, trying to unearth some intellectual property gem that could be developed into a product or service to be sold in the commercial marketplace.

Steve Schlosser provided ideas about improved automated test equipment. Lou Ray had devised a new way to write and evaluate software. Others in the company had ideas, some mundane, others far-out. One by one, I examined them all, looking first to see if the technology was solid and unique, and if it was, performing due diligence on the size of the market and the costs and speed of entering that market. I prepared a report on each concept, ending with my conclusions and recommendations. George and I met to discuss each potential business scheme. We rejected all of them. Prospects appeared dim.

Even the CADCOM division presented a problem. Our computer-aided design software was running on Apollo workstations, and we were selling it unbundled from the hardware for $60,000. The price point was comparable to those of our competitors, namely, the pioneers of the CAD world such as Computervision and Auto-trol.

Then in 1982, seemingly out of the blue, a new name appeared on the competitive horizon—Autodesk. A Silicon Valley start-up, it offered a CAD package of limited functionality for around $17,000. It was called AutoCAD, and it precipitated a great deal of chortling in our industry.

"This thing is a toy," we laughed. "Who would want to buy something that has less than 70 percent of the functionality of our software?"

It turned out that many customers were more than happy to accept a more modest, no-frills product at a 70 percent discount on our price. Small companies and architectural offices for whom CAD software had been prohibitively expensive in the past could now afford to automate their design work. The rest of us stopped laughing. We reduced our prices, but it was too late. Autodesk had captured a huge segment of the market. While CADCOM still had a viable product for the large, sophisticated user, its future prospects were limited. It failed to meet the requirements of the spinout I was seeking for ManTech.

Then, as had been the case so many times in our years together as business partners, "Dr. John," as John Gebhardt was known among CADCOM's technical staff, came to the rescue. John had visited a ManTech facility that was producing operating and service manuals for M.A.N. Corporation, a major German manufacturer of buses and trucks. M.A.N. had won a bid to sell its trucks to NATO and, as part of the contractual requirements, had to provide such manuals in English. It had subcontracted that task to ManTech.

"You wouldn't believe this operation," John exclaimed when we met in his Annapolis office. "There's a hangar with rows and rows of about a hundred people. About eighty of them are typing. Another ten are drawing pictures—line drawings showing how to change a tire or how to pull a spark plug. Then, the last ten people in the back of the huge room are cutting and pasting together the text and drawings, making up the pages of the manuals."

"Wow!" I said, anticipating John's suggestion.

"If we could convert CAD2D from software for engineers and draftsmen to software for illustrators, we could replace all those artists. And if we could marry the word processing with the illustrations into a single package, we'd have a hell of a product for publishing. There's your idea for a new commercial business!"

John sat back and waited for my response. I knew nothing about the publishing world, but I found the concept exciting.

"There must be a huge market out there," I said. "Just about any publication that combines line drawings with text—car owners' manuals, product instructions, product bulletins, all sorts of specs and manuals. There's almost no limit! But is it technically feasible? We know how to do the graphics, but how about the text?"

John had done his homework. "There are companies out there now, like Interleaf, TeXet, and a few others. We could strike a deal with one of them and integrate their text processing with our graphics capability."

I presented the idea to George Pedersen. He bought it immediately and we began to strategize. We would structure a ten-person software development group with John Gebhardt as its head; we would organize it as a division of ManTech with me double-hatted as its executive director; and we would begin an effort to raise money for it.

"What we'll do," announced George, "is find outside capital from angel investors or venture capitalists, and we'll spin this baby out with ManTech owning a third of it."

It was my job to write the business plan that would serve as a sales document to attract these investors. The old CADCOM software products—CAD2D, essentially a drafting system, and CAD3D, newly developed computer-aided design software with three-dimensional capability—would become property of this new division, as would the Illustrator software that we would begin to develop for the publishing market. We placed the arbitrary value of $1 million on the entire package—and we called it "Intercad."

As exciting as the new venture seemed at the start, it proved to be full of frustrations, as George and I spent the next eighteen months searching for funding. A spreadsheet of venture capitalists and private investors I had contacted contained more than 120 entries by the spring of 1983. Several of the names had transitioned from possibilities to hot leads. But, whenever we found an interested party, we came up against the same single barrier.

We held several productive meetings with one of the largest and most prestigious venture capital firms on the East Coast, New Enterprise Associates. NEA's iconic partner Frank Bonsal, liked the technology and the prospects of a large market. He insisted that I become part of the deal and be the CEO of the spun-out company. I was excited by the prospect of once again running a firm, especially one funded by a top-notch VC firm. We held our third meeting in the CADCOM division's Annapolis office, where John Gebhardt and the nine other members of the Intercad division resided. John made a presentation consisting of the current state of our technology, and George and I provided more information about marketing and sales strategies.

Everyone was smiling and appeared to be on the same page as we descended the stairs on the way to Frank's car in the parking lot. Suddenly, Frank tugged at my arm, pulled me close and whispered, "You get ManTech out of this deal, and we're ready to go."

As he, George, John, and I walked outside, I processed his words. He was telling me that ManTech's insistence on owning one-third of the new company was unacceptable to NEA. He wanted them out altogether and was not even suggesting a negotiation of a smaller piece for the current owner. As Frank drove out of the parking lot in the direction of Baltimore, I knew the deal was dead. I was becoming more and more disheartened by the impasse we always reached when it came to the issue of equity distribution. At the same time, I was getting more restless. Every suitor wanted me to come along as the head of the spun-out venture. These gestures went beyond stroking my ego; they reawakened in me a desire to strike out once more as an entrepreneur.

Next, we held an extended "mating dance" with Atlantic Ventures' managing partner, Buck Bennett. We met countless times. Each time we seemed to be getting close to a deal, Buck and George butted heads about the same issue: ManTech's future involvement.

"I've had it with these venture capitalists," George finally announced over lunch. "Let's see if we can find a corporate investor who might have a strategic reason for getting involved. Maybe Intercad's products would expand their markets or they would help them sell their existing products."

When I told John Gebhardt about the new thrust, he suggested Honeywell. Their workstations were not gaining much acceptance in the marketplace. If we could port our CAD and future Illustrator software over to their computers, Honeywell would have a brand new, huge market. The idea made sense to me, and apparently, it excited the large company's management as well.

We began serious discussions with one of its vice presidents. When we reached a point at which we appeared to be near a deal, the VP had a heart attack and died. We started all over with another vice president. Incredibly, following several weeks of positive discussions, he, too, passed away. Although by now, Honeywell's top management must have considered discussions with us to be the kiss of death, they introduced a third, live VP into the negotiating process. John and I flew to frigid, wintry Minneapolis, Minnesota, where Honeywell was headquartered. We were a day early, so we drove to Lake Minnetonka, where we watched huge ice boats sailing at breakneck speeds across the lake. It proved to be the only fun we would have on the trip.

George Pedersen joined us the next day. We met with VP number three in a fancy conference room overlooking a city that resembled the capital of Siberia. The new man knew nothing about the previous discussions we had held with Honeywell and was totally ignorant about Intercad and our business. We started from the beginning, repeating the same presentation we had given the previous two late executives.

"Sounds interesting," he said when we finished. "I'll get back to you in a few days."

We walked out of the place deflated and angry. We would be starting from scratch.

"Let's forget this whole thing," said George as we drove toward the airport. "I'm sick and tired of this shit. Honeywell is a dysfunctional company. And venture capitalists are a bunch of jerks. It's over. Let's just run Intercad as a division of ManTech and stop this other nonsense."

John and I found it impossible to argue. The Honeywell experience had been a time-consuming, frustrating farce. Venture capital was out of the question due to ManTech's insistence on maintaining a significant ownership. There seemed to be no way to achieve our original plan.

Yet by now I had become obsessed with spinning out Intercad and being an entrepreneur once again. I longed for the freedom of running a start-up once more, without the shackles of corporate bureaucracy. I decided to pursue other possibilities on my own, without consulting George, until something real appeared on the horizon.

Les Wright, one of a trio of "co-conspirators" who used to meet with Dick Pomroy and me to bitch about ManTech and to discuss our mutual problems, had left the company. He became vice president of a firm called ERC International, headquartered in Tysons Corner in Northern Virginia. ERCI was in the same business as ManTech—primarily a "Beltway Bandit," providing services to the federal government. However, it differed from ManTech in that it had recently gone public and thus offered a much greater financial upside to its management via stock options. ManTech, on the other hand, continued to be very much a private firm, with all of its stock held closely by CEO George Pedersen, President Franc Wertheimer, and a few outsiders who had helped to get the firm started in New Jersey. Although Les was now a competitor, he, Dick Pomroy, and I continued to meet for lunch every month. We had become friends and mentors to one another. Of course, Les and Dick had been following the saga of our attempts to spin out Intercad. They were aware of my frustrations with ManTech's intransigence, the resistance of the investment community, and the dysfunction of large companies like Honeywell.

"I've talked to Jack Aalseth about Intercad," Les informed me during lunch in October 1983. "He's very interested. After the IPO, ERCI has a lot of cash, and it's looking for some sexy technology to jazz up its image. I'll be glad to introduce you, if you want."

Of course, I wanted. A week later, Jack Aalseth, ERCI's CEO, John Scanga, the company's senior VP, and Les and I met for lunch at the Pook's Hill Marriott in Bethesda, Maryland. Two hours into the meeting, Jack was prepared to do a deal.

"Do you think ManTech would be willing to sell the Intercad division outright?" he asked me.

"I don't know, Jack," I replied. "George Pedersen's insistence on holding onto a third of the spun-out company has been a detriment to several potential deals so far."

By now, I had fallen under the spell of Aalseth and Scanga. Their description of how life would be for my colleagues and me in a newly public company was enticing. Instantly, I felt myself switching allegiances—from ManTech to ERC International. I became a conspirator on the side of ERCI, trying to make this deal happen.

"I think it's possible that George is so tired of all the crap we've experienced in trying to get this thing funded that he might entertain a deal, if the price is right," I said. "Let me run the idea by him and I'll get back to you."

Driving back to ManTech headquarters, I became more and more apprehensive about the forthcoming conversation. By now, George, his wife Marilyn, and Sue and I had become good friends. The Pedersens bought a condo in Annapolis, I sponsored George for membership at the Annapolis Yacht Club, we dined and sailed together, and I convinced George to buy his first boat: a ten-foot sailboard. (Some years later, after ManTech became a half-billion-dollar company, George would buy his second boat—this one more than ninety feet long, with a permanent captain onboard.) But I was also aware of George's volatile temper. He had once slammed his fist through the plaster wall of my office in a fit of anger. I expected the worst this time. But my redheaded friend surprised me.

"Do you really want to do this?" he asked after I told him of ERCI's interest.

"I do, George."

"You could have your choice. Stay in your current VP position or run and build the Intercad division within ManTech. I wish you'd think it over." In the coming months, I would think about George's suggestion often, and I would wish that I had listened to him.

"George, there's really nothing to think over. I need to get out and run an autonomous company. ERCI would just be a stockholder in Intercad, and we'd be on our own. You're an entrepreneur, probably the best one I've ever known. I'm sure you can understand. On top of that, John Gebhardt and I would have equity positions in a public company. That's something we can't have at ManTech."

"Okay, let's pursue this. I don't know Aalseth very well, but I know John Scanga. He's a great guy; in fact, I've tried to hire him several times. Let me talk to him. If it sounds like something we should do, I'll get with Jack Hughes and decide on a price to put on Intercad."

Pedersen and Scanga talked, and negotiations soon began. Jack Hughes, ManTech's chief financial officer, recommended a valuation of $650,000. George called Jack Aalseth and named his price: $400,000 now, $250,000 at some later date.

"If they come back and start nickel-and-diming me," George said to me, "I'll know they're not serious. We'll find out soon."

The following day, the "nickel-and-diming" began. ERCI offered $550,000—$300,000 now and $250,000 over four years. George was not happy but continued talking. Aalseth offered several variations on his original bid, but none were acceptable.

Five days later, George called me.

"This is getting to the silly stage," he said. "I've called around and I have an offer from another company. They'll pay $750,000 for Intercad. The only reason I'm still talking to ERCI is that you and John Gebhardt deserve to do what you want."

Despite the fact that Pedersen now held a trump card, Aalseth refused to move off his position. In fact, he lowered his offer by $50,000. Pedersen was furious. I was despondent. The deal appeared dead.

Then, out of the blue, a potential solution to the impasse arrived. Several months before, I had contacted Pete Linsert, president of a Small Business Investment Bank (SBIC) within Suburban Bank. Created by the US Small Business Administration, SBICs are privately owned venture capital firms that make equity and debt investments in small companies using their own funds as well as money borrowed with an SBA guarantee. My last conversation with Linsert had been so long ago that I had forgotten about it. Now he was on the phone, telling me that he would like to pursue the deal. I explained that there was an ongoing negotiation between ManTech and ERCI.

"That's even better," he said. "Maybe we and ERCI could get together and put in enough money to pay off ManTech and provide you guys with enough operating capital to get you to break even."

Wow! I thought. *This could be a hell of a deal. With Suburban as a major shareholder, ERCI wouldn't feel as if it owned us. We would really be independent!*

The next few days saw a flurry of activity. ManTech was offered, and accepted, $750,000, matching the bid George Pedersen claimed to have in hand. ERCI would make a straight equity investment of $250,000 and Suburban would put up $500,000 in the form of a loan that could be converted to equity. Operating capital for Intercad would come in through a financing vehicle called R&D Limited Partnership (whereby individual investors purchased technology from a company and received tax deductions; over time, when the company began selling products based on the technology, it purchased back its technology from the investors). Lawyers and accountants scurried to generate memoranda of understanding, letters of intent, a sale and purchase agreement, the incorporation of the new Intercad Corporation, employment agreements with the eleven employees of the new company, and various other documents.

The first two weeks of December 1983 were spent revising and signing contracts, fighting over details, producing and reproducing financial forecasts, keeping the Intercad team informed and happy, and waiting. All that was left was final approval by Suburban's board. Our goal had been to close the deal before Christmas. It was December 19. The board met that evening. At 11 p.m., Pete Linsert called me at home.

"Charlie, I'm terribly sorry. My board turned down the deal. I won't go into details, but there's nothing I can do. I'm really sorry."

Stunned, I called Jack Aalseth. He had returned from vacation in Australia a few days before and was still somewhat jet-lagged, but he was surprisingly unconcerned.

"Let's talk in the morning," he said.

By the time he and his CFO, Tom Bennett, called me on December 20th, they seemed to have everything figured out. ERCI would simply pick up the piece of equity that had been intended for Suburban. The only problem: ERCI would now own 51 percent of Intercad. Additionally, if we failed to meet various milestones, they would receive more. We would not be independent. But, at this late stage, what choice did we have?

We closed the deal before the end of the year and leased office space in a one-story building on Admiral Cochrane Drive in Annapolis. Intercad Corporation was open for business. Once again I was a CEO—and this time I was about to face a different kind of entrepreneurial terror.

CHAPTER FOURTEEN

Rise, Betrayal, and Fall

As an entrepreneur, I was always outwardly optimistic, giving the impression to those around me that everything would turn out great. Inwardly, though, I have had a wild fear throughout my life that something would go wrong—no doubt a result of the terror I had experienced as a hidden child in Nazi-occupied Czechoslovakia. Throughout those formative years, I had little reason for optimism. In my chase of the American Dream, the tribulations were less frequent and far less calamitous, but they happened. Although I attempted to hide my feelings from my colleagues, my fear was never far away. In the case of the ERCI "marriage," I had good reason to be apprehensive, despite the fact that things started well.

We strengthened our founder team by bringing in a seasoned vice president of marketing and sales, Jim Starnes, and a fastidious and perceptive chief financial officer, Pam Ayers. Several Wall Street high rollers, investment bankers who had been involved in bringing ERCI public, invested personally in Intercad. This provided us with additional operating capital.

We struck a crucial deal with Apollo Computer, a company in Billerica, Massachusetts, with the largest share of the burgeoning computer workstation market. Soon, we became a major Apollo reseller, packaging our Illustrator software with Apollo's hardware and selling to early adopters. However, there was a problem—one that we failed to recognize at the time because we were so enamored with our early success. While the rest of the computing world was using an operating system (OS) called Unix, Apollo had its own proprietary OS. Our software had to be written in such a way that it was compatible with that OS. This meant that we were tied inexorably to Apollo, which would prove costly in the future because we could not easily port the software to customers' non-Apollo computers or to new-to-market workstations, such as those of Sun Microsystems and Hewlett Packard.

A year into our life as a separate company, Jim Starnes decided to leave in order to start his own company. This caused an immediate void, and we initiated a national search for his replacement. We selected an energetic, ambitious young man whom I will call "Stan Nolan," who came to us from an established computer-aided design firm, a subsidiary of a large, multinational energy company. Stan began to build a national sales force. I made contact with an old friend from my native village in Czechoslovakia, now living in Sweden. Vratislav Böhm signed on as our European representative, and together we contracted with F.A.G. Corporation, located in Lausanne, Switzerland, to be our overseas distributor. (We had lots of fun with that company's acronym!)

Midway through 1984, our former parent ManTech decided to abandon the computer-aided design software business and to have its CADCOM division concentrate exclusively on providing services to the Department of Defense. Consequently, they released us from our non-compete agreement, and we were able to return to our roots and add a CAD product—one we called MASTERCAD—to our arsenal.

While we were busy building our business, ERCI continued to grow via acquisition. They purchased a firm called IEAL, which provided services to the nuclear industry. John Gray, president of IEAL, was named chairman of the board of ERCI, which was reorganized into groups. Intercad became part of the Computer Systems Group, headed by another IEAL manager, a man named Jack Young. He and I would have a roller-coaster relationship.

Intercad's product development was going well, the infrastructure was in place, and we were establishing important relationships. But sales were slow, hovering just below $2 million annually, and the rest of ERCI was underperforming, as well. At our weekly management meetings at the parent company's headquarters in Vienna, Virginia, CEO Jack Aalseth repeatedly emphasized the pressure he was under from Wall Street analysts.

In January 1985, Aalseth informed me of his unhappiness with Intercad. We had missed the deadline for completion of a solid modeler (three-dimensional CAD) and our beta test of MASTERCAD was late. He called his watchdog, Vice President Jack Young, into the meeting, and both informed me that they wanted Intercad to enter the market of computer-aided design services—using our CAD products to perform designs for customers.

"Guys," I said to the two Jacks. "We're a software product company. It's very difficult for a small company to sell both products and services. I strongly disagree."

A long discussion resulted in an impasse. We ended up not entering the service business. However, this marked a major fissure in my interaction with Jack Aalseth. My relationship with the guy designated to oversee us, Jack Young, was already strained. Young, who came from the nuclear energy industry, had no clue about our business and had no interest in learning it. His often inane comments and suggestions infuriated me, but, in the spirit of teamwork, I controlled my feelings and outwardly showed him respect.

A month after the meeting about CAD services, Young called me.

"You guys are doing a pretty good job of setting yourselves up for the commercial market," he said, "but you're not paying attention to a huge opportunity right on your doorstep."

"What opportunity is that, Jack?" I asked.

"The federal government. For God's sake, Charlie, you know from your ManTech experience that there are huge opportunities with the feds. And they're right down the road—the low-hanging fruit."

"I can't argue, Jack," I said. "But we've built our sales staff for the commercial market. They don't have any experience selling to the government."

"I have the answer for you," Young replied. "We have a marketing guy at ERCI who can do that for you. I'll introduce him to you, and you can decide if you want him to transfer to Intercad."

The next day, Albert Pines came to see us. Stan Nolan, John Gebhardt, Pam Ayres, and I met with him. He seemed knowledgeable about the Washington scene and appeared to be an intelligent, pleasant man. We hired him and put him in charge of sales to the US government, reporting directly to Nolan. Pines sat in on our management meetings, and he began to outline a strategy for attacking the federal market. But something was wrong. He seemed to be spending a great deal of time away from the office, presumably speaking with Washington customers, yet nothing seemed to come from these meetings. A few weeks after joining us, Pines asked to speak to me privately.

"There is something I need to tell you," he said.

"What's that?" I asked.

"I came here as an ERCI guy. But I really like you guys, and you've made me feel like a part of your team. I want you know how much I appreciate it."

"That's great, Al," I replied, wondering what this was about.

"So, I have to tell you that I was sent here to spy on you guys and to report to ERCI about your 'real' technical progress, sales strategy, and your leadership. All those Washington meetings I told you I've had actually were meetings at ERCI."

Our relationship with the parent company had deteriorated, but I had no idea that it had come to this. Did they send a spy in order to gather evidence to fire me? Stunned, I walked out of the office and got myself a cup of coffee, leaving Pines sitting there. I returned a minute later.

"Why are you telling me now, Al, and what do you propose we do?"

"I'm telling you because I feel like scum." He bit his lower lip and looked down at the red carpet. "It's dishonest, and I don't want to do it anymore. I'm gonna tell Les Wright that it's over. Whether or not you want to keep me here is up to you."

"Les Wright?" I asked, incredulous that my old friend from ManTech days, and the person who had facilitated the Intercad ERCI introduction, had turned against me.

"Yeah, he's the one who came up with this. I report to him, and I guess he then passes the information on to Jack Young. And by the way, everything I've told Les about Intercad has been positive. I keep telling him that all you need is time."

"Al, thanks for being so forthright," I said. "I'm sorry these guys put you in such an awkward situation. You go tell Les that you're finished with espionage work, but don't mention the fact that you've told me. At my end, I'll tell John Gebhardt but no one else so that your loyalty won't be doubted. We'll keep you here, but you'll devote your full-time efforts to getting us into the federal government."

This was the spring of 1985, and nearly every week, the news media carried a story about another computer revolution, one as important as time-sharing had been a few years back. The computer was moving to the desktop. The local press reported that Westinghouse had just purchased several hundred personal computers for its engineers. Black & Decker was putting PCs on the manufacturing floor. And so it went. The handwriting was on the wall.

"John," I said to my partner, John Gebhardt, "we need to port our software to the PC. Pretty soon, the workstation is going to be obsolete. Nobody will want a computer the size of a refrigerator anymore."

John had been thinking along the same lines and agreed. I asked him to work on a plan to rewrite our software so that it would run on an IBM PC. He and his staff came up with a number: $750,000. Together, John and I prepared a slide show that I would use to attempt to persuade our investors—ERCI and the Wall Street bankers—to provide the funds.

I went to New York to make the pitch. I included what I considered convincing proof that this was the wave of the future and the way for us to go. I showed potential sales and profit figures. Everyone seemed impressed until I hit them with the amount needed to make it happen.

"Three quarters of a million!" said one of the bankers. "You've gotta be kidding. Why the hell would it take so much money just to move a program from one computer to another one?"

I provided a detailed list of costs involved in the effort to no avail. Our investors had seen a list of our prospects for the existing MASTERCAD and Illustrator products. It was impressive. We were in serious discussions with GE, Sperry, Raytheon, Motorola, and Bell South. Within the government, the Navy, FBI, NSA, and FEMA were considering our software. And we were active overseas, with potential customers in Australia, England, Germany, and Japan. Why should we be looking at a new product that would require high development costs? I was told to "stick to your knitting."

I considered this a terrible mistake, one that would cost us dearly in the future as our competitors would jump into the low-end desktop market. To me, it was a reaffirmation of the fact that the current relationship was a dead end for Intercad. I decided to embark on a clandestine effort to buy our way out from ERCI's repression and visited two venture capital firms in Boston, Graylock Partners and Morgan Holland. Both expressed interest in making an investment in that revolutionary field we had begun to call "electronic publishing." Through our company attorney, Mike Cromwell, I held discussions about raising private capital, or perhaps a public offering, with the investment banking firms Alex Brown and Baker, Watts & Co. Additionally, I spent many days meeting with a wealthy individual investor, Steve Bank, whose family owned the Joseph A. Bank retail clothing chain.

Once we had a few informal proposals in hand, Mike Cromwell and I decided that he, as a neutral party, would approach Jack Aalseth.

"He seemed interested in selling ERCI's interest in Intercad," Mike informed me following the meeting. "He'll get back to me in a few days. Aalseth is a dealmaker. He likes to do a deal, just for the sake of doing a deal. I think we'll be able to move ahead."

But Mike was not counting on the other guy at the top of the organization, chairman of the board John Gray.

"Aalseth called me," Mike told me a week later. "He told me that he was ready to unload Intercad, but John Gray wouldn't go along with it. So that's that."

We were stuck in our present situation and would have to make the best of it. While I was contemplating the future of our company as an ERCI subsidiary, as well as my own as a captive of our parent, an old friend came to visit me. Dr. Rudolph P. Lamone was the dean of the College of Business and Management at the University of Maryland. We had known one another socially for some time. I unloaded on Rudy about our struggles and my personal frustrations.

"Why don't you say to hell with it and come back to academia?" Rudy asked. "I know how much you enjoyed teaching. Come to the University of Maryland."

I laughed. "Rudy, I'd love to do just that, but I can't just walk away from all this and leave my people. They're counting on me to make this thing go. Now that I know we can't get out from under our masters, I need to get my ass back in gear and generate some sales."

I cracked down on our technical team. They had missed too many development deadlines, and I felt that they were adding too many unnecessary "bells and whistles" to our software products.

"John," I said to Gebhardt, "we're not writing a PhD dissertation. We can't keep on changing, improving, and playing with the software and delaying releases. We need to get products out into the market." John and his team responded by setting realistic goals and deadlines.

At our staff meetings, our sales and marketing VP Stan Nolan presented his weekly pipeline reports—multipage, handwritten spreadsheets of potential customers. As is characteristic of most salespeople, Stan's forecasts were wildly overoptimistic, creating expectations that went unfulfilled.

"Stan, get real," I instructed him. "I don't want to see any more suspects in your reports—only real prospects. And get more realistic about the probability of turning these prospects into paying customers."

Additionally, I had to make certain that our relationship with Apollo Computer would continue into the future. It was a difficult time and I was on edge when I arrived in Billerica to negotiate a new contract with Bill Poduska, Apollo's CEO. I was in the middle of a difficult discussion about the terms of the agreement when Bill's administrative assistant walked in to say that I had an urgent call. When I came out of the conference room, I was told that it was my assistant Geri Logue. *She knows how important this meeting is. What could be so critical that she would call me out of it?*

"I'm sorry to get you out of your meeting, Charlie," she said. "But I have an urgent problem on my hands."

"What is it?"

"You know that Lenore is responsible for taking out the mail twice a day?"

"Yeah, so what?" I asked, perturbed to be pulled out of a critical meeting for something so trivial. Lenore was the daughter of our best friends, Don and Sue Griffin, and she was working for Intercad during her summer vacation from the University of Alabama.

"I opened her desk drawer this morning and found it full of one week's outgoing mail," she said. "One of the letters there is to Apollo, telling them that we'll be returning a computer after a thirty-day trial. Because the letter is still here, we've missed the deadline. John Gebhardt says that now we'll have to keep the computer and pay $11,000 for it."

"Wonderful," I replied, knowing that we were on a knife's edge of profitability and even such a small amount could throw us into the red for the month.

"I'm calling you about this because I know how close you are to the Griffins. I need your permission to let Lenore go," Geri said. "I don't have any choice, but I need your okay."

I swallowed hard, but now I was the one who had no choice.

"Geri, I told you before we hired her that you'll have total discretion in these matters. You do what you think is right."

With that, I hung up and returned to the negotiation table. Later in the day, when I got to Logan Airport, I drank two fuzzy navels at the bar. The first drink was a solitary celebration of having negotiated a good agreement with Apollo. The second was intended to help me forget, at least temporarily, that I would have to explain to my best friend why my company had fired his daughter—one who had called me "Uncle Charlie" since she could speak. When I arrived at home that evening, I called the Griffins.

"We're not allowed to speak to you," said Clayton, the oldest child. He hung up.

The following afternoon, while in the office, I received a call from my wife Sue.

"I ran into Sue and Melissa Griffin in Pris' Paper Parlor," she sobbed. "When I walked over to them, Sue told me that she never wants to speak to me again."

Lenore sent me a note in which she gave her side of the story, claiming that she had done nothing wrong. She wondered how I could have allowed Geri to fire her. I wanted to explain my side to Lenore, Sue, and Don in person, but no one would speak to me. So I wrote them a long letter, hoping that we could meet and reconcile. I told them that I did not think this incident should destroy our long friendship. But all communications stopped there. Our friendship was over.

The next time I would see our former friends would be years later at a sad event, the funeral of the boy who had been my favorite, only one small step below our own David—Clayton Griffin. He died tragically, much too young. The second time I would see Sue and the girls would be at the funeral of my former best friend, Don, who would pass away from a mysterious malady. We attempted to resume our friendship with Sue Griffin after that, but it was too late to repair the damage.

By the end of 1985, Intercad settled into slow but steady progress. We were not yet profitable, but we were getting close. Yet ERCI management was still unhappy. The pressure on a public company to show profit and growth each quarter is intense. It overrides everything and often makes for short-term decisions that have negative long-term results. In mid-January 1986, I was ordered to institute across-the-board pay cuts, to freeze all hiring, to close our California and Minneapolis sales offices, and to suspend all major purchases.

These pressures were wearing me down. I had to get away for a few days. Sue was on vacation from school, so we decided to go on a cross-country-skiing holiday in Vermont.

We spent a wonderful week at the Trappe Family Lodge, skiing over miles of trails above the town of Stowe. The night before our scheduled departure, northern Vermont was buried by a three-foot dump of fresh snow. I called our airline and was told that Burlington Airport was closed. Desperate to get home due to a business commitment and Sue's need to be in front of her kindergarten class, I asked the hotel receptionist for advice.

"You might check Logan airport," she suggested. "The roads south of here may not be as bad, and maybe you can drive to Boston and get a flight out of there."

I checked with the highway patrol and was told that the roads to Boston were "treacherous but passable." I switched our reservations and scheduled us to fly out of Logan late that afternoon—Tuesday, January 28, 1986. We stowed our bags, clamped our skis to the rack of our rented car, and headed out. The snow had stopped, the sun came out, and the snowplows had cleared a single lane of the road out of Stowe. As we made our way ever so slowly southeastward, the road conditions continued to improve. We stayed tuned to a Boston radio station, not only to monitor the situation ahead of us, but also hoping that it would carry a broadcast of the space shuttle launch scheduled for that morning. I had a personal interest in the flight because the shuttle pilot, Mike Smith, had been one of my students and advisees at the Naval Academy some twenty years earlier. We got our wish and, around 11:15 a.m., the station picked up the broadcast from Cape Canaveral.

"We have liftoff!" announced a familiar voice just after 11:35. A short time later, the same calm voice said something about "a major malfunction." Seventy-three seconds into the flight, space shuttle *Challenger* blew up and disintegrated over the Atlantic Ocean.

"Uh-oh!" were the last words heard from *Challenger*. They were uttered by former midshipman Mike Smith, just before he and his six fellow crew members—including Christa McAuliffe, who would have been the first teacher in space—died in the explosion.

At one o'clock on Monday, February 3, nine days after we had celebrated my fiftieth birthday in Vermont and six days after the *Challenger* catastrophe, my own life blew up. I was in the middle of my typical "executive" lunch, chewing on a sandwich at my desk with my nose buried in work. I was putting the finishing touches on a joint venture agreement between Intercad and a Boston firm named Xyvision when my phone rang. The interruption annoyed me because I had told Geri Logue to hold all calls except from my short list of family, close friends, and "captors," an endearing term I used for the management team of ERC International.

"I'm sorry, Charlie," Geri apologized. "Jack Young is on the line, and he says it's very important." I swallowed the remainder of my ham and cheese on rye.

"Hello, Jack, how are you?" I said, attempting to sound friendly.

"Well, not so good, Charlie," he replied. "I'm home with a terrible cold. This is the reason I couldn't drive over to Annapolis to give you the bad news in person."

"What bad news?"

"We have decided to ask you to resign as CEO of Intercad."

Jack and I had carried on a continuing battle for many months over matters big and small, from corporate strategy to stock options for my employees. Yet, despite our differences, I had not expected this. In stunned silence, I stared out the window at white cumulous clouds floating toward the Chesapeake Bay.

"We don't want you to leave the company. We'd like you to be senior vice president of ERCI's computer systems division," Jack said, after a long pause. "Stan Nolan will take over as president of Intercad."

Stan Nolan! I screamed silently, quickly brought out of my trance. *I tried to fire that son-of-a-bitch just two weeks ago. Now I understand why they didn't let me do it.*

"Jack," I said, attempting to remain calm. "I need an explanation for this. But not now. I'll call Jack Aalseth and set up a meeting with him. Goodbye."

Although we had had our spats, Aalseth and I had developed a decent professional and personal rapport. I found it difficult to believe that he would agree to my firing and, even if he did, surely he would not have the message delivered by his lackey, over the telephone.

I crossed my office and slumped into one of the soft chairs at my small conference table. As if in a hypnotic state, I stared at a schefflera plant, its large green leaves filling a corner of my office and its straight trunk reaching the tiled ceiling. Tears rolled down my cheeks as I recalled the day in 1969 when my parents presented me with a six-inch plant in a small clay pot and wished me good luck upon starting our first company, CADCOM. Now I thought about the fact that the plant had experienced eighteen years of entrepreneurial terror with me. Questions came rushing at me like atoms colliding in a nuclear reaction.

What am I going to tell Sue when I get home? How will I break the news to my parents without causing them pain? How can I face my partners and employees? What am I going to do with my life? Who is going to take care of all the unfinished business here? Surely not Stan Nolan! I've been working a hundred hours a week for eighteen years. Now what? How can these bastards take away from me what I've built so painstakingly, piece by piece? Shall I tell them to stick their offer where the sun doesn't shine or shall I give myself time to think about it?

Most of all, I felt humiliated. Throughout my professional life, I had been considered an overachiever, a rising star. Now, I had failed. How could I live with this? What would people say about me now?

First things first. At that moment, I needed to compose myself, and then I had to get the hell out of the building. I walked to my desk and pushed a button on the intercom.

"Geri, please come in," I said to my executive assistant.

The pert, pretty blonde who had been my loyal right hand for the past two years walked in with a steno pad in one hand and pen in the other.

"I'm afraid you won't need those," I said. "I just got fired."

"You're kidding me, aren't you?"

"No, that's why Jack Young called," I replied.

"But why? How could they do this? You *are* the company!"

"He didn't give me a reason, and I didn't ask."

Convinced now that I was not pulling her leg, Geri began to sob. I stood up, walked over to her, and put my arm around her shoulders. She gained control of her emotions and, out of the blue, her normally professional demeanor disappeared.

"And that son-of-a-bitch Young didn't even have the decency or courage to say this to your face!" she practically screamed. "The goddamned coward had to do it on the phone!"

At that moment, I realized that Geri's job, too, was in jeopardy. The new president had his own secretary, who would no doubt be moving up with him. She was Stan's faithful servant, having protected him and covered for him many times when I showered my wrath on the underperforming and devious vice president of marketing and sales. Should I decide to accept ERCI's offer to be a senior VP, my office probably would be in Washington. I did not think that Geri would be interested in making the commute. I resolved that protecting her job at Intercad would be one of my agenda topics when I met with Jack Aalseth.

After Geri left my office, I picked up the phone, called Aalseth's secretary, and arranged a meeting in his office in Vienna, Virginia, for the next afternoon. I cleared my desk, put on my overcoat, grabbed my empty briefcase, and headed out the door. I assumed that none of the employees were aware of the cataclysmic change at the top of their company, and I intended to walk out the front door without any indication that this might be my final exit. Entering the hall, I glanced into the office of Stan Nolan, the president-to-be. Out of the corner of my eye, I spotted a large bouquet of flowers in the vestibule of his secretary. I stopped to take a closer look. Next to the vase were a bottle of champagne and a large card that read, "CONGRATULATIONS!"

The bastard knew long before I did, and so did his sidekick! For the first time since Young's fateful phone call, I became enraged. I suspected a conspiracy. My immediate impulse was to walk into Stan's office and punch him in the mouth and, on my way out, pick up his assistant's IBM Selectric and throw it at her. I felt my face burning and my fists tightening as I stood there, transfixed. But common sense took over, despite the fact that my fury had not dissipated one bit. I walked through the lobby, out the door, jumped into my Audi, and drove home.

Sue had just returned from a morning of teaching at the Naval Academy Primary School. She was standing at the kitchen sink, surprised to see me in the middle of the afternoon. I explained what had just taken place.

"I don't know how they could have done this to you after all you've put into the company," she said, tears streaming down her cheeks. After recovering, she added, "But I'm sure everything will be just fine. You'll make the right decision."

The following day, I met with Jack Aalseth. In weeks past, he welcomed me to his office with a smile, a slap on the back, and an offer of a drink from his hidden treasure trove, followed by a dirty joke. He was a different guy on this day. When I asked him to explain why I had been asked to resign, he handed me a typed sheet. It was a dossier containing eleven of my deadliest sins, the majority having to do with underperformance in sales.

"Primarily, it's because you weren't making your numbers," he said.

"Jack," I replied. "During the last quarter, we were within two percent of our forecast. Is that so terrible?" When he failed to respond, I asked, "And you decided to make Stan Nolan president? Just two weeks ago, I was here in your office, pleading with you to let me fire him because he wasn't closing sales and because he was lying about the pipeline. You agreed with me. What happened?"

"John Gray and Jack Young felt there wasn't anybody else in your company capable of running it," Aalseth replied.

"How about John Gebhardt?" I asked. "He's my co-founder, he knows the business better than Nolan, and he's certainly more respected by the people than Stan."

"John's a technology guy, not a businessman," he said. "We didn't consider him a candidate."

"I presume that your decision is irreversible—that this is a done deal?" I inquired.

"Yeah. Let's not even talk about it anymore."

"What about the offer to make me senior VP of your computer systems division? What's that job all about? And what happens to Geri Logue, does she go with me?"

"Damned if I know. That's something you need to discuss with Jack Young. But I hope you'll stay. I'd also like you to stay on the Intercad board. We need your knowledge, contacts, and reputation."

I wanted to laugh and tell my former friend where he could stick his offer. Instead, I managed to control my temper and say that I would think things over.

On the long drive home in rush-hour traffic on the Washington Beltway, I contemplated that dossier of my perceived deficiencies. Most surprising was number eleven. It stated simply: "Nepotism: niece cost company $11K—caused company to go negative for a month." My first reaction was *What the hell is this? I don't have a niece!* Then I realized they were referring to Lenore Griffin, to whom

I was "Uncle Charlie." Her failure to send a letter had cost CADCOM $11,000 and Lenore her summer job. The price I paid was considerably higher. First, Lenore's parents had cut ties with Sue and me over their daughter's dismissal. Now, her transgression had been used as part of the justification to fire me from the company I had co-founded and led.

I thought about all that I had lost as my car crawled along the Beltway. My emotions alternated between humiliation and anger. When I reached Route 50 and aimed the car toward Annapolis and home, I decided that I needed to deal with my new situation in a calm, practical manner. By the time I pulled into our driveway, I had decided to remain on the board of Intercad and to accept ERCI's offer, regardless of the job description. It would allow me to draw a salary while contemplating my future. Of course, I did not say this to Young as we negotiated the terms over the next several days. Although our discussions never yielded a precise definition of my duties, I was able to work out a financial package that was even better than the one I had as Intercad's CEO. The major downside was the location of my office. I was asked to work out of the infamous Watergate Building, next door to the Kennedy Center, in downtown Washington.

The following week, assisted by Sue and David, I cleared out my office at Intercad in the middle of the night, so that I would not have to face any of my former colleagues and employees. We removed all my personal belongings, including files, books, and— most importantly—the beautiful schefflera, which would continue to accompany me on future journeys.

CHAPTER FIFTEEN

Shifting Gears

I showed up at the Watergate offices of ERCI, where Jack Young introduced me to the staff and showed me a small office with windows looking out over the Potomac River into Northern Virginia. *Nice, but no thanks,* I thought. The Watergate, where Richard Nixon's henchmen had committed a crime that led to his resignation, may be appropriate for the thieves of ERCI, but it was not for me.

The following day, having signed a new employment agreement with ERCI, one that did not specify the location of my office, I did not show up for work. Knowing that I had the upper hand in the discussion that would follow, I called my fearless leader.

"Jack, I'm not making the commute. From the little I know about my new job, there's no need for me to be in Washington, except for staff meetings. I can do the rest from an office in Annapolis. Why don't you just give me an office at Intercad?"

It took thirty minutes to convince Young that there was no way I would make the daily commute to the Watergate. After he exhausted his arguments, he told me that he would get back to me. He called the next day to inform me that he had discussed the situation with Jack Aalseth, and the two of them had decided that I could work out of Annapolis. However, locating me at Intercad was out of the question. I would be a "disturbing influence."

"People who used to work for you would be coming to your office to bitch about Stan Nolan. We can't have that," he said. "You'll work out of the CAD/Infoshare offices. And you won't need a secretary. Geri Logue will stay at Intercad."

CAD/Infoshare was an architecture firm we had acquired and moved from New York City to a small office building on Forest Drive in Annapolis. The company had seemed like a good match for our computer-aided design software, which they would modify for their industry and sell to architects throughout the country. For a variety of reasons, the merger had not worked out and we sold the firm back to its management. They departed for New York and left behind an entire floor of empty desks, drafting tables, chairs, and filing cabinets.

The next morning, I arrived dressed in a suit and tie, carrying a leather briefcase. When I unlocked the front door and entered, I was struck by the absurdity of my situation. Here was my office—all three thousand square feet of open space—occupied by no one but me. I hung up my jacket and spent the first hour selecting a spot near a window, moving the best desk and chair there, and stocking up with pads, pens, pencils, and paper clips. I went back to my company-owned Audi and brought out three cartons of hanging folders, which I proceeded to arrange in a filing cabinet. As a final act of arranging my new home, I placed family photos on my desk and unwrapped my ever-present wooden Pistol Pete, mascot of my alma mater, Oklahoma State University. The schefflera remained at home in our sunroom. This would be a temporary situation.

Finally, I sat down at my desk. I looked around and smiled when it occurred to me that I might have the largest office in the country—bigger than that of the president of the United States. Then it hit me. I also had the loneliest office. There would be no human contact, except by telephone. As CEO, I had always believed in "managing by walking the ship," spending time to stop by people's offices to hear ideas, thoughts, complaints, personal problems, and to engage in small talk. Now, I would be alone, day after day. I thought of Napoleon and his exile to the island of Elba. My single hope was that my former colleagues from Intercad would swim to my island to visit me occasionally.

During the days that followed, I fulfilled my contractual duties to ERCI. I managed the relationship with Intercad's European distributor, and I took care of various pieces of unfinished business from my CEO days. The problem was that I had become accustomed to working ten- to twelve-hour days, and now I was completing my work before lunch. The saddest part of my exile was that only three of my former Intercad colleagues paid me regular visits. Geri Logue and an administrative assistant named Karen came often, occasionally bringing me candy or cookies, as well as gossip from the company. One of Intercad's managers, whose name I have forgotten (and to whom I apologize profusely if he happens to read this), came almost every day, usually to share a sandwich during the lunch hour. But no one else dared to provoke Stan Nolan's ire by associating with me.

In some ways, the four months I spent in that godforsaken place on Forest Drive were good for me. I had more time for family, friends, skiing, and sailing. Even the duties I was performing for my employer were relatively stress-free. But I found my situation demeaning and ego-shattering. For the first time in many years, I did not feel that every action I took was a matter of life or death. I knew that I would collect my salary even if I failed to perform, but I could not savor this way of life. If it had been otherwise, I would have carved out a career at some large company or the government instead of choosing to live on the edge as a serial entrepreneur.

By early May, I had to escape "the island prison." I considered becoming a venture capitalist and spoke with old friends Frank Bonsal of New Enterprise Associates in Baltimore and Buck Bennett of Atlantic Ventures in Virginia about the possibility of joining their firms. I turned down an offer to be COO of a new Silicon Valley software company run by Nolan Bushnell, the famous founder of Atari and Chuck E. Cheese Pizza-Time Theaters. Several friends who ran Washington-area high-tech companies met with me about joining forces. I had choices. For the first time in weeks, I was feeling good about myself and about my prospects for the future.

I recalled a meeting with my friend Rudy Lamone a few months before. Rudy was the dean of the business school at the University of Maryland. I had told him then that I was experiencing entrepreneurial burnout and that my life was becoming too stressful because I was not in full control.

"Why don't you say to hell with it and come back to academia?" Rudy had asked.

With his words echoing in my head, I dialed his number. That call changed the course of my life. Dean Lamone promised to "look around" the university to ascertain if there might be an opportunity for me. A few days later, he called back.

"There is an interesting opening," he said. "The Engineering Research Center is looking for someone to develop a program for faculty to do applied research that would result in new products for Maryland companies. You should check it out."

For the next couple of days, while continuing to pursue the opportunities on the table, I pondered whether or not I was ready to take a major haircut in pay and to jump into the internal politics that come with any university job. On the third day, late in the afternoon, the phone rang in my cavernous office.

"Dr. Heller?" said the voice at the other end. "This is John Slaughter. I'm chancellor of the University of Maryland."

"Of course, I know who you are, Dr. Slaughter," I said, trying to disguise my surprise. "To what do I owe this honor?"

"Rudy Lamone told me that you're trying to decide on your next career move. When he reminded me about the ERC position, I knew it would be a perfect match for you."

"How so?" I asked, wondering how he came to know anything about me.

"I know that, in the past, you had some bad experiences trying to get an agreement to license some of our university's technologies to your company. You've been critical of us, and rightly so. Now, you can come help us fix the problem."

Assuming that the chancellor was offering me the job, I asked what would transpire if I accepted. He must have been smiling at my naiveté as he introduced me to life at a state institution. He explained that this, like all hiring, had to be a competitive process and that I would have to apply. Dr. Slaughter gave me the phone number of Dr. David Barbe, the executive director of the Engineering Research Center, and suggested that I call with any questions about the application process. I thanked him and hung up, thinking that I had reached a stage in my life and career where I did not apply for jobs. Either I started my own companies or people sought me out and asked me to join their executive teams. No way was this former CEO going to become an ordinary job applicant!

That evening, I explained the University of Maryland situation to Sue. While describing it, I realized that I was checking off all the benefits, as if trying to convince her—as well as myself—that I should become a Maryland Terrapin. My wife, who had shown her love throughout our marriage by tolerating the crazy ups and downs of a life of entrepreneurial successes interrupted by moments of entrepreneurial terror, responded in her usual way.

"Do what will make you happy."

The following day, I phoned Dave Barbe, who gave me more information about the position and promised to send me application materials. I applied and, three weeks later, I received a letter offering me the position of director of industrial research at a salary—oh, my God!—40 percent less than my current pay from ERCI. I called Dave and asked if the amount was negotiable.

"It's not," he said. "But you'll get an annual cost-of-living increase plus a merit raise. And, most importantly, remember that you'll get one day a week for consulting. Think of the university salary as being for a four-day week."

"Okay, I'm in," I said, fearful that with time to think about the economics I might turn down the offer. "I'll see you on Monday."

Having accepted, I felt a surge of excitement. Someone out there actually thought I could be a major contributor to an important effort! Instead of pretending that I was working, as I had been for the past four months, I would be tackling a new challenge. Feeling confident and free, I decided that I might even have sufficient leverage to improve my financial situation by finessing ERCI.

On June 24, 1986, I submitted my resignation in the form of a proposal to the company. I would honor the non-compete portion of my employment agreement for one year, but only if I would be retained by ERCI/Intercad as a consultant with guaranteed payment for a minimum of eight hours per week for one year, and if the company would buy 670,000 shares of Intercad stock from me, leaving me with 100,000 shares. Since this constituted a savings of more than $50,000 for the company and, at the same time, removed any threat I may have represented to Stan Nolan and his cohorts, management gladly accepted my offer.

I was free to move on to my next career, with a nice income for doing little in the next twelve months and a cash bonus for stock which, I feared, would be worth little or nothing after a few months of Nolan's leadership. For good measure, I threw in the condition that the company must sell me the company-owned auto I had been driving—a jet fighter on wheels, disguised as a silver Audi 3000 Quattro—for a price equal to its wholesale value. No doubt happy to get me out of their collective hair and save money in the process, ERCI bought the entire package without negotiation. It was a win-win.

Jack Aalseth, CEO of ERCI, called me at the university a couple of weeks after we signed the agreement. He asked me to come to Virginia to have lunch with him. I assumed that he wanted to discuss my upcoming consulting assignment. But, as soon as we toasted one another with glasses of Chardonnay, I discovered that he had something entirely different on his mind.

"Charlie, I owe you an apology," he said while looking down at the tablecloth.

"For what?" I asked.

"The main reason you were asked to resign was that, month after month, your sales were so far off your projections. As CEO of a public company, I was including your numbers in my informal forecasts for the analysts, and you were making me look bad."

"I know that, Jack," I responded. "And I told you at the time that I couldn't understand why it was such a tragedy that we were a couple of percent below our projected sales."

"That's just the point," he said, looking sheepish. "I've discovered that I wasn't seeing *your* numbers. Every month, Jack Young was feeding me Stan Nolan's numbers, which hadn't been scrubbed. They were off regularly by twenty to twenty-five percent! I never saw your numbers."

We looked at one another, and each of us shook his head sadly. After a long silence and a sip of wine, Jack finally spoke.

"How do I make this up to you?"

A longer pause followed as I recalled our weekly Intercad staff meetings at which Marketing and Sales VP Nolan presented the team with his sales forecast. His numbers were consistently overly optimistic, and we "scrubbed" them until the final projections became more realistic. At the end of each month, I delivered this refined report to Jack Young of ERCI. Now, the other Jack—CEO Aalseth— was telling me that all along, he had been receiving from Young the original, "unscrubbed" sales numbers, which contained a wish list in addition to a real sales pipeline. After an initial flash of anger, I said to myself, *To hell with it. Let it go!*

"Jack, I have to tell you that I suspected a conspiracy for some time." I said. "But, I don't want you to make it up to me. The fact that you know, and that you know what kind of people you're dealing with, is good enough for me. I'm very happy in my current situation. Let's just stay friends."

Jack seemed relieved. We toasted our friendship and parted company. It would be the last time I would see Jack. He would die of a heart attack on September 5, 1990, in Fort Lauderdale, after having sold ERCI to Ogden Corporation for $80 million. I sat in church at Jack's funeral next to George Pedersen and cried while Bette Midler sang "Wind Beneath My Wings," Miki Aalseth's final homage to her husband.

CHAPTER SIXTEEN

From the Real World to Academia

My first day as director of industrial research at the University of Maryland was a clear case of culture shock. My new life began as I climbed the stairs to the second floor of the Wind Tunnel Building and entered the offices of the Engineering Research Center (known today as M-TECH). I was greeted by Dr. Herb Rabin, the center's director, and Dr. David Barbe, its executive director. Dave escorted me around the office suite, introducing me to my new colleagues.

Culture shock number one: I was introduced as "Dr. Heller." For years in the informal, entrepreneurial, high-tech world, I had been "Charlie." Now, I was entering an arena in which those who lacked the magical PhD were addressed by their first names, while those of us who had earned the degree were treated with reverence and called "doctor."

Eventually, Dave turned me over to a neatly dressed, red-haired lady named Shirley Nestor, whom he identified as the ERC's executive secretary.

"Let me show you to your office," Shirley said and walked a few steps from her desk through a nearby door. I followed and she waved her arm, pointing out a large wooden desk, a comfortable-looking green chair, a side chair, a filing cabinet, and a bookcase. She completed her scan near the door where, on a small wooden table, stood a white box with a small screen, inscribed with the letters "IBM." Under the table sat a large, rectangular metal box, with a blinking green light. It, too, was labeled "IBM."

"What's that?" I asked Shirley.

She looked at me incredulously, apparently thinking I was joking. Finally, smiling, she replied, "Why, that's your computer."

"*My* computer?" I asked, equally unbelieving. "What am I supposed to do with it?"

"That's where you'll type your memos and your letters. You can also do spreadsheets and even prepare your presentations," she answered, still looking dubious.

"Shirley, I don't even know how to turn it on, much less how to use it."

"But I thought . . ." She stopped in mid-sentence and said no more. Immediately, it hit me. I knew what she was thinking: *They told me this guy had been founder and CEO of two software companies before coming here, and he doesn't even know how to turn on a PC!*

Little did Shirley know that, as CEO, I had not written a computer program for the last seventeen years. I had been busy running companies; I had employees who wrote code; I had an administrative assistant who took care of my correspondence. The first moments in my new office brought about a shocking realization. For the first time in years, I would not have anyone to type my letters, my notes, and my presentations. It became instantly clear that I had better learn not only how to turn on the PC, but how to use the damn thing. And I had better do it quickly.

I spent my first morning reading introductory materials and filling out a variety of university forms. When noon approached, Dave Barbe walked into my office and invited me to join him and Herb Rabin for lunch. We drove to a favorite student hangout called R. J. Bentley's, one that I would visit often in the coming years and whose owner, John Brown, would become a friend. Herb, Dave, and I chatted over tasty sandwiches named after old cars—Duesenberg, Stutz Bearcat, and such—as we became better acquainted with one another. Culture shock number two arrived with the check. Dave examined it and announced,

"Let's just split it into thirds. That will be $6.25 each."

I hadn't considered the annual cost of lunches when I calculated the difference between my past and present salaries. I had not purchased lunch with my own money in seventeen years! The midday meal had been one of those hidden perks that add up to real money. Only half a day had passed, and I had already discovered that my post-CEO life would be vastly different. Yet as I sat at my desk during the afternoon, learning more about my new organization, my new job, and my computer, I realized that I was happy. Deliriously happy, considering the trauma I had suffered during recent months.

As director of industrial research, my charge was to make university researchers—those in engineering and computer science—relevant to companies in our state. This was no easy task. Many professors viewed applied research—pioneering work leading directly to commercialization—as both beneath their dignity and of little help in furthering their careers. Promotions and tenure were rewards for the publication of papers in learned refereed journals, based upon basic, theoretical research. At the same time, outside the campus, managements of Maryland companies viewed the University of Maryland as an ivory tower with little interest in assisting them in the development of new products. Those few who had tried to purchase intellectual property from the school were turned off by an unwieldy, time-consuming licensing process. Like me in years past, they decided that dealing with academia was not worth the aggravation and effort. Now I would have to try to find ways to help change the culture of the university and to convince industry that we could be its invaluable research arm.

Herb, Dave, and I spent many hours devising a strategy to bring our faculty's brainpower together with the marketplace. Finally, we came up with a skeleton of a plan. We would ask the state government for money, which we would use to incentivize both sides. Companies would tell us their needs and we would match them up with the appropriate faculty expertise. We would provide matching money for the firms' contributions to the projects, with the funds going to professors performing the work in the form of laboratory equipment, research assistants, and travel funds. We would call the program Maryland Industrial Partnerships—MIPS.

Although I had not returned to the grind of hundred-hour workweeks, I was putting in at least sixty hours and having fun. The only day that I left the office early was Wednesday. During the late spring and summer, I was on our sailboat by five o'clock, ready to compete in Annapolis Yacht Club's Wednesday Night Series, something I had done for many years in two different boats. During the winter, I substituted indoor tennis for sailing, playing competitive doubles every Wednesday evening at the Big Vanilla Racquet Club.

One such Wednesday night in 1987, the phone rang when I returned home from tennis. It was my friend, Rudy Lamone, dean of the Maryland Business School.

"Charlie," he said. "I have a problem. As you know, I got $2 million from Mike Dingman to start an entrepreneurship program and center. I hired a guy from Cornell to run it and found a job for his girlfriend."

"So, what's the problem?" I asked.

"The guy was supposed to arrive here today, and we have a press conference announcing his appointment scheduled for tomorrow. Governor Schaeffer is coming to make the announcement. The press and a lot of dignitaries from the state and the university will be there."

"That sounds great, Rudy," I said, anxious to get out of my sweaty tennis clothes and into the shower.

"Well, it's *not* great. The guy called me this afternoon. His girlfriend wants to stay in Ithaca, and he turned down the job. I'm stuck." My friend sounded despondent.

"That's terrible. What can I do to help, Rudy?" I asked.

"You can come to the press conference tomorrow, and I'll announce you as the new director of the Dingman Center for Entrepreneurship," he blurted out. "I'll take care of all the bullshit that goes with doing a search and hiring you after the fact. Don't worry about it."

It took me several minutes to process the offer which had just been made to me. It took me less time to formulate an answer.

"Rudy," I said, choosing my words carefully, such that I would not offend my friend. "I can't do that. I've only been at the ERC for a few weeks, and those guys are counting on me to get MIPS off the ground. Not only that, but I can't just give them a few hours' notice. Herb and Dave did me a huge favor when they rescued me from a miserable life, and I just couldn't treat them this way. I'm truly sorry, but I can't help you."

Rudy did not attempt to persuade me. He realized that the idea had been ill-conceived. After a pause, he admitted that he had known what my answer would be.

"It was a desperate move on my part. I guess I knew it wouldn't work. Thanks for listening. I'll work it out—somehow."

The next day, the press conference went off as scheduled. Governor William Donald Schaeffer announced the formation of the new entrepreneurship center and its focus on both entrepreneurial education of students and outreach to early-stage technology companies in the region. Then he introduced the *acting director* of the Dingman Center—Dean Rudolph Lamone—who would manage the organization until a permanent director was found.

Now it was February 1987, and I was tasked with filling in the details and closing the loopholes of the Maryland Industrial Partnership concept. The product of my work would be a proposal submitted to the Maryland State Department of Economic and Employment Development or DEED (known today as DBED, with "Business" replacing "Employment" in the name). Due to the state's budgeting schedule, I had three weeks to get it done. In the academic world, twenty-one days is equivalent to the blink of an eye; in the entrepreneurial arena from which I had come, it is forever. Preparing the proposal in time was no problem.

I considered the University of Utah a pioneer, and best role model, for bringing together university researchers and industry. My friend Pete Garity was vice president in charge of the acclaimed program at U of U. I called Pete and scheduled a series of meetings with him and his colleagues for the following week. Not so coincidently, it was the height of the ski season in Utah's Wasatch Mountains, my favorite place to ski, in the deepest and driest powder in the world.

It was the start of one of the most productive and fun weeks of my life. In Salt Lake City, I got up early each morning to catch the first ride up the mountain at Solitude, Brighton, or Alta. I had a blast skiing alone in the bowls and on the trails, while—on chairlift rides—I formulated ideas for MIPS. Each day, I stopped skiing at two o'clock and returned to my temporary home at the Embassy Suites, where I worked until midnight. By Friday, I had built a detailed plan around the skeleton concept we had hatched back in College Park. Upon my return, Herb and Dave provided their input, and we submitted the proposal to DEED. Thanks to Herb's political skills, the state committed to the requested funds, and we were off and running by early summer 1987. I became the first director of MIPS, a program which, I am proud to say, is relatively unchanged today and successful beyond my initial dreams.

Building a new, exciting program and its organization provided me with a thrill I had not experienced since working with my fellow co-founders to build CADCOM from nothing. I hired good people, including Lou Robinson as associate director, Judy Mays as marketing manager, and Peggy Elder as my administrative assistant. (Yes, I had a secretary again, although the word "secretary" was passing out of the business lexicon at the time). Together, we embarked on a public relations campaign both inside the university and in corporate Maryland. We made our first MIPS awards, which included a variety of projects from producing better electric hand tools in our injection molding lab for Black & Decker, to designing touch screens for a home security and entertainment system, to developing an oyster farm on the Eastern Shore of Maryland. We were on our way.

By 1989, MIPS was off and running. We had managed to convince a large number of faculty members about the value of the program to them personally, to the university, and to Maryland companies. By now, we had sponsored enough projects to capture the attention of the press and to gain the confidence of firms around the state. Maryland's government seemed to get it too, and it promised continuing financial support.

The MIPS process was in place; the MIPS team was terrific; things were running smoothly. The entrepreneur's work was done. I felt fulfilled, but I was bored. I had recovered from entrepreneur burnout and felt that I had paid back those who had rescued me from it. It was time to go off and start another company.

Re-enter Rudy Lamone. He had managed to replace himself as acting director of the Dingman Center for Entrepreneurship and had hired a man named Jerry Feigen as the Center's first permanent head. One day in the fall of 1989, Rudy invited me to lunch at Chef's Secret restaurant, not far from campus.

"How's it going at the ERC?" he asked after we toasted one another with our wine glasses.

"It's going great, Rudy," I replied. "I've really enjoyed my three years there. But now it's time for me to move on."

Rudy's eyes lit up. "Really? I know just the right place for you to move on to."

"You do?" I asked, expecting to hear about an executive job with a company from the dean's extensive network.

"Yes," he said. "Things haven't worked out as I had expected at the Dingman Center. We've agreed to part company with the current director, Jerry Feigen. I need you to come run the Center."

I took a sip of my cabernet sauvignon and stared out the window for a few moments before responding.

"Rudy, I really appreciate your confidence and your offer," I responded. "But my answer is the same as last time, although for different reasons. I've enjoyed my stay at the university. It's been fun and a great relief from entrepreneurial terror. But, I have my second wind, and I'm ready to go off to start another company."

Lamone argued that building the entrepreneurship center would be the same as starting a new company, with the added advantage of a head start provided by $2 million from a guy named Michael D. Dingman.

"Rudy, it wouldn't be the same at all," I said. "First, there's the difference in financial upside for me. Second, the Dingman Center is part of the University of Maryland. Frankly, the one negative of my last three years has been trying to deal with the bureaucracy and politics of a university. I don't need that crap anymore."

"Charlie, you'll be reporting directly to me," he answered. "You'll not only have complete autonomy, but I've been in this job a long time and I know how to deal with all the bureaucratic bull crap. There's nothing to worry about. As far as the financial part goes, I have a lot of contacts, and I'll get you plugged into some lucrative consulting deals."

We continued the back and forth through an extended lunch. Before we parted, Rudy extracted a promise from me: that I would give it some thought over the next couple of weeks. I arranged to meet with Jerry Feigen to learn more. Although I had met him previously, I did not know Jerry well. I found him affable and knowledgeable. He had done an admirable job of getting the Center off the ground by holding a series of seminars and workshops, assembling a small group of entrepreneurs-in-residence (EIRs) to assist start-up firms in the university's incubator, introducing several entrepreneurship courses into the school's MBA curriculum, and affiliating the Dingman Center with a national group of private ("angel") investors.

When I attempted to probe into Jerry's side of the story regarding his pending departure, his answers were somewhat elusive. Judging from his responses, and reading between the lines, I surmised that one of his major obstacles had been a lack of buy-in by the business school faculty. Later, I voiced this concern to Dean Lamone, but he assured me that it was untrue. But he must have suspected that I remained unconvinced because, a couple of days later, I received a phone call.

"Dr. Heller," said a woman's voice tinged with a slight Australian accent. "My name is Judy Olian, and I'm a professor at the College of Business and Management. I'd like to arrange a meeting with you, along with a couple of my colleagues."

I met three members of the business school faculty for lunch at the historic Rossborough Inn on campus. Judy Olian looked unlike any professor I had ever met. A pretty, petite, shapely blonde, she was dressed more like a fashion model than an academic. Soon I would find out that this chic, energetic lady was a respected scholar and an outstanding teacher, despite the fact that she defied the physical stereotype. She and her husband, Pete Liberti, would become good friends of Sue's and mine. Eventually, Judy would leave to become dean of the business schools at Penn State and UCLA.

Ken Smith was a former entrepreneur who decided to earn a doctorate and become an academic; his primary area of expertise was business strategy. Steve Carroll was the elder statesman of the trio, a pleasant man with a soft voice who, like the others, was a member of the Management and Organization Department.

"We're the search committee for the director of the Dingman Center," Steve informed me. "We'd like to try to convince you to apply for the position."

Search committee? I said to myself. *What the hell is going on here? I thought Rudy was offering me the job. Now I find out that this is a competitive process?* I said nothing out of concern for my friend Rudy. If he was trying to go around his search committee, it would not be politic for me to rat on him.

Later, when I questioned Rudy about the search committee, his response was quick and to the point.

"Don't worry about it. The university has its rules, and I know how to deal with them. Just apply—please!"

As I had not yet come up with any innovative ideas for starting another company, I thought, *What the hell. Maybe I can do this for a short time while I try to figure out what to do with the rest of my life.*

"Rudy," I said on the phone a few days later. "I've decided to apply. But, if I'm selected, I can only commit to you for one year. After that, I don't know what I might do."

"That's great," he replied. "I'll accept that. I know you're gonna love it and will stay a lot longer than a year."

CHAPTER SEVENTEEN

Time of My Life

In November 1989, I received a formal letter that informed me I had been selected by the search committee, and I was extended an offer of the position of director of the Michael D. Dingman Center for Entrepreneurship. I walked into Dean Rudolph Lamone's office in Tydings Hall and presented him with a written response: a list of fifteen demands. Following a lengthy negotiation, Rudy accepted all but two.

One he rejected was my request to bring with me Peggy Elder, my administrative assistant at MIPS. Rudy informed me that the Dingman Center already had an admin, but that she was out on extended sick leave and that she had filed a workman's compensation suit against the school. While this was pending, there was no way to bring in a new person. Reluctantly, I backed off.

The second pertained to the position of director itself. The business school was not only offering me a staff, and not faculty, appointment, but also one of a contract employee. At a university, titles and perceptions of status are very important. I knew that if faculty members perceived me as one who was inferior to them in the hierarchy, my job would be difficult and the Dingman Center would be considered a second-class organization. I informed Rudy that this was a deal-breaker. His dilemma was that a regular position counted against his allotted headcount while a contractual one did not. He had no room for me. I told him that I understood but would have to decline.

A couple of weeks before Christmas break, I received a revised offer, one that met my demands. I became a believer: Dean Lamone really did know how to get around "the bureaucratic bull crap."

I parted amicably with my colleagues at the ERC and took over the Dingman Center on Monday, February 5, 1990, four years to the day from my exit as CEO of Intercad Corporation. I walked down the dark, dank hall of the basement of one of the shabbiest buildings on the College Park campus—LeFrak Hall, named after an alumnus who was a successful, but somewhat disreputable, New York City builder. As I approached the room that would become my office, I spotted a familiar figure. A guy whom I recognized as CEO of one of the start-up firms in the university's incubator was sitting on the floor, leaning against my office door. When I came near, he stood up.

"One of your EIRs is trying to rip me off," he said without a greeting or preamble. "Your Center is supposed to be offering free mentoring, and this guy not only wants me to pay him a consulting fee, but he wants a piece of our equity. All this, just to help us write a business plan and introduce us to an investor."

The entrepreneurs-in-residence were experienced businesspersons who volunteered their time as mentors to young companies. I promised to look into the problem as soon as I became situated. Finally, I was able to open the door and walk into my new office—or I should say "our office." The small room contained two desks, and a young lady was sitting at one of them.

"Hi, I'm Charlie Heller, the new director of the Dingman Center," I introduced myself. "And who are you?"

She identified herself as one of the Center's graduate assistants, a second-year MBA student, who would be sharing the office with me.

Holy shit! I thought. *What have I gotten myself into? They've put me in a dark corner of the basement of this hellhole, and they didn't even give me a private office?*

I spent the morning meeting my staff, made up solely of graduate students and a mysterious administrative assistant who, as a result of an injury and her subsequent lawsuit against the university, had not been seen in six weeks.

It became clear to me almost immediately that there were two students upon whom I would lean the most in trying to get through a start-up period that was looking rocky. They were Susan Green, a second-year MBA, and Phil Bundy, a first-year. In Susan, I saw someone who was serious, process oriented, and meticulous. She would become my "Miss Inside," someone who would help me organize the Center and make it functional. Phil, who had come to UM straight from Wake Forest, where he had been a member of the NCAA championship golf team, was energetic and extroverted, a guy with obvious sales and marketing skills that would be critical in building the Center's outside image.

I tasked Susan with working through the university bureaucracy to get us immediate clerical relief by bringing in a temporary administrative assistant, and asked her to find another place for my office-mate so that I could have a private office. I cornered Phil and told him about my encounter with the CEO earlier that morning. Phil informed me that there were five entrepreneurs-in-residence and that each worked independently under few, if any, constraints and with no supervision. I asked Phil to call all of them and to tell them that, effective immediately, I was dissolving the EIR program. It was not yet noon of my first day on the job, and I had already pissed off several people. In the afternoon, I provoked the ire of another.

"A reporter from the *Washington Post* is on the line and wants to interview you," said the voice of a business-school public relations woman. "I'll connect you."

The reporter asked about my prior life as an entrepreneur before questioning me about my goals for the Dingman Center. I responded with a pitch that would become my party-line: to provide the kind of assistance I wish had been available to me when I was starting my first company, including mentoring from "been there, done that" entrepreneurs, education and training, and assistance with raising capital. I said that our goals were to become the focal point for entrepreneurs in the mid-Atlantic region and to develop a top-ranked entrepreneurship curriculum within the school's MBA program.

When I read the next morning's *Post*, I was astonished by a statement attributed to me. The reporter had written something to the effect that I was starting from scratch and that nothing at all had been accomplished at the Dingman Center prior to my arrival. Naively, I called the reporter and asked for a retraction, only to be told that he had heard me say those exact words and that no retraction was in order. Next, I called my predecessor, Jerry Feigen, and told him that I had not made the statement attributed to me and apologized for the fact that the article reflected negatively on him. It was clear that Jerry was skeptical and, when I hung up, I knew that I had failed to convince him. As a result, our relationship would be frosty for the next several years.

I convinced Rudy to provide the Center with additional offices in the dingy basement so that my staff would not be forced to hot desk. I organized a work party to make the place brighter and friendlier. I bought several gallons of paint in non-institutional colors and one evening all of us, along with our respective wives, husbands, and significant others, converted a virtual cave into a welcoming workplace. After midnight, with everyone gone, I inspected the premises. The rooms looked great, except for the unsightly wires that hung down from the ceilings. So, Sue and I walked around and cut them off. The next morning, I discovered that we had blown up the building's Ethernet network. My list of enemies was growing. Rudy called me into his office.

"What the hell are you doing over there?"

"I'm building you an entrepreneurship center."

"Okay, but walk a little more gently, will you?" he implored.

"No problem, Rudy. I will." I was really thinking, *You hired an entrepreneur to run your entrepreneurship center. I have no intention of slowing down.*

I convened a meeting of the center's board of advisors and discovered that several of them had resigned because they were friends of my predecessor and were unhappy with the change in leadership. I replaced them with my own friends and colleagues: Ed

Broenniman, president of The Piedmont Group; Bill Cole, partner at Ernst & Young; and Rogers Novak, a venture capitalist.

When I attended my first meeting of the management team of the Robert H. Smith School of Business, consisting of department and center heads, I could feel the chill in the air when Rudy introduced me. It was not long before I discovered that the faculty saw the Dingman Center as a threat, believing that it was competing with them for university funding, and that they did not consider entrepreneurship an area worthy of serious study and research. I realized that I had some tough work to do, not just outside the university, but inside the business school, as well.

I would have to overcome a number of obstacles if I was going to turn the Dingman Center into a serious player in the world of entrepreneurs. On the home front, I would have to convince the business school faculty not only that entrepreneurship was an area worthy of academic study and research, but also that my center would not compete with their departments for university funding. In order to accomplish the latter, I would have to find more outside sources of money. The current annual budget consisted of the interest on Mike Dingman's endowment, five percent of $2 million. That was $100,000, an amount that did not even cover my salary and left nothing for new activities and programs or salaries for a small staff.

Several MBA-level entrepreneurship courses had been developed prior to my arrival and ably taught by Ken Smith, an entrepreneur-turned-academic, and others. As we began planning additional courses pertaining to starting, financing, managing, and growing high-growth startups, I was determined to have them taught by "been there, done that" entrepreneurs rather than by academics whose knowledge came from texts and journal articles. I knew that I would have to apply gentle persuasion to get my colleagues to accept this philosophy.

Perhaps the most daunting task would be that of convincing the region's business community that the Dingman Center could deliver real, practical assistance beyond the boundaries of the College Park campus. I knew the world from which I had come. Its denizens viewed universities as ivory towers, inside which there was no interest in the world of commerce and contempt for the word that defines the ultimate goal of any private enterprise—"profit." At Dingman, we had set as our objective to become "the focal point for entrepreneurship in the mid-Atlantic region." In order to accomplish that lofty goal, we would have to earn the entrepreneur community's trust by providing services and programs of value.

Amazingly, I found myself facing the same enormous undertaking that I had encountered three times before: starting a "company" from scratch. Except this time, I was doing it within the constraints of a state university. My ability to multitask was tested immediately. I was creating and designing new programs, I was recruiting a cadre of volunteers, I was schmoozing the faculty, I was traveling around the region in order to promote our brand, and I was raising money. It was back to the hundred-hour workweek. And I was loving it!

What appeared to be some low-hanging fruit on the fundraising front was an effort started by Dean Lamone prior to my arrival. Rudy had connected with a Japanese billionaire named Koji Kanazawa, who wanted an affiliation with the Dingman Center, one that would help him begin to develop an entrepreneurial culture in his country. He was going to pay $350,000 for the privilege.

I was brought into the negotiations with Kanazawa's US representatives, and we held several meetings that seemed to lead nowhere. I examined the correspondence between the two parties, and it confirmed my view that the Japanese were changing the rules of the game with each meeting and letter. Having dealt with Japanese companies as a CEO, I recognized the tactic, and I wanted no part of it. I needed money now, and I did not have time for games.

"Rudy," I said to my boss. "These guys are just playing with us. Let's tell 'em to shit or get off the pot."

"I see that you're learning to speak like an academic," Rudy laughed. "I don't agree. We just have to let this play out. It's the way things are done in Asia. We need their money, and they have all the leverage."

The following day, I decided to defy my friend. I dictated a letter to Peggy Elder, whom I had been able to get transferred to the Dingman Center after several weeks of fighting the bureaucracy.

"Dear Mr. Kanazawa," it began. That was the extent of courteous language. In the next paragraph, I told him to shit or get off the pot using words only slightly less profane. I told him that I had a job to do, that it was urgent, and that I did not have time to play games. I picked a magic date in the life of every American—April 15—and stated that if Kanazawa's money did not arrive by that date, the deal would be off. Peggy typed and mailed the letter.

"You're out of your mind!" Rudy shouted when I brought him a copy. "You can't speak to the Japanese this way. With them, everything has to be polite and indirect. You've just blown your chance to have some significant start-up money. I put a lot of effort into this, and now you've blown it."

"I'm sorry, Rudy," I replied, embarrassed that I had acted hastily. "I have so much on my plate, and I just felt that I had to bring this thing to a close."

I pushed the incident out of my mind and continued to work on getting the Center off the ground and on finding money elsewhere. On Friday the 13th of April 1990, I walked into my office and found a pink telephone message slip on my desk. "Call the University Foundation Office," it stated. I dialed the extension and identified myself to the lady on the other end of the line.

"We have a check here made out to 'Dingman Center/University Foundation'," she said. "It's for $350,000. What do you want us to do with it?"

She did not have to tell me who had written the check. It would be a year after I deposited the check before Rudy and I finally would meet Koji Kanazawa. His caravan of five white limousines picked us up at our hotel in Albuquerque, New Mexico, and whisked us off to dinner in an otherwise empty Japanese restaurant his people had rented for the evening. I had never seen anyone consume as many glasses of alcohol as our Asian hosts seated around the sunken table. In three or four hours, there were toasts to everything from the health of each individual present, to cooperation between our organizations, to friendship between our countries, to peace in the world. Each toast was followed by the downing of a shot of sake. Fortunately, I was seated in front of a large potted cactus, and I was able to sneak my shot glasses under the table and to keep the tropical plant well fed. I hope it survived. Had I not been able to play gardener with much of my sake, someone would have had to carry me out the door.

The next time I saw an image of Koji Kanazawa was a year later in a photograph accompanying an article in *Business Week* magazine. The piece described the recent crash of Japanese markets and it singled out Kanazawa because the failures of his real-estate ventures had taken down two of the nation's largest banks. Now bankrupt, he attempted to get back the money he had donated to us, only to be told that, once money is contributed to a University of Maryland endowment, it cannot be returned. I was happy to have his cash, but I felt sad for Koji, who was a nice man.

Those early days of 1990 marked not only a happy transition in my professional career, but also a titanic change in my personal life. My native country, Czechoslovakia, cast away forty-one years of oppression under Communism and became free. Having obeyed my father and forgotten everything that had happened to me on the other side of the Atlantic, I thought I had also followed Papa's order to "become one hundred percent American."

To my surprise, during the Velvet Revolution of November 1989, I was mesmerized by the words of free Czechoslovakia's new leader, Václav Havel, who spoke words so eloquent and so full of hope that I felt my past unexpectedly come rushing at me. I experienced a surge of pride in my native country and a sudden need to reconnect and reconcile with it.

Rudy Lamone recognized my need to return to Prague. Pretending that it was important to the university, he arranged for me to attend the first major conference on doing business in the "new" Czechoslovakia. To convince me that the trip had value to the business school, Rudy registered to attend along with me. Unbeknownst to me, he had no intention of going and cancelled at the last moment. Quite simply, he was doing me a favor.

On October 20, 1990, my first night in Prague, after sitting in my room and fighting jet lag, I decided to go for a walk, despite the fact that it was nearly midnight and I had not slept in more than twenty-four hours. Once outside the Hotel Diplomat, I felt as if a magnet was pulling me in a single direction. It drew me toward Hradčany, the castle on the hill above Prague which has been home to kings and presidents for hundreds of years. The castle's panorama is dominated by a great cathedral, whose soaring spires have served as inspiration for the Czech nation's writers, poets, composers, and exiles like me.

As I walked up the narrow streets toward Hradčany, I noticed that the small, baroque, hundreds-of-years-old houses were gray. I remembered them having had bright colors, mostly yellow and beige, when I was a kid. Under the dim light of street lamps, I could see that the stucco façades were filthy, shabby, and crumbling. Like everything that had no immediate utility to them and their party, the Communists had allowed my city to fall apart.

My city? I startled myself. *Did I really say that?*

Emerging from a passageway, I was overwhelmed by the sight of St. Vitus Cathedral, the spiritual center of the nation for six hundred years. The burial place of former Czech kings and home of the crown jewels, the Gothic tower soared toward the night sky. As I stood there alone and stared at the statues of saints looking down at me, I felt as if I had been struck by lightning.

How much these old gentlemen of stone have seen! Just in my fifty-four years of life, how much oppression have they observed? I counted the years of Czech freedom in my lifetime: 1936, 1937, 1938, 1945, 1946, 1947, and now 1990. *Only seven years out of my entire life! Incredible! How could God let this happen to one small country?*

I dropped to my knees and began to weep, uncontrollably and for a very long time, alone in this sacred place. I cried for my country, for my fellow Czechs, for my murdered family, for my exiled parents, for the friends I had left behind, and for myself.

When, finally, I got up and made my way back from the castle, I was shocked by the metamorphosis I had just experienced. I realized that I had not succeeded in erasing my childhood memories after all. I had only hidden them from myself. For the first time, I wanted to connect with my past in every way possible.

My visits to Prague became more frequent as I got deeply involved in the training of Czechoslovak businesspeople about life in a free-market economy. At the same time, with the help of our attorney, Jiří Bedrna, and good friend Jitka Thomasová, I began to recover my family's properties. Eventually, I got back our clothing factory and a couple of single-family houses through the government's restitution process. Our seven-story building in Prague, which had been taken over by the Communist Party, was another matter. Mother and I sued the Party, and I took over the building following a settlement.

More than anything during these visits—often accompanied by my wife Sue—I enjoyed walking the streets of Prague with Mother's best friend from years past, Aša Hahnová, the wonderful lady whom I called *Teta* (aunt). I delighted in hearing the sound of the Czech language, particularly when spoken by children. When I spotted them pouring out of school doors, I stopped, listened, and laughed along with them. Hearing my native language spoken by innocent children was like a concerto emanating from the strings of Itzhak Perlman's violin. The sight and sound transported me back to another time, a time when my boyhood best friend, Vlád'a Svoboda, and I had roamed the streets of Prague after school.

Seeing familiar buildings and streets in Prague gave me a sense of belonging. I had been robbed of my heritage, but now this beautiful city in the heart of Europe seemed to be saying, "Welcome home, prodigal son. You're still my son."

Franz Kafka learned of her power long ago, when he wrote: "Prague does not let go—either of you or me. This little mother has claws. There is nothing to do but to give in. We would have to set her on fire from both sides . . . only thus could we free ourselves."

Back in America, we got off to a fast start at the Dingman Center. We saturated the region with seminars, roundtables, and workshops for entrepreneurs. I kept in mind the two things I needed more than anything else when I was starting companies: seed funding and advice from experienced entrepreneurs. Neither was available in the mid-Atlantic area, so we set about correcting the situation. We started a network of angel investors and called it the Baltimore-Washington Venture Group. I contacted twenty-five friends who were successful high-tech entrepreneurs and asked them if they would be willing to volunteer the equivalent of a day each month to mentor newbie founders of companies. To my surprise, all signed on. I was totally shocked when, a few months into the program, nearly two hundred more volunteers—entrepreneurs, corporate executives, accountants, and lawyers—joined as mentors. Just like that, we were a major player in the conversion of our region from a black hole for entrepreneurs to a hotbed.

Our efforts did not go unrecognized. We received a lot of press because our events played to full houses. In 1992, I received the Maryland "Entrepreneur of the Year" award for services to entrepreneurs. The award was sponsored by Ernst & Young, Merrill Lynch, and *Inc.* magazine, and our connection to these powerhouse organizations boosted us in such a way that we were suddenly a national model, one to be emulated by universities throughout the country. I was joined at the hip with Dean Rudy Lamone, who supported me in every way. For his efforts on behalf of the region's entrepreneurial community, he, too, would be a recipient of the Entrepreneur of the Year award a few years later.

The Kauffman Foundation, the largest funder of entrepreneurial activities in the world, invited me to its headquarters in Kansas City, where I was introduced to the directors of centers similar to ours from Harvard, Babson, University of Pennsylvania's Wharton School, Baylor, University of Southern California, UCLA, and Ball State. The Foundation anointed us the leaders of the entrepreneurship movement among American universities. We formed a small coalition that held conferences dealing with best practices for university centers and other issues. Long after my departure, as entrepreneurship finally became fashionable at universities, this group grew into a consortium of more than two hundred schools.

We were flying high. Mike Dingman added $4 million to his original $2 million endowment, and I started a group called the Inner Circle—corporations and individuals who made annual contributions to the Center. I had enough money to surround myself with a strong team. Susan Green received her MBA and stayed on as associate director, now married to her classmate, Scott Simpson. Following Susan's eventual departure for Colorado, Sandra Nola took over the number two position, Angela Tandy joined us and eventually became assistant director, and Tonya Brockett directed some of the programs. We created a scholarship program that brought bright MBA students called Dingman and Lamone Scholars into the Center to manage several programs. Some truly outstanding young people passed through and made lasting contributions. There were Phil Bundy, Robin Samuelson, Andy Enfield, Jeff Grinspoon, Cathy McNeil, Mike Preston, Michael Wolf, Chris Campbell, and many others to whom I owe a debt of gratitude and an apology for not including their names.

We assisted hundreds of young technology companies throughout Maryland, Washington, and Northern Virginia with advice and training. We helped entrepreneurs build their teams and to find start-up funding. Our impact expanded when we took over the management of the Small Business Development Center network for the entire state of Maryland. While becoming the focus for entrepreneurship in the region had been a pipe dream when I took over directorship of the Center, the business press and—more importantly—our constituents were now using similar words to describe the University of Maryland's Michael D. Dingman Center for Entrepreneurship.

I continued to toil impossible hours and to put hundreds of miles on my car's odometer, yet I managed to balance work with fun activities. Sue, David, and I raced our sailboat regularly and successfully on the Chesapeake Bay. We bought a mountain condo in beautiful Canaan Valley, West Virginia, where we skied in the winter and hiked and played golf in the warmer months. I wrote a weekly column for *The Capital* newspaper, a monthly column for the *Washington Business Journal,* and I freelanced for sailing and skiing magazines. Grudgingly, I admitted to myself that I was enjoying myself more now than I had as an entrepreneur CEO and that I was finding greater satisfaction from having built the Dingman Center than I had in creating two software companies. Moreover, as a person who has never denied having an ego, I was pleased by the celebrity status I was receiving in the press, in the business community, and—yes—even among my faculty peers.

My life was good even on the financial front. While I had taken a substantial pay cut when I came to the university, my salary now was quite generous. Some years, I made even more money on the outside, from consulting, teaching, and serving on boards of directors. One of the more interesting board appointments came as a direct result of my association with the business school.

Bill Mayer, an alumnus who had been president of First Boston Corporation, succeeded Rudy Lamone as dean when Rudy decided to step down after cancer surgery. Rudy was now working with me at the Dingman Center. Bill was on the board of Hambrecht & Quist, the nation's top investment bank for high-tech companies in the go-go 1990s, located in San Francisco. H&Q had a venture capital arm that invested in technology start-ups. Bill told me about one such investment in Fort Washington, Pennsylvania. The company was called ESPS, and it developed software for the pharmaceutical industry.

"These guys have a hot product, but they're a bunch of techies who can't manage their way out of a paper bag, and they're fighting among themselves," Bill told me. "They need some adult supervision and someone has to convince them that they need to bring in a strong CEO from the outside. You'd be perfect to make that happen from a position on the board."

I agreed to drive up to check things out. I spent a couple of hours with the CEO and was impressed by his depth of knowledge of the market and the technology. But when his co-founder asked for a private meeting with me, I smelled trouble. I found it. Very quickly, it became obvious that there were two factions in the company, each led by a founder, and that they were feuding with one another. As I drove home that evening, I wondered if I really wanted to dive into this can of worms. Besides, I had been told that the company would not be able to pay me in cash, and that my director fee would be solely in the form of stock options. I had enough worthless stock options at home to wallpaper a bathroom, and I wondered if I needed more.

The next day, I contacted H&Q's representative on ESPS's board, Standish O'Grady, intending to decline. But Standish convinced me that together we would not only set the company on the right track, but that, once we did that, we would take the company public. My options would be generous and my gain would be lucrative. I signed on. We managed to get rid of one of the feuding founders and to convince the remaining one to accept a new CEO. We brought in Terry Brennan, an experienced pharma executive with sales and marketing savvy, to run the company, and we were on our way. In those early days of the "dot com era," ESPS was an anomaly. While the internet companies going public were losing millions of dollars and had little hope of ever turning a profit, we were making money and growing our sales at a steady, controlled pace.

When we announced that our company, renamed Liquent, was

considering an IPO, the investment banks came after us like a bunch of starving hyenas. I must confess that I made more money than I deserved to make during the decision period, under conditions that were legal, but only marginally ethical. While they were competing for the underwriter position, three of the banks opened personal investment accounts for me. Every week, each of these outfits was taking several companies public and the IPOs usually took place on Fridays. Sue and I played golf in a couples' twilight league at our club each Friday evening and, invariably, I would receive calls on my cell phone on the way to the course. They would go like this:

"Hi, this is Pete from XYZ," the voice would announce. "We bought five hundred shares of Geewhiz.com for you this morning in an IPO. We sold them this afternoon. You made $3,500." And so it went for several weeks, while I wrestled with my conscience. The latter lost.

The Liquent board went through a procedure called "bake-off," a competition to determine which firm would be most appropriate as an underwriter. I never totaled my profits in those "investments" in companies of which I had never heard, and I have no idea if other board members were receiving the same treatment as I was; I did not ask. Regardless, the intended bribes had no effect on my decision or anyone else's. We voted unanimously for a firm that did not participate in the granting of favors—at least for me—Hambrecht & Quist.

Standish O'Grady, who had been replaced on the board by H&Q Ventures' Chris Hollenbeck, had not lied to me. I had received very generous stock options, and now they were about to have value. I had the option to purchase thousands of shares of Liquent stock, mostly at eight cents per share. The options had to be re-priced because they would be deemed too cheap by the SEC, but my profit would still be huge because we contemplated going public at around $10 per share. There was only one hitch. I had to exercise the options—that is, buy the shares—prior to the IPO, and I would only be allowed to sell a small portion in the initial offering and would be restricted from selling the remainder for some time. The real problem was that, since I was an outside director (rather than an officer or employee of the company), my options were deemed "nonqualified" by the IRS; I had to pay income taxes approaching $400,000 *without* having sold the stock. And I certainly did not have that kind of cash on hand to send to Uncle Sam. What to do?

I convinced the underwriters to allow me to sell enough shares in the IPO to pay off the taxes, plus a little profit, a process called the "green shoe." That was great, but I still had to come up with $400,000 to pay the IRS immediately, before the offering could be filed. Where was I going to come up with that kind of money?

Fortunately, these were the go-go years and even some commercial bankers were willing to drop their usual staid, conservative approach. Especially if one had a bank president for a friend. I was lucky enough to have such a friend. I will call him Bruce. He ran a community bank in Annapolis. I told Bruce my story and promised him that a loan of $400,000 would be paid off as soon as Liquent went public. He scratched his chin while I sweated in my seat.

"What if the IPO doesn't happen, for whatever reason?" he asked.

"That's a reasonable question, Bruce," I answered. "Frankly, I haven't thought about that scenario. I guess the answer is we'd both be in deep shit. But I think you know me well enough to believe that, eventually, I'll pay back every cent."

Bruce looked away from me and stared out the window, no doubt wondering how his board would react in case of such a catastrophe. Finally, he picked up the phone and asked his loan officer to join us in the office. Bruce explained that the bank would make me the loan and then proceeded to nearly floor me with his instructions to the loan officer.

"Since there's no collateral, I want you to make it look like a second mortgage on Charlie's house. Don't do anything else. No appraisal, no actual lien, no nothing. Just leave the file open as 'pending' in case the regulators see it before the loan is paid off. If the public offering should fall through, we'll turn it into a real second mortgage."

The loan officer smiled and left the office, only to return a few minutes later with a check for $400,000. I placed it in my briefcase, hugged and thanked Bruce, and practically walked on air down Main Street toward the Annapolis Yacht Club, where I celebrated with a Mount Gay and tonic.

The IPO went off as scheduled, although at $7.50 per share rather than the desired $10. I sold enough of my shares in the offering to pay off the bank loan, and I was poised for the stock price to take off as I prepared to wait the SEC-mandated period before I could begin selling off some of my remaining thousands of shares. But disaster struck quickly because management paid more attention to the stock ticker each day than to running the business and generating sales.

As the first quarter of Liquent's life as a public company was coming to a close, Terry Brennan, the CEO, injured his knee while trying to jump onto a moving train. The injury caused an infection that led to the need for a heart valve replacement. Terry, the company's most effective salesman, was out of action for many weeks. Liquent failed to make its numbers, and Wall Street was unhappy. The stock price dropped, other management problems sprang up, and the CEO was replaced. Eventually, the company was sold for less than thirty cents a share. Instead of millions, I made a few thousand dollars. In the end, it was another adventure that seemed to come with the territory in my ten years as head of the Dingman Center.

By 1998, I had been managing the Center for eight years. During that period, we had been instrumental in helping to change the Baltimore-Washington-Northern Virginia region from a land of government contractors, known as "Beltway Bandits," to a mecca for high-technology start-ups. Our organization had nurtured several hundred of these young companies. We established close ties with the area's growing community of venture capital firms, and I was even elected to the board of directors of MAVA, the Mid-Atlantic Venture Association—the only non-VC on that governing body.

The institutional investors benefitted from their ties with our Center. Although most of our client start-ups were much too early (and thus too risky) for VCs, there were exceptions. Occasionally, we came across firms with such exciting technology or such an impressive management team that venture capitalists found them worthy of an investment. This was particularly true at the beginning of the Internet age, in the mid- and late 1990s. After assisting "dot-coms" and other such entrepreneurial firms with their strategies and business plans, we introduced them to our VC friends, who bet on some of them in hopes of major financial gains down the road.

Perhaps it was greed, or maybe I had become restless again and needed another world to conquer, but in the fall of 1998, I decided to leave the University of Maryland and go into the venture capital business myself. My ten years at the Smith School of Business had been the most fulfilling period of my professional life, but it was time to move on. I would explore the opportunities, but I would not reveal my plans until I could see more clearly the road ahead.

CHAPTER EIGHTEEN

Ego Trip

L ike entrepreneurs, venture capitalists were the rock stars of the go-go, dot-com years. The VC world was an exclusive club, one to which many aspired and very few ascended. For me, the lure of the "dark side" was less about the chance to make big bucks than another mountain to climb and—perhaps—another way to gain respect.

I decided to attempt to ascend the mountain on my own. I saw an unfulfilled niche in the financing food chain for young firms. At a company's inception, there are high-net-worth individuals called "angels" who are willing to risk relatively small amounts of seed money on bright new ideas. Often, they are cashed-out entrepreneurs. Even more often, they belong to a group derisively called the "3Fs"— friends, family, and fools. They may not understand the technology behind the start-up, but they are willing to risk a few thousand dollars to help a relative or a friend. Some do it to feed their egos.

"Hey, let me tell you about the Internet company I've invested in," they can boast to their friends at cocktail parties.

Venture capitalists are professional investors who run limited partnerships funded by institutions such as pension funds, insurance companies, banks, and family offices. They invest considerably large amounts—often several million dollars—but usually only in young companies with services or products that have been validated by the marketplace. The companies must have some sales and should be within a year or two of cash-flow breakeven in order to appeal to VCs. Most importantly, they need to have promise of high, and relatively fast, growth in order for the investors to have a reasonable expectation of a profitable exit.

The void in the chain that I identified came between the original, small seed investment and ultimate eligibility for traditional venture capital. There was a good reason for this void. The amount of investment generally required during this phase—known as the "A-round"—was too high for angels and 3Fs and too risky for institutions. So I decided to step into this abyss and to raise a venture capital fund that would invest in such early-stage companies. I was confident that I had sufficient experience, both as an entrepreneur who had taken his own companies across this chasm and as one who had spent the past nine years helping others who were at this stage, to make such a fund a success.

I brought in two friends as partners. Ed Broenniman was president of The Piedmont Group in Northern Virginia, an experienced businessman and a former entrepreneur-in-residence at the Dingman Center. Arthur "Jib" Edwards was a fellow Annapolitan whom I had met through tennis; he had taken over his father's successful real-estate investment firm and had become interested in, and knowledgeable about, high-tech start-ups. Together, we drafted a Private Placement Memorandum, a sales document with which we hoped to raise our first fund of $25 million.

We contacted a number of high-net-worth individuals and received a few commitments. But after several weeks, we were a long way from $25 million. I had not called on the wealthiest person on my list of candidate investors because I was hesitant to tell him that I was planning to leave the Dingman Center.

Over the years at the university, I had come to know, and to admire, the benefactor of my center. Following a successful career on Wall Street, Michael D. Dingman had run a number of companies including Wheelabrator-Frye, Signal, Allied Signal, Fisher Scientific, and the Henley Group. Currently, he was living in The Bahamas and operating Shipston Group, an international investment firm. Most important to me personally, he had become a good friend and loyal supporter.

I wondered how Mike would react to my decision to leave the organization that bore his name. We were anxious to gain some traction and needed a big name that would become a magnet for other investors. So, with a lump in my throat, I telephoned Mike at his office in Leyford Cay on the island of New Providence.

"Mike," I began. "I haven't told anyone because I wanted you to be the first to hear it. I'm planning to leave the Dingman Center." I held my breath as I awaited his response.

"Really?" he asked. "What are you going to do, start another company?"

"Well, sort of," I said. "I've learned a lot about venture capital firms after doing so much business with them, and I've discovered an uncrowded niche in the market. I've decided to take a crack at being a VC and to start a fund."

"What're you going to invest in?" asked Mike. To my great relief, he sounded interested and not at all angry about my plans to leave the Center.

"There's a real gap in the financing of high-tech start-ups." I explained the void to him and pressed on. "At the center, we see a lot of new companies with great potential die because they're starved for that early-stage capital infusion. At that point, they need someone who comes not only with money, but who can also provide mentoring based on 'been there, done that' experience. That's where I want to be."

"That's a pretty risky business, isn't it?" Mike did not wait for an answer before he continued, "Charlie, you've done a hell of a job building the Dingman Center, and I want you to know that I appreciate everything you've accomplished. I think if anyone can pull this off, it's you. I wish you nothing but the best."

Grateful that the Center's benefactor would not resist my exit, I felt emboldened to ask the next question.

"Mike, do you think you might be interested in investing in the fund?"

"I don't know. I have lots of things going right now, mostly in Russia," he said. "Do you have anything in writing about the fund that I can look at and pass on to my finance guy?"

"Yes. We have a PPM. I'll overnight it to you. I'll appreciate you taking a look at it."

Knowing how important an investment by Michael D. Dingman would be—both in terms of helping us toward our fundraising goal and for his drawing power—my partners and I spent an anxious two weeks waiting for a response. When it came, it hit me like a thunderbolt.

"Charlie, I've decided to do it," he stated on the phone, and I nearly wet my pants. "I'll put in twenty-five."

The smile disappeared from my face, and my pants remained dry. Twenty-five thousand was a drop in the bucket. Surely, he could do better.

"But, Mike," I finally sputtered. "The minimum investment for individuals is a hundred thousand."

"You don't understand," he answered. "I meant twenty-five *million*. I want to do the whole thing. My conditions are that this will be just you and me. There won't be any other investors, and you won't have the partners listed in the PPM. In effect, I'll be like the Limited Partner and you'll be like the General Partner. You'll find and vet the deals, you'll make the investment decisions and run them by me for approval, and I'll make the money available as it's needed. We'll work out your compensation and operating budget before we get started. I'll let you and my finance guy finalize all the details."

I was blown away. I muttered something about appreciating Mike's confidence and looking forward to being in business with him. After hanging up and having had time to grasp what had just taken place, I began to worry about having to inform Ed and Jib that they would not be part of the revised fund. Both were friends as well as business colleagues. I worried about ruining our friendships. I had built my entire career on integrity and loyalty, and now I was in a position to violate both. Yet, what choice did I have?

My partners were not happy. But they seemed to agree with me that without Mike Dingman or someone like him, we would be unable to raise sufficient capital anytime soon. Reluctantly, they wished me luck and left me to inform those few investors whom we had "soft-circled" that plans had changed.

Thus began the Chesapeake Venture Capital Fund. I contacted Baltimore venture capitalist Bill Gust, who had been managing partner of a now-defunct fund of the same name, and received his blessing to use the name of a body of water that was near and dear to my heart.

For some time, I had been tracking the progress of a network security company in the University of Maryland Technology Advancement Program, an incubator for high-tech start-ups. Having already performed a great deal of due diligence, I proposed the deal to Mike Dingman as our first investment, a total of $250,000 up front, with an additional $250,000 to follow if certain milestones were reached. Mike agreed, and I turned to my attorney friend, Ernie Stern, for the preparation of a term sheet, defining the terms and conditions of the investment.

Immediately after that, I left the country as part of a State of Maryland trade mission to Israel. I was going there as a representative of the university, and my tasks consisted of initiating faculty and student exchange programs with Technion University in Haifa, learning about the country's incubators, and looking for other opportunities for cooperation. At the same time, I could not help but occasionally wear my Chesapeake Venture Capital Fund hat and to look for investment opportunities. Israel is a hotbed of entrepreneurship, with the highest number of start-ups per capita in the world, and I was brought in front of several interesting companies looking for financing. I met the managing partner of a small Israeli venture fund, and we agreed to look at co-investing in one or two of these firms.

After a whirlwind week in Israel, I flew home satisfied with the results of the mission. I had accomplished all my objectives for the University of Maryland, and I had kick-started the fund by discovering several potential investments. I was on a roll.

I was working two jobs now, but I was flying high—doing something that challenged and excited me. Ernie Stern had completed the term sheet and, after a few edits, I presented it to our first potential portfolio company. While waiting for a response, I began doing due diligence on the best of the Israeli deals.

Then, a figurative bomb blew up my new world. I was in my home office early on a Tuesday morning, only a few days after my return from Israel, when the phone rang. It was my partner, Mike Dingman.

"Charlie," he said. "I'm in Russia. And I have bad news. I'm involved in some big oil and gas exploration deals over here. These Russian bastards are robbing me blind and mismanaging my money. I have to stay over here for a while to run things. I'm about to lose a ton of money. I'm afraid that I'm out of the venture capital business."

I do not recall what I uttered into the phone as I saw the Chesapeake Venture Capital Fund, and my dreams, go up in smoke. Stunned, I sat in my office and stared at the walls for a couple of hours before my mind began to clear. There was work to be done. I had to unwind everything that I had started. Immediately, I called the CEO of the company to whom I had presented a term sheet. I apologized profusely when I informed him that the offer was off the table. I sent messages to my newly established contacts in Israel, advising everyone that the fund had lost its major investor and was not going to be investing in the immediate future. I informed Ernie Stern that I would be paying for his legal services to the fund out my own pocket.

When Sue returned home from teaching at the Naval Academy Primary School, she knew from my facial expression and body language that all was not well.

"The venture fund is dead," I told her. "Mike Dingman called me from Russia and said that he is losing millions there and that he has to pull out of our deal."

"I'm so sorry," she answered. "What are you going to do?"

"I haven't had time to think about that yet. I've spent all day undoing all the things I had going with the fund. It was damned embarrassing. Now it's time for me to think logically about the future."

For the next few days after Mike Dingman torpedoed my plans, I found it challenging to think rationally about my immediate future. I had difficulty sleeping, and during the day I sat at my university desk and stared out the window, seeing nothing. It took a couple of weeks before I began to consider the possibilities. I could contact Ed Broenniman and Jib Edwards, tell them what happened, and ask them if they were interested in resurrecting the old plan. I could try to raise money for Chesapeake Venture Capital Fund on my own. I could forget about the idea of becoming a venture capitalist—at least for now—and continue my work at the Dingman Center. After all, I had earned a certain amount of recognition and I was happy there.

For the first time in a long while, I took the time to contemplate my situation. Prior to coming to the University of Maryland, I had been CEO of two software companies for eighteen years. Although I derived satisfaction from having led the teams that built CADCOM and Intercad from scratch, I had to admit that neither was a smashing success as measured in terms of monumental sales, sizable profits, and ample returns to shareholders. My fulfillment had come primarily from having pioneered and advanced important technologies, from having created companies known for their integrity and dependability, and, most importantly, for having put together tightly knit teams of talented, wonderful people, all of whom I considered more as colleagues than employees. But building CADCOM and Intercad had not given me the kind of general personal prominence that my entrepreneur's ego demanded.

Now, after eight years of building and running the Dingman Center, I had to acknowledge the fact that I had achieved the kind of preeminence that had eluded me when I was managing companies. My time spent assisting hundreds of start-ups, educating and training scores of entrepreneurs, and playing a major role in making the University of Maryland the focal point for entrepreneurship in the region had not gone unnoticed. Much to my delight—which I attempted to hide in order to appear modest—the press called me "Mr. Entrepreneurship." I was a frequent guest on TV and radio shows, I was quoted almost weekly in various publications, I wrote articles about entrepreneurship and new venture creation, and I turned down many requests for guest speaker and panelist appearances as I just didn't have the time.

My ego really became inflated when the *Wall Street Journal* not only wrote about me, but even printed a dot portrait of me, a rare honor in the 1990s, usually reserved for CEOs of Fortune 500 companies. I was named Maryland's Entrepreneur of the Year, a magazine included me among "The Fifty Most Influential People in Southern Technology," and the University of Maryland appointed me its first-ever Professor of Practice in 1999. The financial rewards were substantial, as well. I took advantage of the university's policy of allowing faculty members to spend one day per week consulting. Large companies were willing to pay me as much as $350 per hour to teach them to be more entrepreneurial. Young high-tech companies sought my presence on their boards of directors and most paid me in stock options, some of which turned into real money when the firms went public. I was earning more money, and generating more respect, than at any time in my life.

Fortunately, I had not announced my intention to leave to anyone at the university, and I was certain that Mike Dingman had not discussed it with anybody in College Park. Thus the decision to stay at the Dingman Center was not difficult. However, my taste of life as a venture capitalist had me keeping my eyes open for other opportunities to get to the "dark side."

CHAPTER NINETEEN

Bahamas Adventure

With the arrival of 1999, I had so much on my plate that I had no time to lament what might have been, had the partnership with Mike Dingman worked out. Mike had donated $2 million to the College of The Bahamas in order to start an entrepreneurship center there, and he asked Rudy Lamone and me to help the Bahamians get it off the ground. Before his problems in Russia began, Mike had committed an additional $2 million to the creation of a seed venture capital fund to assist Bahamian start-ups.

Rudy and I made a number of trips to Nassau on the island of New Providence. With assistance from my Dingman Center colleagues, Sandra Nola and Angela Tandy, we got the COB entrepreneurship center going and helped select its first director, Michael Rolle. Now, my task was to raise additional money for the newly created Bahamas Seed Venture Fund. I was practically commuting to The Bahamas—not an altogether unpleasant task because my home away from home was the fabulous Atlantis hotel on Paradise Island, where I always managed to find time to enjoy the beach, the pool, the river ride, and a few hours in the casino.

Along with fundraising, Rudy and I conducted a number of seminars for Bahamian entrepreneurs. These were major events, with television coverage and stories on the front page of the *Nassau Guardian*. Entrepreneurs from many of the country's islands—New Providence, the Abacos, Grand Bahama, Andros, Eleuthera, Great Exuma—attended our workshops and roundtables. We were celebrated by everyone from the governor general and prime minister to waiters in restaurants. I made many friends in Nassau and developed a taste for conch salad, grouper, and Kalik beer, particularly when served at my favorite restaurant, Greycliff. My trips to Nassau became so frequent that the Greycliff maître d' greeted me with "Welcome home!" each time I entered.

Raising money for the seed fund was another matter. Mike Dingman introduced Rudy and me to some of The Bahamas' wealthiest residents, most of whom lived in the same gated community as the Dingmans, Leyford Cay. But they were reluctant to put money into a fund that could not promise high returns similar to those of US VC funds. In America, venture firms bet on high-growth companies that provide an exit through either public offerings of stock or acquisition by larger firms. Bahamian companies, on the other hand, were neither high tech nor high growth. They tended to provide products or services to the travel industry or to focus on the islands' only other large market, fishing. They were typically unglamorous and offered slow growth and no promise of an exit for investors.

Sir John Templeton, founder of the hugely successful Templeton Funds, put his finger on the problem.

"This isn't really a venture capital fund," he said as he rejected my fundraising plea. "It's a pot of money for economic development."

He was largely correct. And he and other ex-pats living in The Bahamas did not feel the same obligation to assist the nation's economy as did Michael Dingman. Our pursuit of institutions such as commercial banks, insurance companies, and the Inter-American Development Bank yielded the same negative results after months of wasted effort. Eventually, the idea fizzled and the fund was dissolved. In a few short months, I had been CEO of two nonstarter venture capital funds. Was there a message there? Perhaps, but I didn't receive it.

Looking back at my 1999 calendar to refresh my memory of the events from that year, I wonder how my body and mind survived the rigors of constant travel. In the first four months of that year, my journal shows four visits to The Bahamas; twelve trips to Liquent in Fort Washington, Pennsylvania; board meetings in Los Angeles, Miami, and San Francisco; conferences in Atlanta, Kansas City, and Houston. There were also two visits to my mother in New Jersey. In addition to all this, I ran frequent Dingman Center evening events for entrepreneurs in Northern Virginia, Washington, and Maryland's Montgomery County.

Interspersed among these business trips were three vacations: golf in Myrtle Beach and skiing in Sun Valley and Canaan Valley. It was these vacations, as well as other diversions with family and friends, that kept me both sane and grounded, not only during those first months of 1999, but throughout my career. Among the many lessons I pass on to entrepreneurs is to "have a life." One must have interests and hobbies outside the business, and—as difficult as it might seem to most entrepreneurs—family, friends, and one's own self are more important than the company.

CHAPTER TWENTY

Crossing to the Dark Side

*H**oly crap!* I thought as I stared at the man who walked through the door of my Dingman Center office. *It's Sean Connery!*

I knew that Connery no longer looked like the James Bond character he had played in films some twenty years back. I had seen the Scottish actor in The Bahamas only a few months before. He was a near neighbor of Mike Dingman, and I had stood next to him in the pro shop of the Leyford Cay Club golf course while buying a visor. Now he was in Maryland? Well, not quite.

Rudy Lamone had told me in October 1999 that a friend of his had requested a meeting with me. Not only would this introduction lead to another phase in my professional career, but it would be the start of a long and enduring friendship.

The movie-star lookalike was actually one J. Phillip Samper. Like the present-day Connery, Phil was tall, elegant, and rugged-looking, with thinning gray hair and a gray beard. He had the same wry, charming smile as the former 007. After we would become friends, Phil would regale me with stories of how he had been mistaken for the actor hundreds of times—and how much he enjoyed the notoriety that comes with the mistaken identity. But I found out very quickly that Phil did not need to pretend that he was a famous movie star. He had an impressive record of his own and was something of a legend in business circles.

Phil was raised in Colombia, South America, and came to the United States at an early age. A graduate of the University of California Berkeley and the MIT Sloan School of Management, his most recent positions had been those of chairman and CEO of Cray Research, president of Sun Microsystems Computer Corporation, and before that, CEO of Kinder-Care Learning Centers.

"Tell him about Kodak," Rudy prompted as we continued to become acquainted.

"I was vice chairman, responsible for 70 percent of Kodak's worldwide operations," Samper explained.

"When?" I asked. There was a reason behind my question.

"In the 1980s."

"I have to ask you something, Phil," I said. "In 1985, when I was running Intercad, we were slowly capturing a good piece of the electronic publishing market with our Illustrator software. We were running on Apollo workstations. We had been courting Kodak for months and thought that we were close to a huge sale that would have brought in big bucks and, with the visibility it would have given us, would have made us number one in our space."

From the smile that evolved into a grin, I had the feeling that Samper knew where the story was leading.

"Then," I continued, "while we were waiting for Kodak's approval of the big purchase from us, we were hit by a blockbuster announcement. Kodak was about to invest $20 million in Sun Microsystems. Since Sun and Apollo were fierce competitors, we knew that we had been blown out of the water. You said that later on, you became president of Sun. I have a feeling that you may have been familiar with this deal."

"I was the one who made the investment in Sun," said Phil.

"Wow! If it hadn't been for you . . ." I stopped, smiled, and said simply, "You damn near put us out of business and me out of a job. It's still great to meet you."

Samper said he had asked Rudy to introduce us because he had heard about my work at the Dingman Center. He explained that he and a partner, Rick Bolander, had started a venture capital fund, Gabriel Venture Partners, and were in the final stages of raising $100 million for it.

"We're based in Redwood Shores in Silicon Valley, but we want to be a bi-coastal firm," he explained. "My wife and I have homes in both San Francisco and Annapolis, but I don't have connections in the venture capital or entrepreneur communities here. I know that you have a great network and reputation in this region. We'd like you to become involved with us."

He went on to tell me that they had created a category called "venture partner" intended for people who would help Gabriel source deals and serve on boards of directors of portfolio companies. Rudy informed me that he had signed on as a venture partner and that he hoped I would join him, along with a few others they were recruiting.

"You could do this part-time and use your extensive network to help us find deals, connect us to local VCs we'd want to co-invest with, and you'd serve on a couple of boards. There's no salary, but you'd get a piece of the carry on the companies you'd be involved with."

"Carry" is short for "carried interest," the portion of the profit general partners of venture funds receive upon a successful exit— via acquisition or initial public offering—from a portfolio company. I was intrigued. Perhaps this could be my stepping stone toward finally crossing over to the dark side.

"I'm definitely interested," I informed Phil. He proceeded to tell me more about Gabriel and the position being offered.

A couple of weeks later, Samper introduced me to the other founding partner of Gabriel, Rick Bolander. A tall, solidly built, swarthy man with brown hair and a ready smile, Rick was considerably younger than Phil, but he, too, had an impressive resume. An engineering graduate of the University of Michigan with an MBA from Harvard, Bolander had been a rising executive with AT&T. He left the firm in order to form a real-estate investment firm, Blue Sky Ventures, in Chicago. He got his start in venture capital at Apex Investment Partners, where he had been a general partner. Phil Samper described Rick as "the savviest VC guy I know."

Following my meeting with Bolander and Samper, I signed on as a venture partner, and I made an investment in Gabriel's first fund. I informed both men that I would be interested in becoming more involved should the opportunity present itself in the future and should our relationship work out.

Phil and Rick raised the hundred-million-dollar fund based on their personal reputations and on branding Gabriel as an organization with operating experience, one that would not only provide capital to young entrepreneurial companies, but also would be hands-on in providing the young firms' management teams with mentoring and "been there, done that" advice. This differentiated Gabriel from most VCs—the others were usually financial types, often from Wall Street. This was an attractive proposition for our investors, who were made up of pension funds, corporations such as General Motors, and a few wealthy individuals. Gabriel Venture Partners Fund-I was oversubscribed by some $30 million. The founding partners could not accept the additional capital because the fund was limited to a hundred million by the GP/LP (General Partner/Limited Partner) agreement, and they reluctantly turned down the excess amount.

In the meantime, I informed the University of Maryland Smith School of Business of my intention to resign, and I promised to remain until a national search produced my successor. As my tenure as director of the Dingman Center was coming to an end, I was busy doing a "victory lap" through the Mid-Atlantic region. Everywhere I went, I was bathed in kudos for having helped to create an entrepreneurial community where one had not existed previously. My ego was being stroked continuously.

The search committee tasked with finding my replacement was closing in on its choice. Associate Dean Judy Olian, who chaired the committee, and Ted Muendel, head of the search firm that had unearthed the candidates, asked me to meet with the top choice, Don Spero, and to provide my input before the final decision was made. Don, a tall man with an athletic build, came with an impressive record. He had been founder and CEO of Fusion Systems

Corporation, a company whose core technology was based on post-doctoral research Don had done at the University of Maryland in the development of high-intensity lamps. His athletic achievements were even more impressive. Rowing for the New York Athletic Club, Spero won a gold medal at the World Maccabiah Games, was the 1963 national champion in single and double sculls, and competed in the 1964 Olympic Games. Only a few years younger than I, Don looked as if he could still win a regatta.

I liked Don immediately and was impressed by his knowledge and enthusiasm, although I was a bit concerned about the fact that he made frequent references to his desire to start a venture capital fund within the Dingman Center. I had gone through a thorough investigation of such a possibility a couple of years back and concluded that, while such a fund would fill in the single missing piece of the center's offerings to the region's entrepreneur community, it would be difficult to pull off. The fact that we were part of a state university created all sorts of problems having to do with ownership of stock, distribution of profits, conflicts of interest—not to mention the petty jealousies that arise at academic institutions whenever someone tries to do something out of the ordinary, especially if that something is about money. I reported to the committee that I was in favor of hiring Don, but I suggested that they should try to discourage him from attempting to start a venture fund. A second reservation I voiced to the committee had come from Don's comment to me that he would not be interested in spending as many evening and weekend hours at entrepreneurship events as I had. Despite those reservations, I informed Judy and Ted that I was in favor of hiring Don as my replacement.

Spero took over as director of the Dingman Center on February 4, 2000, ten years to the day after I had assumed the position. Having promised Howard Frank, dean of the Smith School of Business, that I would help Don transition into the job, I took on the title of entrepreneur-in-residence and agreed to chair the center's board of directors. As board chair, I watched Don succeed in forming an early-stage venture fund, although, some months later, I would be proven correct in predicting that it could not exist within the university due to conflicts of interest and other issues. The fund became independent of the University of Maryland.

Following my resignation, I devoted three days per week to Dingman and was paid 60 percent of my former university salary. This seemed like a good deal to me. I figured I could make up for the compensation shortfall with a few consulting gigs, and I hoped that, with a bit of luck, I would transition from an unpaid venture partner role to one of a full partner at Gabriel.

Immediately after the public announcement that I had joined Gabriel as a venture partner, I was swamped with business plans from start-ups in the area. Not realizing that I intended to spend only three or four hours a week on Gabriel work, the entrepreneurs were unhappy with my slow responses. At the same time, I began introducing Gabriel to the area's venture capital community. It would be important to us in the future to have close relationships with VC firms because institutional investors often prefer to invest alongside other VCs, rather than to go it alone. It spreads the risk and increases the amount of due diligence and scrutiny. Also, venture firms specialize in different sectors, often depending on the expertise and experience of their respective partners. If they come across a deal outside their area of interest, they refer it to a firm that invests in that sector. For us, the building of such relationships was critical, and I was able to initiate many of them.

I had my first opportunity to observe the two managing partners, Rick Bolander and Phil Samper, in action when I joined them in New York City for a presentation. Ranch Networks, an Internet infrastructure start-up with an exciting new technology and a potentially huge market, pitched their idea to us in the hope of convincing us to make a major investment. I watched and listened carefully as Rick and Phil ham-and-egged their questioning of the company founders, finding and exploiting weaknesses in their strategy. Most entrepreneurs (myself included, when I was raising money for our companies) have an overblown opinion of the value of their businesses, and I was impressed by the way the Gabriel guys applied the "velvet hammer" while driving down the entrepreneurs' expectations. At the same time, I developed a suspicion that the company might not have legal rights to the intellectual property (IP) behind its product. The inventions had taken place while the principals were employed by Lucent. I asked a number of questions about the origins and ownership of the IP and, after the meeting, I expressed my concern to Phil and Rick. In the next couple of months, our due diligence would show that Lucent would have a good case if it decided to claim ownership. Consequently, we would walk away from the deal.

Prior to boarding a train for home, the three of us had drinks in a hotel cocktail lounge.

"Charlie, we're really happy to have you on our team," Rick announced as we clinked glasses. "Phil and I would like you to take on four of our present and future portfolio companies as a board member."

Although I was fighting a nasty cold, I was elated. *I must have impressed these guys. I'm finally in the venture capital business! And I'm associated with a group that can't lose!* Anxious to please and bursting with enthusiasm, I agreed.

When I woke up the next morning, I began to evaluate my situation. I was committed to spending 60 percent of my time on Dingman Center business. I needed to make up a shortfall of more than $60,000 per year with consulting assignments. Now I had signed up for four board seats with Gabriel companies, in addition to all the uncompensated work I was already doing for the fund in sourcing and evaluating deals. I was in a bind. Immediately, I wrote a long email to Phil and Rick, explaining my predicament. In order to relieve me of the time-consuming tasks of reading and evaluating business plans which were bombarding me at an alarming rate, I suggested that we hire two second-year MBA students who had worked for me at the Dingman Center and who were finishing up their studies. We could bring them in as part-time interns to screen business plans and to do some basic, first-level, due diligence in order to improve our throughput. Consequently, we brought on Michael Wolf, a bright and personable young man from Philadelphia whom I had entrusted to work with companies in our center's angel investor network, and a Romanian student named Raluca Angelescu, who had shown great promise as an analyst. Samper and Bolander agreed, and Michael and Raluca helped me sort through the plans and to select those rare cases which met our Gabriel requirements.

This provided some relief, but it was no panacea. Sue, David, and our daughter-in-law Bobbi had been after me for months to "get a life"—to stop the hundred-hour workweeks and spend more time with family and doing fun things.

When I had submitted my resignation as director of the Dingman Center, I informed my family that things would soon be different. Things were different, all right. I was working longer hours than ever before—and being paid considerably less. So much for getting a life!

By the end of February 2000, I knew that this could not continue. I spoke about it with Phil Samper. A couple of days later, Phil got back to me.

"Rick and I have discussed things," he said. "And we'd like to make your life easier."

He informed me that they would like to change my status from that of an unpaid venture partner to that of a part-time salaried member of the firm. Everything seemed to be falling into place for my gradual transition to the venture capital world.

"We'd like to bring you in as a principal," Phil continued.

By now, I had come to know the firm's two principals, Mahesh Kanumury and Scott Chou. Both were young, bright guys in the West Coast office. Mahesh was a Harvard MBA who had come with a sterling record from McKenzie & Company, a prestigious global management consulting firm. Scott was a brilliant technologist with degrees from Cal Tech and MIT who had previous experience in a high-tech start-up. I had met both of them on a visit to Redwood Shores, and I was impressed. Yet I had a problem.

"Phil," I responded. "I'm flattered by your offer. But, as bright as Scott and Mahesh are, I have years' more experience than they do. It may not be VC experience, but I've run companies. I've mentored the types of companies we'll be investing in, and I've established myself in the Mid-Atlantic in a way that will be critical to our success here. I can't see myself coming in as anything less than a partner."

"Charlie, I understand and empathize," Phil replied. "But, it's impossible. The first Gabriel fund is set up in such a way that it can't have more than two partners. Once we go out to raise our second fund, it will be a different story."

"I understand, Phil. But this causes me a real problem, and I don't know if I can live with it. I need time to think it over."

Nearly all American venture capital funds are limited partnerships, governed by a General Partner/Limited Partner agreement—a "GP/LP," in VC jargon. It is a long, complex, agreement between the general partners, or those managing the fund and making investment decisions, and the limited partners, who are the outside investors. It defines management fees, carried interest, types of investments, and the investment process—all the details defining the operations of the fund, the relationship between investors and managers, and the distribution of profits upon exit from an investment. The contract also defines the hierarchy within the GP organization. For the first Gabriel fund, the two managing partners constituted the top echelon. Principals were the second-level managers, and associates were typically newly minted MBAs who screened business plans and did the bulk of due diligence on potential portfolio companies. Partners received carried interest, while principals were in line to receive "effective carry," an amount considerably smaller than that of the partners.

I understood why I could not be a partner in the first fund, but I had difficulty with accepting an offer to be put into the same category as those who were many years my juniors, in terms of both age and experience. This would be a momentous decision, and it was not about the money. It was about pride. I had spent nearly forty years building companies, assisting hundreds of other firms, and polishing my reputation; I had an engineering doctorate. Like most entrepreneurs, I was driven by ego and, like most immigrants, I was constantly searching for respect. Now my ego was bruised, and I felt that my past accomplishments were not being respected. I was in a wrestling match between these deep personal feelings and fulfilling a desire to be part of a fund with such a pool of talent and expertise that it could not possibly miss. Ultimately, logic won out over vanity. *I'll tell Samper and Bolander that I'll accept a position as principal, as long as I'll be named partner in any future Gabriel funds.*

Before I had the chance to announce my decision, luck intervened. Phil called.

"As you know, we can't make you a partner in the first fund," he said. "Rick and I have decided to offer you a position that will be lower than partner, but higher than principal. We'll give you the title of senior principal. That will elevate you above the others and will signal that you have a special standing in the organization. What do you think?"

I smiled and announced without hesitation, "We have a deal. I'm in!"

I would begin at half-time on April 1, gradually cutting down on my involvement with the Dingman Center and increasing my Gabriel work—with corresponding increases in salary—until I would become a full-time Gabriel guy on September 1, 2000. Finally, I was a real venture capitalist and, over on the dark side, the sky was the limit. Or so I thought.

CHAPTER TWENTY-ONE

Masters of the Universe

When we moved into our house in Rugby Hall in September 1971, David was seven years old. The room next to our master bedroom became his private cave. Over the years, it transitioned from a kid's playroom full of toy trucks and children's books to a jock hangout filled with weights, balls, and sailing posters, and eventually to a study where David reluctantly worked on homework and school projects. A few years later, he bought a condo and moved out; I painted the walls an industrial gray and shifted my home office from a smaller room to the one David had vacated. At first, while still running companies, I spent little time in that home office—primarily using it to pay bills and to store personal files. Then, while at the University of Maryland, I took advantage of school policy that allowed faculty to work one day a week at outside consulting and spent most Thursdays in my gray cavern.

Now it was the spring of 2000, and we announced to the world that Gabriel Venture Partners had an East Coast office. Its address was 1211 Hillcrest Road, Arnold, Maryland—our home address. A flood of business plans followed, overflowing our mailbox. Day after day, a pile of Gabriel mail was stacked by the front door when Sue and I returned home from work.

Despite the whopping deal flow, only two of the plans passed through the selective Gabriel screen. Toward the end of March 2000, we decided to gather the entire investing team in Annapolis to listen to presentations from them and three other East Coast start-ups unearthed by our Silicon Valley colleagues. One of the companies Michael, Raluca, and I had investigated, Bid4Assets, had an interesting online auction business model. The other was a firm named TrainingServer.

The sessions were scheduled for March 29 and 30 in a suite at Loew's Hotel. It was the first time the full Gabriel team—Rick Bolander, Phil Samper, Mahesh Kanumury, Scott Chou, and I, plus two of our venture partners—were together in one room to evaluate potential investments. One of the venture partners was my old friend, Rudy Lamone. The other was Jim Ramich, a former top executive at Corning and a friend of Phil Samper, now living in retirement on Kiawah Island in South Carolina.

This would be my first time in such a venue among all my partners, and I was nervous about my performance. I wanted to make a good impression, but at the same time I hoped to be unobtrusive as the new guy in the firm. Despite my accomplishments as an entrepreneur, I had no experience as a venture capitalist. I had high hopes that my new colleagues would show me respect for the attributes I was bringing to Gabriel, and that they would overlook my lack of deep knowledge of venture investing. For years, I had become accustomed to being one of the "smartest guys in the room." Now, I had to swallow my pride and recognize the fact that I was facing a steep learning curve.

As an entrepreneur raising money, I had presented to many VCs. Most had been arrogant, some were disinterested and dismissive, and a few were helpful and kind. The venture capital culture I had seen from my former vantage point consisted of too many ego-stoked overlords with lofty opinions of themselves. Because they managed large sums of money, and the entrepreneurs who knelt at their thrones desperately wanted some of that money, they exuded power and arrogance. Many forgot the human element. Writers reporting on the Silicon Valley phenomenon often referred to VCs as "Masters of the Universe." I had joined Gabriel in the belief that my partners and I would be different. Now I was anxious to find out if my expectations would be met.

Our first presenter was Ted Bayer. The previous year, while I was still running the Dingman Center, Bill Cole—a partner at Ernst & Young, a member of my board and a good friend—had introduced me to Ted, CEO of a successful Baltimore company called SYSCOM, with several million dollars in sales and two hundred employees. Ted and I hit it off immediately and soon thereafter he invited me to join the SYSCOM board. I did and Ted and I developed a close friendship. Along with our wives, we went out to dinner several times and discovered that we had many interests in common. Ted and his wife were planning to move to Annapolis, and both of us looked forward to spending more time together, sailing and playing tennis.

In early 2000, SYSCOM decided to spin off an education company called TrainingServer. When Ted asked me if Gabriel would consider making an investment in the new firm, I resigned from the SYSCOM board in order to avoid a conflict of interest prior to presenting the deal to my Gabriel colleagues. The new spin-off met the most important criteria we had set out for investment at Gabriel: a likely exit and return of all capital within eighteen months, a potential to return more than ten times our investment, and—most importantly— best-of-class management talent.

Ted Bayer's pitch followed the standard format: overview of the company's product and market, the technology behind the product, marketing and sales strategies, management team and staffing plans, the competitive landscape, and a financial forecast. My partners asked excellent questions, and Ted's responses left no doubt that he knew his stuff and that this company had a real chance of being a homerun for us as investors. All seemed to be going well until Rick Bolander took over the discussion. Rick took issue with nearly every aspect of the presentation. He questioned the sales projections, disagreed with the sales strategy and did not believe the projected size of the market. By implication, he questioned Ted's ability to manage a business, seemingly ignoring the fact that the man had already built one profitable, multi-million-dollar company. I squirmed in my seat and avoided eye contact with Ted. After a final unpleasant exchange of words, Ted departed. When the door closed behind him, Rick

announced the obvious: He had no interest in pursuing even the first
level of due diligence on the company. It took only one negative vote
to kill a deal.

"I couldn't believe the shit I just heard," said a shocked Rudy
Lamone outside in the hall as we headed for the men's room.

I was speechless and chagrined. Ted was my friend. I had
presented myself as the senior principal at Gabriel, and of course Ted
had known me as a successful, and often outspoken, businessman.
Yet I had sat there like a little boy during his first day in school and
said nothing. I was ashamed of my temerity.

The next day, I phoned Ted's office in order to inform him of the
decision to decline investment and, more importantly, to apologize
for the way he had been treated. His administrative assistant told me
that Mr. Bayer was not available, but that she would ask him to call
me. He did not call. I tried at least three more times, but Ted did not
phone me back. Finally, I handwrote a letter to Ted apologizing and
expressing my hope that this incident would not affect our friendship.
Again, Ted stonewalled me. Our friendship was finished and I have
not seen, nor heard from, him again.

Surprisingly, no other presenter was treated as rudely as Ted,
despite the fact that two of the companies unearthed by our West
Coast colleagues failed to come close to meeting our investment
criteria. The session resulted in Gabriel's selection of only one of the
presenting companies. Called Rentmaker, the Boston firm was number three out of five on my list when each of us ranked the companies
according to his order of preference. But again, I was the new guy, so
I dared not protest.

Rentmaker's business was providing an online market for the
rental of construction equipment, from huge cranes to small bobcats.
The co-founders of the firm were friends of Rick Bolander's from
their Harvard Business School days. The biggest surprise came when
I was told that Rentmaker would be "my" company. If we decided to
invest, I would join its board as Gabriel's representative, along with
Rudy Lamone, and be responsible to my partners for the company's

performance. With Scott Chou doing most of the heavy lifting, we completed our due diligence and spent several weeks seeking strategic co-investors. Jerome Meyer, the Rentmaker CEO, helped to convince Phelps Dodge, Bechtel, and several smaller firms to join Gabriel in the first round of funding.

Soon, I was fully immersed in Gabriel's frantic activities. Although I had made a commitment to the University of Maryland to dedicate half my time to the Dingman Center at the beginning of my phase-out period, I was not living up to my promise. I kept track of the hours I spent on each job and discovered that I was averaging six times as many hours on Gabriel business as on work for the Dingman Center—hardly a fifty-fifty split. The university was paying me nearly $100,000 a year for a dozen hours of work each week, and I felt guilty. Something had to change. I spoke with Phil Samper, and we decided to accelerate my departure from Dingman. Don Spero and I had gotten on well and his transition into the director job had gone smoothly. Instead of waiting until Labor Day, I would go full-time with Gabriel on July 1, 2000.

I met with Howard Frank, dean of the Smith School of Business, and associate dean Judy Olian, in order to inform them that I would be cutting all ties with the school.

"You'll be back," Howard said with a smile. "You love this too much."

Little did I know that Howard's parting words would come back to haunt me.

My departure from the Dingman Center received a great deal of press. Newspapers and magazines carried stories that stroked my ego by giving me credit for building the center into one of the best in the nation. I received letters and emails from all over the world, thanking me and wishing me good luck in my new endeavor. As much as I had craved respect throughout my career, I was astounded to discover how much of it I had earned.

The most surprising piece of correspondence came from a man whom I loathed even now, some fourteen years after he had betrayed me. Jack Young, one of the two men who had cooked my company's numbers in order to convince the board of directors to depose me as its CEO, wrote in part,

"I don't know if you remember all the guys from ERCI that were 'helping' you. I was one . . . just wanted to say it looks like you did an outstanding job at Maryland, and I am pleased. Congratulations." I was tempted to respond by thanking him for having "helped" by conspiring against me. Young had since retired and Intercad had been renamed Intercap Graphics Systems. I had no interest in either, and I had more important things to do than revisit old wounds.

At Gabriel, help was on the way. We offered a full-time associate position to the winner of the intern "play-off," Michael Wolf. I helped Raluca get a position with friends at a Washington, DC, law firm and thus hoped that she did not feel unappreciated for the help she had provided us during her internship. Michael and I had developed a great working relationship and genuinely liked one another. Unfortunately, my colleagues on the West Coast failed to recognize Michael's skills, intelligence, and value. Consequently, they low-balled his offer. I argued, explaining that many of Michael's fellow MBA graduates were receiving offers of twice the salary we were proposing, but to no avail.

Venture capital is an exclusive "industry." *Forbes* magazine compares it to professional baseball. There is approximately the same number of VCs as there are guys playing baseball for money. Consequently, each year, very few young people are offered entry-level positions and the competition for these sexy positions is fierce. While the starting compensation may be lower than that paid to MBA graduates by large corporations and financial institutions, the upside for venture capitalists appears much higher. Students read the stories of fabulous riches amassed by investors in start-ups like Apple, Facebook, Google, and Microsoft, and they have stars in their eyes. They believe the myth that all VCs make fabulous amounts of money.

Michael was not happy with his offer, but he was one of only two Smith School graduates selected by a VC firm. He accepted.

In years past, despite long hours at the office and at various evening functions, I had always set aside Sunday as family day. Other than reserving Sunday nights for writing my newspaper column, that day was reserved exclusively for activities with Sue, and with David when he was younger. Our home had been our sanctuary. With our house serving as the "East Coast headquarters" of Gabriel Venture Partners, this was no longer the case. The phone rang till midnight seven days a week, and faxes and emails rolled in nonstop.

"This has to end—and very soon!" Sue announced after suffering through this onslaught for several weeks. She was correct, of course, and I informed Phil Samper that we had to speed up our search for a *real* East Coast office, even if it meant renting temporary space somewhere.

When our discussions about a permanent office location began, I discovered one of many differences between Silicon Valley and eastern VCs, and between me and my California partners. Since I lived near Annapolis and Phil Samper, who would be splitting his time between the two coasts, had a home there as well, it made sense to find an office in the state capital. Furthermore, because we were managing our operating funds carefully, I wanted to find space that was relatively inexpensive. That plan did not play well with Rick.

"In the venture capital business, image is critical," he lectured me. "Not only do we have to have a first-class office that impresses our investors and entrepreneurs, but it has to be where VCs generally hang out. In your area, that means Northern Virginia."

Interestingly, I had received the same marching orders some years back from our board of directors when we were starting CADCOM. To the board's surprise, we demonstrated that customers, vendors, and investors much preferred to visit us in Annapolis than they would have wanted to come to the concrete jungles of DC, Northern Virginia, or Maryland's Montgomery County. On many occasions, when I had offered to fly to Chicago, New York, Los Angeles or another city, the person at the other end of the phone line would say, "Oh no, let me come to Annapolis to see you. I'll bring my wife, and we'll make a weekend of it." We saved a lot of travel money by having our headquarters in the beautiful and quaint resort town on the Chesapeake Bay.

On this occasion, I told Rick and Phil that I would call some of my Washington-area VC friends to get their opinions. In my unscientific phone survey, I asked, "If you were starting a venture fund in this region now, and forgetting where you personally reside, where would you want to locate it: Tysons Corner (Northern Virginia), BWI airport area, Baltimore, College Park, or Annapolis?"

I called eleven VCs. The score was eleven for Annapolis to zero for all the others. The result convinced Phil, who managed to turn Rick around. We would locate in Annapolis, but only if we could find a place that had "image."

We engaged a commercial real estate firm and, while they were searching for a permanent home for us, they rented us their own former office at the Annapolis City Marina in Eastport. It was a quirky little structure, situated on a dock on Spa Creek, underneath the outdoor patio of Carrols Creek restaurant. By now, Michael Wolf had joined us as a full-time associate, we brought in Jana Fisher as office manager, and Phil Samper began spending some of his time in Annapolis. Entrepreneurs who came to make their presentations and VCs who visited remembered us for having the most unique office of any venture firm in the Mid-Atlantic. From the scraping of chairs above our ceiling during lunch and dinner, to the wet carpets during unusually high tides, to the bikini-clad girls wiggling by our windows on their way to the sightseeing sailboat *Woodwind*, we were different. I loved it, but our West Coast partners did not. They could not wait till we moved to a prestigious location and an office with luxurious furnishings. Eventually, we moved to such a place on the other side of Annapolis, far from the water and the bikinis.

In addition to working with the companies already in our portfolio, we were on constant lookout for potential investments. After all, we were committed to our investors to place $100 million, less our expenses, in a relatively short time. Jeff Grinspoon had been one of our star graduate assistants at the Dingman Center while working on his MBA. We had become friends after his graduation, and I had also befriended his father, Les, a successful entrepreneur. Les and his partner, Vic Hess, had started a company called ComputerIO, which produced a server containing the company's middleware for the Internet. The company was generating more than $8 million in annual sales and had forty employees. A Virginia-based venture firm called SpaceVest had funded the company's first round and now they were looking for another VC firm to lead the next round, which would accelerate ComputerIO's growth. One of the SpaceVest partners, Stephen Rochereau, was a long-time friend of mine and contacted me to inquire about Gabriel's interest in leading the B-round. I presented the ComputerIO case at our next regular Monday conference call, and a decision was made to invite the company's principals to make a presentation in our Redwood Shores office. I would accompany them to the West Coast.

Les and Vic made an impressive pitch and, judging by the questions asked by my partners and their apparent satisfaction with the responses, I thought there was a decent chance of our giving serious consideration to investing. Then, shades of Annapolis! Rick Bolander began his onslaught. Questioning every assumption and forecast, he came close to bringing the two entrepreneurs to tears. One had to admire Rick for his insights but not for his style.

"Guys," I said as I walked Les and Vic to the front door of the Gabriel suite, "I am so sorry. There's no excuse for the treatment you just got. I hope most of it was an act, and that we'll decide to pursue an investment. I'll call you as soon as I get home."

I was dead wrong. Rick dismissed the deal as being overpriced and the technology as being obsolete.

"A custom job-shop" was his description of ComputerIO.

We voted, and only two of us were in favor of pursuing the deal. The others agreed with the valid points and objections Rick had made and, in fact, provided criticisms of their own. But their way of expressing doubts or disagreements was considerably gentler than Rick's.

That evening, when I arrived at the San Francisco airport to fly home on the red-eye, I spotted Les and Vic near the gate, waiting for the same flight. I sat down at a nearby gate in order to avoid being seen by them and having to report that they had wasted their time and money. I was even more embarrassed when I boarded with the first-class passengers, while my friends were destined to spend the night cramped in the economy section of the jet.

CHAPTER TWENTY-TWO

On Thin Ice

I discovered quickly that the life of a venture capitalist was not an easy one. There was the travel, of course. One had to log thousands of miles on airplanes, hundreds of miles behind the wheel of a car, and spend many lonely nights in hotel rooms while looking for potential investments. On top of that, we were a bicoastal firm, with members three thousand miles apart. When conference calls did not suffice, those of us in Annapolis traveled to California or our Silicon Valley partners came east.

But that was something I had expected. I had done my homework and was prepared to manage my travel in such a way that I would still have a personal life. What I had underestimated was the complexity of the job itself. I brought to the firm my network and reputation in the region, attributes that we hoped to turn into high-quality and high-quantity deal flow. Most importantly, at least in my mind, I brought a "been there, done that" history to Gabriel. In my experience, the best venture capitalists were those who had themselves been entrepreneurs. More than anyone, they understood the issues and difficulties faced by young firms. I believed that the Gabriel team would recognize my value as an experienced entrepreneur and put it to use.

I had an engineering doctorate and a solid background in technology. However, it had been thirty-two years since I had practiced engineering or written a computer program. As CEO of high-tech companies for eighteen years, I had spent the majority of my time managing people, marketing, and raising money. I had participated in technical planning and discussions only at a fifty-thousand-foot altitude. In my years at the Dingman Center, I worked with many start-ups, but intimate knowledge of their respective underlying technologies was not required of me. In short, I was many years removed from having been a techie. Yet now, as a venture capitalist, it was necessary for me to have a thorough understanding of the technical details of a candidate company's product or service in order to begin to evaluate the firm's potential. Moreover, this knowledge could not be confined to a certain narrow discipline. On any given day, I might be reading the business plans or listening to presentations of companies in computer network security, web-based videoconferencing, telecommunications, heuristic data mining, and nanotechnology. It was part of a day's work—and I was expected to understand it all.

With twelve-hour workdays in the office and on the road, there was little time to educate myself. Most nights, I fell asleep in bed with an incredibly boring technology or science primer for the next day in my hand. It was like teaching the Engineering Materials course at the Naval Academy all over again—staying one lesson ahead of the students in a course I had never taken. Except that now, instead of undergraduates, I was dealing with experts—both the entrepreneurs and my partners—who knew more than I did. There were no answers in the back of the book, and there was a lot more at stake.

Then there was deal structuring. When we started CADCOM, I had no background in finance or accounting. I was an engineer and a computer guy. I had to learn by doing about cash flow, income statements, and balance sheets. I became intimate with financial forecasts, budgets, and strategic plans. In dealings with venture capitalists, both as CEO of companies and director of the Dingman Center, I had been exposed to some of the VC methodologies in determining the valuation of a company. However, now I was on the inside looking out, and I had to become an expert in structuring investments that would be appropriate to the deal and to our firm's goals and objectives. I had to learn about pre- and post-money valuations (how much a company would be worth before and after our investment), the staging of investments, computing our potential return on invested capital, the use of preferred stock and warrants, and new terms such as burn rate, convertible debenture, and step-up.

When I agreed to join Gabriel, I knew that I would have a steep learning curve; however, I had not realized just how precipitous that curve would be. Phil Samper had told me that Rick Bolander was the best venture capitalist he had ever met in terms of innovative structuring of deals. Consequently, I had looked forward to being tutored by Rick.

But things were moving too fast. There was little time for education. We were under pressure to invest our investors' money in the Gabriel-I fund, so I was spending the majority of my time reading business plans and meeting with company founders in search of a promising deal. Each time I found one, I had to do a preliminary analysis and enter it in Gabriel's deal log. Once in the log, the deal was discussed at the following week's partner conference call. The deal champion had to have sufficient knowledge of the company's technology, market, strategy, and management team in order to be able to convince the other members of the Gabriel team to proceed with the next stage of due diligence. At the same time, we were preparing to go out to raise a second Gabriel fund. This meant lining up potential investors: pension funds, family offices, banks, corporations, and wealthy individuals. Each of us was responsible for bringing in a significant amount of capital as we planned for Gabriel Venture Partners II.

For the first time since my days as a young researcher at Douglas Aircraft, I felt inadequate. While Phil was sympathetic, no one was prepared to come to my rescue by utilizing my strengths and helping me overcome my weaknesses. Perhaps I should have sounded an SOS, but I was too proud and confident in my ability to handle it all. As always, my father's words rang in my ears: "Don't ever let anyone tell you that you're not capable of doing something. Put your head down and go do it! And no matter what you do, don't ever give up!"

In addition to a difficult learning curve, I had to face two issues. One was the towering presence of Phil Samper. He and I developed a great rapport, became friends, and he was a vital sounding board for my complaints and problems. Phil was by far the most astute and experienced operating manager in the firm, and the result of his presence was that my skills in that area were ignored. Phil was the single go-to guy whenever the management team of one of our portfolio companies needed the kind of mentoring only a senior, perceptive businessperson could provide. Consequently, a major attribute I had brought to Gabriel was being snubbed. It was not only tough on my ego, but it diminished my value to the firm.

The second problem was that of parochialism. I was shocked to discover that West Coast venture capitalists, unlike their mid-Atlantic and midwestern counterparts, held a strong bias against those of us who had not graduated from the so-called "elite" schools—Harvard, Princeton, Wharton and the other Ivies, or Stanford and MIT. The great majority of West Coast VCs had attended those schools, and they hired mostly their own kind. It was a vicious cycle. Because they recruited from this narrow range of schools, they increased the chances of students from those institutions to be VCs and, at the same time, they reinforced the reputations of those schools.

One of the things that had most impressed me about America—that is, the America west of New Jersey (the state where our family had settled) and east of Palo Alto—was the democracy of this nation's higher education system. While researching universities as a high school student, I had been drawn to the Midwest and Southwest by the philosophy of those regions: Higher education should be accessible to everyone with a proven academic track record, intelligence, ability, and a solid work ethic. State colleges and universities in a part of the country some easterners derisively called "flyover" put up relatively low barriers in terms of entrance standards and cost. Their notion was "We'll let you in, but then you have to work your ass off to stay here and graduate." To me, this was an essential tenet of the America about which I had dreamed in post-war refugee camps, one where everyone was given the opportunity to be the best he or she could be.

Thus, while the majority of my high-school classmates were applying to Princeton, Harvard, Cornell, Brown, Vassar, and Williams, I expressed my disdain for the academic exclusionism I associated with Europe. My distaste for the so-called "elite" schools was strengthened one day when, as a senior, I was playing in a high-school tennis tournament at Princeton. After my match ended, as I sat in the stands watching one of my teammates play, a well-dressed young man sat down next to me. He introduced himself as a Princeton assistant basketball coach and informed me that he had followed my exploits in various leagues in Northern Jersey.

"Have you considered coming to Princeton next year?" he asked.

"No, sir. I'm really not interested. Besides, my family couldn't afford it."

"If you make the freshman basketball team, we'll arrange an academic scholarship for you," he said.

I was dumbfounded. The Ivy League schools constantly trumpeted the fact that they did not offer athletic scholarships, clearly implying that their hands were cleaner than those of universities that did. Now, I was being told that I could receive an *academic* scholarship to Princeton, but only if I was a good enough jock to make the basketball team.

Once I matriculated Oklahoma State University as a freshman, I did wonder how my education might be different from those of my former high-school classmates at the Ivy League schools. During the spring semester, I was enrolled in Physics: Electricity and Magnetism, taught by a physicist who had been a member of the famous Manhattan Project, which designed the atomic bomb. Prior to coming to OSU, he had been on the faculty at Princeton.

"Professor Perkins," I said to him one day after class. "I had a chance to go to Princeton and I'm curious. Can you please tell me what difference you see between it and OSU?"

"Funny you should ask that, Mr. Heller," he said. "My wife asked me the same thing just the other night at dinner. Here is what I told her. It's much more difficult to get into Princeton but, once you're in, it's almost impossible not to graduate. It's relatively easy to get into OSU but, once you're here, you have to work a lot harder to graduate than you would at Princeton. The other thing is that, if you and I were at Princeton, I wouldn't be teaching this freshman class. You'd be taught by a teaching assistant, not a full professor."

While these two incidents helped me form a negative view of the so-called "elite" schools, I had not given the subject much thought through the years. My bachelor's and master's degrees from Oklahoma State University and my doctorate from The Catholic University of America had not been a deterrent to my career as an engineer, teacher, or entrepreneur. *Once we're out of school, everything depends on our ability, hard work, and our character,* I had thought—and it had been true. But now I was in the venture capital world and discovering that this was not so, at least not on the West Coast.

I witnessed this bias as an official act when it was decided that Gabriel would hire a new partner for our Annapolis office in preparation for raising, and then investing, our second fund. An internal email describing the ideal profile read:

Education:

a. Business school:

Top level: HBS (Harvard Business School), *Stanford, MIT*

Level 2: Berkeley, Wharton, Northwestern, Princeton

Level 3: Others represent a problem

b. Technology:

Cal Tech, MIT, Stanford, Berkeley, Purdue, etc.

Where did that leave Michael Wolf and me? We must "represent a problem." Earlier in the year, I had received the Lohmann Medal, one of the highest honors bestowed on its alumni by the OSU College of Engineering, Architecture and Technology. Now I understood why my Gabriel partners had scarcely noticed.

I had spent the majority of my time as CEO of CADCOM and Intercad raising money, and the same had been true of my ten years at the Dingman Center. But the fact that fundraising had been a dominant activity, and that I may have been reasonably good at it, did not mean that I enjoyed it. As a matter of fact, I hated it. I found it demeaning and not unlike begging. Now I realized that it was another part of life as a venture capitalist that I had been too naive to anticipate. As a partner in our new fund, I had a duty to bring in a significant portion of the capital—and I failed miserably. I met with more than twenty potential investors, including Lockheed Martin, Allied Capital, CS First Boston, and Imperial Bank. No luck. My personal network did not include highly placed people in organizations—like pension funds, family offices, investment banks, and large corporations— that made major investments in funds. Consequently, nearly all my presentations came as a result of cold calls to strangers.

At one point, I thought a cold call would result in my bringing in three times my quota. Following several sessions with the Pennsylvania State Retirement System for Teachers, they were impressed and ready to invest in Gabriel-II. However, in the end, they insisted on too many provisions we found unacceptable. The deal died. My final fundraising tally: zero.

Looking back, I think that this was the point at which Rick may have decided that I had outlived my usefulness to Gabriel. If not, the demise of Rentmaker may have been. When I discovered that the management of that company had been "cooking the books"— showing us deceptive financial information that made it appear the company was making progress while, in fact, it was tanking—I pulled the plug on them at a board meeting in Boston. These were Rick's friends, and Rentmaker was "my" company. When Rick implied that I should have been aware of the deception, I was certain that he blamed me for our write-off of the investment.

After moving to our new offices on Admiral Cochrane Drive in Annapolis, we had a well-equipped conference room with videoconferencing equipment. Late every Monday afternoon, our office manager, Jana Fisher, and her assistant, Jill Hall, set up the conference room in such a way that the East Coast and West Coast groups saw one another on their respective TV screens and spoke to each other via speakerphone. The meetings were scheduled for the convenience of our Redwood Shores partners, three hours behind us, and thus they often lasted late into Maryland evenings.

Besides eliminating any possibility of family time on Monday nights, I began to hate the meetings because Rick managed to create tension between the two offices. He asked intimidating questions about the quality and quantity of our deal flow and, by implication, about our performance as a team. Michael Wolf was scared. I was pissed. Whenever I spoke, I noticed on the television screen that Rick turned his back to the camera at his end. Although I never said a word about it, these snubs infuriated me so much that I often stumbled all over myself while attempting to describe a potential deal or giving a progress report on a particular transaction.

For the first time in many years, I found it difficult to get up in the morning and go to work. I was unhappy and felt that I had lost control over my life.

CHAPTER TWENTY-THREE

Goodbye, Gabriel

The day after Memorial Day 2001, the Mid-Atlantic Venture Association held its Capital Connection, a major annual event attended by nearly all venture capitalists in our region and many others from other parts of the country. For two days, carefully selected young companies seeking investments presented in a large auditorium of the Waterfront Marriott in Baltimore to an audience of some two hundred VCs. Rick Bolander, Michael Wolf, and I represented Gabriel. The morning of the first day, Rick became ill. I drove him to a clinic and he was confined to his hotel-room bed for the remainder of the venture fair.

At breakfast on the second day of Capital Connection, I was attracted by a large photo of a man holding a saxophone in the *Baltimore Sun*. His name was Kim Waters and the article described how this Baltimore native had gained national stature as a jazz musician. He would be performing a few gigs in his home town. I knew that Michael Wolf, too, was an accomplished sax player, though I did not appreciate how good he was until Rudy Lamone convinced me. Prior to returning to school for a doctorate in business, Rudy himself had been a professional musician, touring the country with his own band. Once, soon after we met, I asked if he could play his sax for me.

"I haven't played in years, and I refuse to play unless I'm at my best," he told me. "My sax is staying in its case."

Both Rudy and I heard Michael play a saxophone for the first time at a Gabriel holiday party. I thought he was terrific. But, while I have always liked jazz, I was no expert. The official verdict came from my friend who *was* an authority.

"I gave Michael my saxophone," Rudy told me a few days later. "I haven't heard anyone play so well in years. This guy is fantastic!"

When I saw Michael in Baltimore at the venture fair, I showed him the article in the *Sun*.

"Oh, I know Kim Waters," he said. "We played together a few times in the past."

Later that day, Michael and I were invited to a party hosted by a new venture firm called E4E. As we walked through the restaurant in Little Italy and onto an open terrace, we heard soft jazz being played.

"There he is!" Michael exclaimed. "That's Kim Waters." The man who had stared at me from the *Baltimore Sun* page was entertaining the crowd, along with a combo, from a small stage in the rear of the terrace. We waited until the band took a break and walked over to the stage. Michael and Waters embraced and I shook hands with the musician. After Waters answered Wolf's questions about his most recent exploits and travels, it was his turn to catch up on Michael's activities since they had last seen one another. Michael told him that he had returned to school and earned an MBA from Maryland.

"That's great. What are you doing now?" Kim asked.

Michael smiled and proudly announced, "I'm a venture capitalist."

Among his MBA peers, Michael's response would have elicited envy. Kim Waters stared at him for a long moment before saying quietly, "What a terrible waste of talent."

My initial thought was, *Wow! Michael must be one hell of a saxophone player for a star like this to think he's wasting his talent in venture capital.* As I gazed out at Waters's audience, too wrapped up in discussing deals with their fellow VCs to have listened to Kim's music, a revelation hit me: *Not everybody thinks we're Masters of the Universe!*

A couple of hours later, while driving home, I turned the musician's remark toward myself. Maybe venture capital was a waste of *my* talent! I brought all these assets with me to Gabriel, and they were going to waste. It was the first time the thought of giving up had crossed my mind. However, as always, Papa's instructions to never give up rang in my head and made me even more resolute to work hard in order to become a good venture capitalist.

In 2002, after we reached our initial fundraising milestone for the second fund, we made our first investment out of Gabriel-II—in a company that I had brought to the firm. Network Mantra was a computer network security start-up located in Northern Virginia. Its founders, Suri Bulusu and Suprotik Ghose, were Indian and came with excellent credentials. I spent a great deal of time with the company, refining its strategy, building a management team, and making introductions to potential customers. Network Mantra was making decent progress and generating some sales, although it was still many months from becoming profitable. In early 2002, it became obvious that the company would need to raise additional funds in a new round of venture financing. Called a B-round, such a second round requires a different lead investor than that of the A-round. Since Gabriel was the lead in the latter, we needed to go out to recruit a VC firm to take the lead in the forthcoming round. For this to take place, the CEO—Suri Bulusu—had to hit the road with a presentation that would attract a venture fund. We would make the introductions and open the doors, but the CEO had to make the sale.

Michael and I spent several weeks helping Suri structure and then refine his pitch. In order to test the presentation on a group of venture capitalists, we decided to ask Suri to do a dry run with our Gabriel team of investment professionals as the audience. He came to our Annapolis office and, with our West Coast colleagues having joined us via videoconference, Suri gave his talk. I was disappointed that he came across as uninspired, and thus somewhat unconvincing, but I wrote it off as nervousness. I assumed that the pitch would improve with more practice. My partners asked a number of questions and made several suggestions, but there did not appear to be any major issues. Suri left the room and headed back to Virginia. All hell broke loose after his departure.

"This guy doesn't act like a CEO!"

"In the A-round, you can have a CEO with some flaws, but in the B-round, the company is expected to be more mature and the CEO has to come across as strong. Suri's not that guy."

I stared at the TV screen, taken aback by the strong reactions from California.

I seemed to be the only one, with the possible exception of Michael Wolf, who believed that Suri Bulusu could continue to lead Network Mantra to the next level. After a long discussion, I was given the repugnant task of informing Suri and his partner Suprotik that we would have to put the B-round on hold until we brought in a new CEO.

It is not uncommon for venture capitalists to replace founders of their portfolio companies once these firms reach a certain level of maturity. Often, investors feel that the person who had the original vision lacks the ability to manage the company once it grows beyond a few employees and a low revenue level. Nearly all entrepreneurs resent and resist such a change. After all, these companies are their babies and the visionaries had dreams of taking them to extraordinary heights and becoming the next Bill Gates or Steve Jobs. Having been a jilted entrepreneur myself, I could feel Suri's pain when I informed him of Gabriel's decision. Yet, I had to be a Gabriel team player and try to convince Suri that this move would be good for everyone, including himself.

A couple of weeks later, a brilliant idea came to me—at least I thought it was brilliant. And my partners agreed with me. A few months earlier, we had added an accomplished telecommunications executive to the board of Network Mantra. He also happened to be Indian. He and the company's management team seemed to have excellent rapport and, judging from the interactions I had observed at board meetings, the founders respected the man's opinions and recommendations. I thought that placing him at the head of the company would be more palatable to Suri and his team than the insertion of a complete stranger, especially one of different ethnicity.

The man agreed, took over as CEO and all seemed to go well—for a month. Then the daily calls from Suri and Suprotik started coming.

"He doesn't understand our business."

"He stays in his office and doesn't go out to meet customers."

"He treats us like his employees, not as the founders."

When I met with all parties, it became obvious that the old management team had not accepted the new CEO and the founders were not about to cooperate with him. It was then that a former University of Maryland colleague, an immigrant from India, gave me a brief "Indian culture for dummies" lecture. In bringing together Network Mantra's founders with a fellow Indian, I had been unaware of a culture in which people despise one another because of caste, religion, language, color of skin, and even diplomas from different schools. Any one of such dissimilarities could be a cause of serious friction. We continued to hope that things would change and that everyone would get on the same track toward success. It never happened. The company imploded. We ended up selling its assets and taking our first loss in the new fund.

As 2003 dawned, I realized that my days as a Gabriel partner were numbered. It was clear that Rick did not want me. I had the feeling that Phil agreed, although he was too polite and too gentlemanly to make it obvious. The three of us held an amicable meeting at which we decided that I would take on a new part-time role. My title was changed to entrepreneur advisor, I moved from general partner to retired partner (meaning that, from an economic standpoint, I assumed the standing of a limited partner), and my work was reduced to two days per week with a proportional decrease in salary. At about the same time, Phil decided that he, too, would transition into a part-time mode. He and I had been the oldest partners in the firm, and it was time to help the young guys take the reins.

For the next five months, I sourced and evaluated deals and helped to plug Scott Chou and Phil Summe, whom we had hired away from a New York VC firm, into the Mid-Atlantic entrepreneur and venture capital communities. The only problem was that I had hoped to make up my salary shortfall by consulting, and it was not happening. I found myself spending much more than two days a week on Gabriel business—shades of my early days of transitioning to the firm from the University of Maryland. I requested an increase in salary commensurate with the level of my effort and further asked that my title be changed to that of "special partner" in order to give me a more distinguished standing when representing Gabriel.

When both of my requests were denied, I knew that it was time to cut the cord. With a silent apology to my late father for giving up, I decided to depart and to remain a silent and passive retired partner. In September 2003, I gave notice that I would resign effective December 1. I wanted to make my departure as amicable as possible because, despite the professional issues and disagreements some of us may have had, I considered all my former colleagues personal friends—and that included Rick Bolander. I wanted those friendships to survive my departure. Moreover, from a selfish standpoint, I had a financial investment in Gabriel and thus would continue to have an important economic stake in the firm.

My former partners flew in from the West Coast and all of us got together for my farewell dinner at the Annapolis Yacht Club. They presented me with a small plaque and a Mont Blanc pen and wished me well in my new endeavors. I told them that I considered them among the smartest people with whom I had ever worked and said that, although it may not have always been obvious, I had learned a great deal from them. I expressed my gratitude for the learning experience.

It took Phil Samper, who has remained a close friend and whose wisdom I value and respect immensely, to put my Gabriel experience into perspective.

"You're a proud and thoughtful guy," he told me. "You felt humiliated and frustrated. But one thing you were *not* is a failure. You were much too hard on yourself. You have many terrific attributes, professional and personal. So, don't beat yourself up over Gabriel. Venture capital is 70 percent luck and 30 percent skill. We were a bit unlucky with our timing, and all of us made some mistakes. But we all learned a lot along the way, and we did lots of things right."

CHAPTER TWENTY-FOUR

Never Give Up!

During my slow but steady departure from Gabriel, I thought a great deal about my time there. The breathtakingly fast pace of searching for potential investments, vetting companies, structuring deals, raising money for the next fund, and constantly attempting to demonstrate to my partners that I was contributing had not afforded me the luxury of sitting back and contemplating my situation. Mostly, I had been in a reactive mode and too stressed out by daily pressures to be introspective. But as I reflected on the past three years, much of the resentment I felt began to melt away, and I saw my Gabriel experience in a different light.

I decided that I had been beating myself up unnecessarily, thinking of myself as a failure in the venture capital world. Unlike most of my peers, I had entered the business as an engineer and entrepreneur rather than an investment banker or management consultant. I was not the product of one of the "academic country clubs," which provide access through well-placed alumni. My hard-earned reputation in the mid-Atlantic entrepreneur and investment communities had been largely responsible for Gabriel's ability to establish itself as an important player there. Most importantly, on countless occasions, entrepreneurs told me how refreshing it was for them to deal with a VC who had been there and done that, rather than an investor whose credentials consisted of a fancy MBA and a stint in a large company or investment bank.

"You're too nice a guy to be a venture capitalist," I was often told by founders of companies pitching me in search of investment.

Moreover, as I looked back, I realized how much I had learned. Gabriel was an extremely structured and process-driven firm. Everything we did followed a prescribed policy or format: deal flow, due diligence, investment review, funding decisions, portfolio company reviews, and a variety of required reports. As a "ready, fire, aim" entrepreneur, I had often pushed back against this rigorous system and derided it for having taken away from "real work." In hindsight, it was evident that the Gabriel way had taught me invaluable lessons in investment discipline and rigor.

As I thought about all of this, I came to the realization that I had not been a failure as a venture capitalist, after all. Although, at first and in my frustration, I had intended to walk away from the VC business, I began to change my mind. Why let all this knowledge and experience go to waste? And, as always, my father's admonition to never give up was never far from my mind.

More than anything, what had driven me throughout my life was a search for respect. Perhaps it was a product of having grown up a child of war, disrespected and hunted by the Nazis. The drive was reinforced by my internalized feeling that, as an immigrant in America, I was a second-class citizen. Following the humiliation I had suffered at Gabriel Venture Partners, I felt a need to regain my self-respect. I would find a way to return to the world of venture capital—and I would succeed!

My opportunity came sooner than I expected. While still at the Dingman Center, I had met a man whom I will refer to as Sean O'Hara. He was a hedge fund manager who ran a firm that I will call Lighthouse, and who decided to start a venture capital fund investing in early-stage technology companies. Our Center entered into a contractual relationship with Lighthouse: Our graduate assistants would perform due diligence for a fixed fee on companies he was considering for investment. When Sean discovered that I was about to leave Gabriel, he invited me to lunch at the Annapolis Yacht Club.

"I'm a hedge fund guy," he said. "I really don't know much about the VC business. How about coming in and running it for us?"

He explained that Lighthouse was headquartered in Bethesda, Maryland, and that it was fully invested out of its first two small funds and would need to go out to raise a new fund. He provided me with a few documents and some promotional materials. I told him that I would think it over and promised to visit him at his office within a week to give him my decision. When I told Sue about the opportunity, she was not enthusiastic.

"You'd really want to commute to Bethesda?" she asked. "You were miserable commuting to Rockville twenty years ago. It's about the same distance, and there's a lot more traffic today than there was back then!"

"You're right," I replied after my mind projected a picture of my silver BMW Z3 sitting in bumper-to-bumper traffic and spewing carbon dioxide on the Washington Beltway. "At this stage of my life, I don't need that crap."

"And what about your writing and consulting?" Sue persisted. "You're sitting on a bunch of boards, and you've started a memoir. Don't you want to continue those?"

Again, I could not argue with my wise wife. I would see O'Hara as promised, but I would decline his offer.

Following a one-hour drive to Bethesda, the elevator delivered me to Lighthouse's offices, where I shook hands with O'Hara.

"Sean," I said after sitting down. "I really appreciate your offer, but I have to turn it down. I still intend to get back into the venture capital business, but this job doesn't fit my plans going forward."

"How so?" he asked.

"There are two major issues. One, I've reached a point in my life where I refuse to spend a large part of it sitting in Washington traffic. Whatever I do next, I'm not gonna be a commuter. And two, I have some other things going—including the writing of a book—and I don't want to work full-time. I'm gonna find something that requires only half my time."

O'Hara tried to tempt me into changing my mind with promises of the wealth I would accumulate by sharing in the company's profits.

Finally, he concluded that I was not negotiating. I really was spurning his offer.

"Okay," he said, smiling broadly. "Here's the deal. You'll run the private equity side of the company, working half-time and out of your office at home. You'll need to come here just once a week for a meeting, plus on other occasions when it's necessary. How does that sound?"

"Are you serious?" I was incredulous. "You really think I can manage the business working half-time and out of my home?"

"Well, I'm devoting less than half my time to it now," he said. "And you know a hell of a lot more about venture capital than I do. So, there's no doubt in my mind that it'll work."

I felt as though I had just hit a pure five-iron on a par three for a hole-in-one. I'd be getting back into venture capital, I'd be running the show, and I'd be doing it on my own terms. On an hourly basis, I'd be earning the same salary I had at Gabriel, and I'd be sharing in the carried interest, a share of the profits paid to the investment managers when a VC firm exits an investment as a result of a public offering or acquisition. On top of all that, I liked Sean; I had enjoyed having a drink with him in the past and was sure we would get along well as business partners. The deal seemed almost too good to be true. It fit my personal needs and desires so well that I failed to do any further due diligence before saying yes. I would pay dearly for that error!

"I'm in, Sean," I said enthusiastically.

In the weeks that followed, I attacked work with a renewed energy and verve. It was back to the hundred-hour workweek, but I was accustomed to that, and it was fun again. I dedicated many hours each week to writing my first memoir, which would become *Prague: My Long Journey Home*. I initiated venture capital processes at Lighthouse, unashamedly emulating those of Gabriel Venture Partners. I became involved with my new firm's remaining portfolio companies.

Despite this hectic schedule, I managed to spend more time with

Sue, to enjoy our three grandchildren, to play golf and hike in the summer, and to hit the slopes and cross-country trails when snow fell on our vacation getaway in Canaan Valley, West Virginia. Only half-jokingly, Sue and I referred to Monday evenings as "Un-Gabriel Nights," as a celebration of my freedom from Gabriel's interminable Monday meetings. We spent these evenings together each week, highlighted by a glass of wine with dinner at a restaurant, followed by a movie.

At Lighthouse, it was time to prepare for raising a new fund. Drawing on my Gabriel experience, I began drafting a Private Placement Memorandum (PPM), a document designed to convince potential investors—pension funds, family offices, corporations, and wealthy individuals—to place a bet on our ability to find promising start-ups, purchase an equity position in them, and nurture them to a successful exit (an IPO or acquisition), one that would result in significant profits shared by our investors and Lighthouse.

The most critical selling point of all venture capital PPMs is past performance—how the firm's earlier funds performed and, in the case of new investment professionals, their personal track records. Listing my past accomplishments, as well as those of Sean and of an associate working with me, was relatively easy. The hard part was demonstrating Lighthouse's past success as a VC. I was disappointed that there did not exist a clear and concise listing of the firm's earlier investments. A year into my involvement with Lighthouse, I was unable to respond to the most obvious question people asked: "How have your funds done?"

At Gabriel, and at all good VC firms, a running record is kept of all investments, and monthly or quarterly reports are sent to the limited partners. Partners who hit the road to raise a new fund are thus ready to respond to the basic question with, "Our first fund had an internal rate of return of X percent" or "Fund Two returned Y-times invested capital" or something along those lines. When I repeatedly requested such information from O'Hara, his answers were vague and evasive. I would have to unearth the data myself, although I was unaware at the time how difficult this task would be—and what an unsettling secret it would reveal.

I spent the next several weeks at the Lighthouse offices, combing through files from which I had to dig up information on each past investment, bit by bit. How many dollars were invested and when? How many shares in the company did those dollars buy? What percentage of the company did those shares represent? What, if any, follow-on investments were made and on what terms? Had there been an exit through an IPO or acquisition? If there had been a successful exit, how was Lighthouse's share of the profit distributed among outside investors and Lighthouse? If there had been no exit, should the investment be written off because the company had been liquidated or considered among the "walking dead?" If the company was still in business, what was the unrealized gain or loss on our investment?

The work was tedious, painstaking, and occasionally led to a dead end. But, with the help of Lighthouse's executive assistant, I managed to cobble together a reasonable history. However, as I began to create a summary table for the PPM, one thing did not seem to compute. The money from successful exits that should have been distributed to outside investors failed to match the amount actually paid out. According to my calculations, the investors should have received about $250,000 more than they had gotten. Concerned that I must have made an error in my arithmetic, I showed my tabular summary to Sean O'Hara.

He brushed me off. "Oh, you made a mistake. Check it again."

I did—several times. Same result. When O'Hara refused to go over the numbers with me, I became skeptical. Had I missed something? Had someone made a clerical error? What happened to the money? I had no answers.

The discrepancy was on my mind as Sue and I departed on vacation in the Czech Republic. Two weeks later, upon our return home, I found a letter from the insurance company that carried our Lighthouse-provided health insurance policies. The letter informed me that, since the premium had not been paid for some time, my policy had been cancelled while I was out of the country. Angry that he had failed to warn me, I confronted Sean. His laughter at my concern made me see red.

"And what about the $77,000 in back pay you owe me?" I screamed into the phone.

"Don't worry about it. You'll get it in due time," he said dismissively.

Lighthouse was in financial trouble, its managing director was not being forthright with me, and there was that matter of the large, unaccounted-for sum of money. Ten minutes after hanging up, I made my decision. It was time to get out. I called Sean and resigned.

During the ensuing months, I received three disturbing calls. All were from attorneys representing investors in the early Lighthouse funds—one from Chicago, another from Toronto, and the third from Wilmington, Delaware. All claimed that their respective clients had not received status reports from the funds in many months, that O'Hara was not returning their calls, and that all felt shortchanged in the distributions of funds.

Concerned about my personal reputation, one I had built painstakingly over many years, and worried that I might be implicated in a nasty lawsuit, I assured the lawyers that I had had no involvement in the early funds, I had joined Lighthouse in order to raise a new fund, but I had resigned recently in order to have time for other pursuits. Despite the fact that the attorneys seemed satisfied with my answers, for the next few months I lived in fear of a subpoena arriving at my front door. I was walking on thin ice, hoping to reach the shore before it cracked. Fortunately, I did.

I attempted to collect the money that was owed to me, but O'Hara stonewalled my letters, as well as those of my lawyer. Finally, I decided that it would be best for my mental health to forget about the whole thing and to obliterate the Lighthouse experience from my mind. It was not easy, and the withdrawal pains were acute, but I had to move on.

There was one important take-away from the fiasco. Even at my advanced age of sixty-seven, there were lessons to be learned. This one was that when something appears too good to be true, it probably is. If there should be a next time, I would do my due diligence, regardless of the seeming attractiveness of any proposition.

CHAPTER TWENTY-FIVE

Staying Relevant

One morning soon after my sixty-ninth birthday, I looked in the mirror and saw my father gazing back at me. I was startled by my resemblance to Papa as he appeared during his post-retirement years. Now I was jobless. Did that mean that, like my father, I was retired?

I thought back to Papa's retirement party—a celebration of his career with McGregor-Doniger, where he had begun as a $35-per-week immigrant pattern-cutter only to become one of the top executives of what was now the world's largest manufacturer of sportswear. When he reached the company's mandatory retirement age of sixty-five, he felt that he was still at the top of his game.

I sat in the front row, listening to speech after speech extoling his contributions to the firm, his leadership, his vision, and his influence on others. Everyone present seemed genuinely happy for him and even expressed envy of Papa's upcoming life of leisure. Everyone but me. I always felt out of place attending the retirement parties of friends because I felt nothing but sadness for the honoree.

Yesterday, that friend had a calendar filled with appointments; his or her telephone calls were so numerous they had to be screened by an assistant; his or her e-mail inbox was jammed with messages requiring responses; a barrage of issues—from trivial to earth-shaking—demanded his or her immediate decisions.

Twenty-four hours after the celebration, my father's calendar would be blank; the phone would not ring; there would be no assistant; and the biggest decision would concern tomorrow's tee time on the golf course. Overnight, Papa—like my retired friends who were former corporate leaders like he—would become irrelevant. No one would give a damn.

Having been a spectator at these events as I approached retirement years myself, I became obsessed with a single aspiration: *I will not become irrelevant; I will never retire!* After all, as L. Jon Wertheim wrote so eloquently, "work is often less about what we do than about who we are."

Over the years, I had served on a number of boards of directors, and I had turned down many more offers of directorships than those I had accepted. Now, I decided that one way to continue to be relevant would be to become involved with a number of companies and nonprofit organizations at a high level. I accepted a board seat by the Czechoslovak Society of Arts and Sciences (known as SVU, an abbreviation of its Czech-language name) and became a founding board member of the Chesapeake Innovation Center, the nation's first incubator for cybersecurity start-ups.

The most challenging position I took on was that of trustee at FBR Mutual Funds. As an investor, I had a rudimentary knowledge of mutual funds. However, I had no clue about the inner workings of the funds. Upon joining the FBR board, I found myself on a steep learning curve. My Mutual Funds 101 course consisted of learning the intricacies of expense ratios, trading costs, soft dollars, and 12b-1 fees.

Naively, I had assumed that our board meetings would be similar to partner meetings of venture capital funds, sessions during which the primary topics were investment strategy and specific investments. I looked forward to the shift from privately held start-ups to securities with public markets. However, the mutual fund industry is highly regulated and subject to more governmental scrutiny than any business sector with which I had been associated previously. Consequently, our board meetings consisted overwhelmingly of discussions of regulatory issues. Lawyers talked and trustees listened. Investment issues were left to the advisors of our funds. When a vacancy on the board was created via the retirement of a trustee, I brought in my friend Bill Cole, who had retired recently as partner in the accounting firm, Ernst & Young. Bill and I worked together to learn the mutual funds business.

Eventually, parent company FBR sold its family of mutual funds to Hennessy Funds, a successful investment firm in California. Under the terms of the acquisition agreement, our FBR board stayed on for two years as advisors to Hennessy. After that, it was dissolved.

Lee McGee and I had met on a golf trip to TPC Sawgrass, not far from Jacksonville, Florida. At the time, Lee was chief financial officer of Sylvan Learning Systems, a firm with two business segments: tutoring centers for children at one end and higher education at the other. Sylvan's CEO, Doug Becker, was busy acquiring privately-owned colleges and universities around the world, and the corporation was on a fast track. Eventually, it was split into two separate entities, with the Sylvan Learning Centers comprising Educate, Inc., and the colleges and universities under the banner of Laureate International Universities.

"Have you ever heard of Walden University?" Lee asked me one day over lunch in a Baltimore restaurant.

"No, where is it?"

"Well, it's not exactly 'somewhere,'" he replied. "It's one hundred percent online. The academic headquarters is in Minneapolis and the business headquarters is in Baltimore, but it's virtual."

He went on to explain that, like all Laureate schools, Walden was a for-profit institution, and that it specialized primarily in graduate education leading to master's and doctoral degrees in a variety of disciplines.

"We have a vacancy on the Walden board," Lee said. "With your combination of business and education experience, you'd be perfect for it. I think you'd really enjoy it and would contribute a lot to it."

"Lee, I'm really not a believer in online education," I said. "I don't think you want a skeptic like me on the board."

"Do me a favor and meet with the Walden CEO," Lee replied. "Then decide."

I agreed and a few days later, I sat in the office of Paula Singer, who convinced me, in a short two hours, that Walden, with its outstanding faculty and state-of-the-art computer delivery technology, could teach nearly any course as effectively as a classroom-based institution. She made a persuasive argument about the opportunity afforded by online education to the nontraditional student, one with a full-time job and a family. Moreover, I departed from Paula's office convinced that there was no stigma attached to being a for-profit university as long as it delivered a quality education at a reasonable price.

As I write this, I am in my thirteenth year on the Walden University board, and I must say that it has been one of the most satisfying experiences of my professional life. The erudite directors, who have become my friends, believe in the social change mission of the school and all are passionate about fulfilling it. Paula Singer is one of the most effective and indomitable leaders I have come across. And Walden's president Jonathan Kaplan has, through his navigation of the turbulent waters of regulatory and accreditation agencies as well as the attacks of ignoramuses who paint all for-profit institutions with a broad brush, earned the respect of faculty, staff, and directors.

By the time Paula Singer asked me to join the board of another Laureate college—NewSchool of Architecture & Design in San Diego—I was a dedicated convert to the parent company's business model. I jumped at the chance.

In my obsession with keeping myself relevant, I found myself overcommitted. Like the girl who can't say no in the musical *Oklahoma*, each time someone invited me to serve on a board, I said yes. I was in the impossible position of serving on eight boards. While this may have provided sustenance to my ego, it played hell with my personal life and created a multitude of time conflicts.

"You really need to cut back," said my patient wife one day. I knew that she was correct and reluctantly agreed.

One by one, I departed the boards of the Chesapeake Innovation Center, Tagnetics, World Artist Experiences, SVU, and even our son's company. David had founded an information technology business,

WebTide Technologies; Sue and I were his major investors and I chaired his board. I had always dreamed of someday being in business with my son. This had been as close I would come to fulfilling that dream. Ironically, the Great Recession forced him to shutter the company, and he would become an IT manager at Laureate.

Strange as it may seem, while I was in the process of divesting myself of directorships, I received an offer I could not refuse. Gail Naughton, CEO of the National Czech & Slovak Museum & Library in Cedar Rapids, Iowa, came for a visit. I had met her a year earlier, during my speaking and book-signing gig at the museum.

"We'll be transitioning the board of the museum from a regional one to a national one," Gail said. "I'd like you to be on it."

My initial reaction was to say "no way" and explain my situation. But my interest in maintaining the legacy of Czech and Slovak immigrants to this country won out. After talking it over with Sue, who agreed wholeheartedly that this was something I had to do, I called Gail and not only signed on, but also made a significant financial contribution.

Then there were three: Walden, NewSchool, and the NCSML. Chairing the finance committees of the former two and the mission delivery committee of the latter would keep me busy and—I hoped—relevant.

CHAPTER TWENTY-SIX

One More Time!

Remarkably, I was afforded another opportunity to return to the venture capital business and to apply what I had learned at Gabriel and to avoid the mistakes I had made by joining Lighthouse. John Elstner, former head of the Chesapeake Innovation Center (CIC), the Annapolis-based business incubator for cybersecurity companies, called me one day out of the blue.

"I'd like you to meet a guy who runs an interesting venture fund," John told me.

I liked Gordon Hawke from the moment I shook hands with him. A burly Canadian with blond hair, he looked more like a defenseman for the Toronto Maple Leafs than an investment banker. Gord explained that he was president of Athlone Global Security, a venture fund with offices in Toronto and Tel Aviv. Since both Athlone and the CIC were focused exclusively on homeland security start-ups, they had recently signed a partnership agreement. He said that, as part of the agreement, Athlone would have an office at the CIC in Annapolis.

"We view this as the third leg of a three-legged stool," he told me. "Israel-Canada-United States. But we don't have anyone to run the American part."

"I see," I muttered, the reason for our meeting becoming clear.

"John has told me a lot about you, your experience as an entrepreneur, and your expertise in venture capital. You'd be a perfect fit for us."

He explained that he would like me to join Athlone as a member of its board and to chair the company's investment committee.

"We have people in Israel who have the inside track on a lot of technologies because they have close ties with the defense and intelligence establishments. And the best security technology originates in Israel. Our basic model is to build an R&D team in Israel around a great piece of technology, form a C-corp in the United States and invest in it, and once the technology is commercialized, bring the company's management, marketing, and sales to the United States, where the market is immense."

I was intrigued. On my only visit to Israel up to that point, I had been astonished by the innovative spirit and entrepreneurial activity in this small country. The Athlone business model made a lot of sense. And becoming the company's US connection was an attractive opportunity. However, I was not about to jump into anything without carefully checking it out first. I had learned my lesson.

"Gord," I said after asking several questions, "this sounds very interesting. I'd like to meet your partners and to think things through."

A couple of weeks later, I flew to Toronto. At the Queen Street office, I met the founder and primary financier of Athlone. Stan Barti was a short, slender, middle-aged man who favored flashy clothes and strutted rather than walked when we left the office for lunch. Stan informed me that he was "just the ideas guy" who had come up with the Athlone concept and had no expertise in either venture capital or homeland security. His main business consisted of trading in penny stocks, primarily those of Canadian mining and minerals companies.

In the afternoon, I met a man for whom I would eventually have the utmost admiration, and whom I would consider a dear and valued friend, despite the fact that in the future, we would often disagree when it came to specific investments and the direction of Athlone Global Security. His name was Doron Almog.

A short, muscular man in his mid-fifties, Almog became a national hero while still in his twenties. In 1976, he was the first para-recon commander to land at Entebbe, marking the runway for

Israeli airplanes carrying soldiers who pulled off a daring rescue of 248 passengers on an Air France flight that had been hijacked by Palestinian and German terrorists. Eight years later, Doron participated in the clandestine airlift of seven thousand Ethiopian Jews in another daring undertaking called Operation Moses. In his last posting with the Israel Defense Forces, Doron had been a major general in charge of the Southern Command, a position that brought additional fame because his troops had secured the border of the Gaza Strip against infiltration by Palestinian terrorists. I was in awe of this man and felt honored to be given the opportunity to be his business partner.

"I'm in, Gord," I told Hawke on the phone one day after my return from Toronto.

I was back in the VC business. I was impressed by the people, and they wanted me for my experience and talent. Devoting a couple of days per week to Athlone, I chaired an investment committee that, over the next several months, picked more winners than losers. We invested in start-ups dealing with cybersecurity, physical security of essential facilities, and in a company building unmanned aerial vehicles. All followed the Athlone model. The single variant, despite the opposition of my friend Doron Almog, was an American company that designed and built virtual reality headsets. I discovered the company through my mid-Atlantic contacts.

In 2007, I flew to Israel to attend an Athlone board meeting. For the first time, I met a number of directors whose voices had become familiar to me from various board calls. Barti, Almog, and Hawke had assembled quite a group: a retired Canadian general who had led United Nations forces in the Sinai, a retired British general who had been involved in intelligence, a retired American general who had been the top man in Iraq after the 2003 invasion, the former associate deputy director of the FBI, and the former head of the Mossad.

By any measure, this was a collection of security all-stars. The only problem was that the group had little business experience and no track record in investing. Gord Hawke and I were the only board members with expertise in investing in early-stage technology companies.

For me, the best part of the Tel Aviv meetings had nothing to do with business. Walking through the streets of Tel Aviv with Doron Almog was an amazing experience. As a national hero, he was recognized by many Israelis. I watched in awe as mothers ran up to him and thanked him for having taken care of their sons and daughters, who had served under him. I met Doron's pretty wife, Didi, and learned of their family's work in establishing a village for autistic and mentally challenged children. Sadly, their son Eron, afflicted with severe autism, would die later that year.

Doron arranged special tours for our group. We visited military museums and walked through tunnels beneath the Western Wall, something not available to ordinary tourists.

It was unfortunate that, following our excursions, we had to return to business. Our Israeli contingent had a surprise for some of us—a proposal that would lead to my eventual departure from Athlone. They recommended that we change our business model from that of an investment firm to that of an operating company. Their basic idea was to seek out contractual opportunities, primarily with the U.S. federal government, and to bid on them with Athlone as the prime contractor. Consortia made up of our portfolio companies would be our subcontractors who would perform the technical work, while we managed the projects.

Gord Hawke, Buck Revell (the former FBI executive, with whom I had developed excellent rapport), and I looked at one another in disbelief, as if to say, *Are these guys joking?* Such a major shift would cause problems with our recent IPO filing at the Toronto Stock Exchange. More importantly, to me at least, it made no business sense. I thought we had made some good investments and that now we should apply our efforts to assisting these companies toward successful exits. Furthermore, we had almost no experience as prime contractors to the federal government. (I did, but it was experience I preferred to leave behind.)

Gord, Buck, and I stated our opposition to the proposed shift, but to no avail. Everyone else seemed to think it was an excellent idea. The motion was made, seconded, and overwhelmingly approved.

Because of an upcoming trip to Prague, I had to leave Israel a day before the meetings ended. Since the board discussion lasted into the late afternoon, I worried about being late for my flight. Ben Gurion Airport is famous for its intense security screening of passengers, and I knew that the journey to one's flight could be long and arduous.

"Don't worry," Doron said to me. "I'll take you."

As he drove through Tel Aviv, he described his vision for the "new Athlone," attempting to convince me that the change would be for the best. Realizing that it was a done deal, I did not argue, although I disagreed. When we arrived at Ben Gurion, I was once again reminded of what it meant to be in the presence of Major General Doron Almog in his home country. On our way to the Air France aircraft, uniformed personnel never asked me a question, never checked my carry-on bag, did not require me to walk through a metal detector, and took only a brief, perfunctory glance at my ticket and passport. Doron walked me all the way to the base of the steps leading to the first-class cabin. I was the first passenger to board.

Sadly, the flight home was the beginning of the end of my Athlone journey. For several months, I attempted to be a good team player and to go along with the new business philosophy. But it was difficult. During several board calls, and during a meeting in Arlington, Virginia, I failed to disguise my disapproval and my doubts about the future of the company. When Gord Hawke informed me that he was being replaced as the CEO and downgraded to a lower position, I knew it was time for me to depart.

Unlike my resignation from the firm I have chosen to call Lighthouse, I found leaving Athlone a sad occasion. I had believed in the original business model, thought that we had made some excellent investments, and—most importantly to me—respected and genuinely liked my partners, despite our disagreements.

Thus ended the fourth adventure in the venture capital phase of my career. I had shut down Chesapeake Ventures when its funding disappeared as a result of business problems in Russia. I had departed from Gabriel because I felt overwhelmed, overworked, and underappreciated. I had left Lighthouse when I lost trust in my partner. And now, I departed from Athlone over philosophical differences. Despite the last two escapades, I no longer felt as though I had failed as a venture capitalist. Actually, I had been pretty damned good—and I had restored my faith in myself. Moreover, I had followed Papa's edict to never give up. It was time to move on.

CHAPTER TWENTY-SEVEN

Dreams

I had to blink several times in order to assure myself that I was not dreaming. For so many years, I had obeyed the command given me by my father when we landed in America: "I want you to forget everything that happened to you on the other side of the Atlantic." Yet, following Papa's death, I had often dreamed of going back to the Czech Republic and making amends for having wordlessly renounced my native land. Now I was on the other side of the Atlantic, seated between my translator, Irena Zíková, and my editor, Antonín Kočí, and facing a large audience of friends and strangers in the center of Prague.

Can this be real? I wondered. From the front row, Sue's reassuring smile affirmed that it was. I scanned the hall and spotted the faces of people who were dear to me. There was my only surviving European relative, Sylvia Pustina, who had driven from Germany with her husband Karel. Seated next to Sue was Jitka Thomasová, a close friend of my mother's whom we considered a member of our family. My closest boyhood friend, with whom I had reconnected after forty-one years, Vláďa Svoboda, was seated next to his wife Marie. Gray-haired Jaroslav Kučera, the historian of my native Kojetice, had come with his family and the town's mayor. Our pals from the historic city of Tábor—Stan Kotrčka and Marie Kotrčková—had driven to Prague along with Jana Šípová. On the side, I spotted the blonde hair of Štěpánka Matesová, whom we had befriended while she was an official at the World Bank in Washington. In the crowd, I spotted a former classmate, whom I had seen only once before in the past sixty years, Josef "Pepa" Tomásek.

In the back row, I found Jiří Bedrna and his son Michal, who had been our attorneys throughout the ordeal of recovering family properties and now were also good friends. Seated near them was a short gentleman whose face I recognized but could not associate with a name; later in the evening, I would discover that he was Lubomír Věchet, the son of my favorite nanny during my privileged, pre-war childhood. At a table in front sat Alexander "Saša" Turkovič, who had stayed at our home in Maryland during a Rotary exchange visit; now he was here, representing all the Rotary clubs of the Czech Republic. In the rear of the room, I noticed employees of the Luxor bookstore scrambling to provide more chairs for people I did not recognize: reporters, critics, and casual passers-by. We had a crowd!

All had come to celebrate the launch of my book, *Dlouhá cesta domů* (*Long Journey Home*), a memoir of my life as one of Europe's "*hidden children*" under Nazi occupation, of our escape from Communism, and of my emotional and heart-wrenching reconnection with my native country and my ethnicity.

When it came my turn to speak, I choked up several times while acknowledging the presence of those so dear to me and thanking them for all they had done for our family. I wiped away tears as I expressed my sadness over the fact that my life's heroes—my parents, Ilona and Rudolph—could not experience this special moment with me. And I cried silently while paying tribute to family members who perished in the Holocaust and to our farmer friends—Vladimír Tůma and Marie Tůmová—who saved my life while risking theirs by hiding me from the Germans and their collaborators.

The journey home to Prague had been a long one, indeed. And the odyssey from the first words I wrote to published book had been at times painful, at other times liberating, and often frustrating and slow. Between the covers of the memoir was a tale of the most courageous people I had ever known—my parents.

My father, who escaped from the Nazis in order to fight against them with the Czechoslovak Division of the British army, had contracted malaria in the desert of North Africa. The aftermath was coronary disease that plagued him in his later years. After starting life in America as a lowly pattern-cutter for the largest sportswear manufacturer in the world, he retired a quarter century later as one of that company's top executives. Throughout his retirement, his coronary health worsened. Finally, in January 1988, we made a family decision to have one of the world's most renowned surgeons repair his heart. Papa failed to survive the surgery. He passed away in Houston at the age of seventy-seven.

I was devastated by the death of my hero and shocked when I realized that his was the first natural death of a family member in my lifetime; all the others had been murdered.

Mother, who had stood up to the Nazis and survived life in a slave labor camp, once again exhibited extraordinary courage. She remained in her New Jersey house alone and traveled with her best friend, Dr. Jane Emele, until we brought her to Maryland in 2001. Living a few minutes from us at Sunrise Independent Living, she aroused the curiosity of her neighbors there with her lovely, slightly accented English and her near-regal demeanor.

"Charlie," she said to me one day in 2003, "they want me to give a speech here at Sunrise. They want to know all about my life. But I can't do it."

"Sure you can, Mother," I countered. "You have a great story to tell. You'll blow them away when you tell them what you've experienced in your life and what you've accomplished."

"I'd really like to do it," she said, "especially because I can tell from our conversations that these people have no idea of what it was like during the war and what it took to start all over in America. But I just can't stand up there and speak to a crowd. You give talks in public all the time. Can you please make the presentation for me?"

Little did I know at the time that agreeing to be Mother's stand-in would trigger a new journey—indeed, a new career—for me.

Mother and I met several times in order to construct the story of her life. She talked; I listened and took notes. Many of her tales were new to me: about her happy childhood, about falling in love with Papa, about the disappearance of our relatives, about being questioned and even tortured by the Gestapo, about our post-war reunion and the fruitless wait for family members to return home, and about our struggles starting from scratch in America.

My presentation went well. When it came time for the audience to ask questions, I stepped aside and let Mother take over. I watched with pride as the eighty-eight-year-old, gray-haired, and still beautiful and elegant lady shed her shyness and opened up to the audience. When it ended, Mother's face was flushed from excitement as one after another, her neighbors stepped forward to express their admiration.

For me, the experience was a turning point. Following the ouster of the Communist oppressors, Americans exhibited a sudden interest in Czechoslovakia, that small country in the heart of Europe. They questioned me and invited me to speak to groups large and small. In my sixties, I began to defy Papa's orders to leave it all on the other side of the Atlantic. And everywhere I went, I heard the same refrain.

"You must write a book."

Feeling that our story was not extraordinary, I had ignored the requests. However, with Mother having filled in so many voids in that tale with remarkable and touching vignettes, I began to change my mind.

Throughout my life, I had been driven by the desire to achieve respect—in my professional as well as personal life. There were hits and misses along the way, and now I would have to let others decide how well or poorly I had done. With no interest in involving myself in another entrepreneurial venture and no desire to continue life as a venture capitalist—yet feeling the need to remain relevant, I decided that I would like to spend the remainder of my time attempting to leave a legacy. I would do this by embarking on the fifth phase of my career—as a writer.

I had written a great deal throughout my life as a columnist for several newspapers, a freelancer for magazines, and the author of a technical book. But I knew next to nothing about writing a book for the mass market. Consequently, I signed up for course after course, read every how-to book I could get my hands on, attended conferences, and joined a writers' group. I spent months doing research: interviewing Mother further about our family history, devouring the words in my great grandfather's journal—one he kept right up to the time he was taken away to a concentration camp—staring at photographs that our friends in the Czech Republic had hidden for us following our escape, studying the history of the Czech lands and people, and fact-checking every episode I recounted.

As a newbie author, I would have to sell a publisher on my project. Moreover, if I wished to get the attention of a major publisher, and I did, I had to do it with the aid of a literary agent. Armed with this knowledge, I embarked on a journey of education about the publishing industry. In an online course, I learned how to write a query letter that would attract an agent. I purchased and read five books on writing a winning book proposal. I attended conferences and absorbed advice from published authors. I studied the basics of self-publishing in order to have this option available as a back-up in case I failed to hook on with a traditional publisher. Mining directories and acknowledgement sections of Holocaust and World War II memoirs, I compiled a list of nearly a hundred candidate agents. I divided them into groups of five and began sending them query letters, one group per week.

Disheartened and frustrated by rejections and no responses, I contemplated my next move as I flew to Dallas for a board meeting in January 2009. That evening, I had dinner with Stephen Eisner, son of the late Tom Eisner, who had been like a big brother to me when I arrived in America back in 1949, a scared thirteen-year-old knowing two words of English. I recounted my sad tale of agent-searching to Stephen.

"Uncle Steve has a friend in New York who is an agent," he said. "She represented my brother Philip." Philip was a Hollywood screenwriter, and Uncle Steve was Tom's younger brother.

Immediately upon my return home, I contacted Steve, who lived in New York's Greenwich Village. He spoke with his agent friend, and she told him to encourage me to query her. I sent my standard query letter, along with two sample chapters, and held my breath. Two days later, I spotted an email from her in my inbox. The subject line read "Bravo!" I jumped for joy. In a moment, I was transformed from an unknown, newbie writer to an author represented by one of the most legendary agents in the business!

During the first six months of our collaboration, her assistance was invaluable. She helped me focus the book and to weave a thread through its plot. When I mentioned her name at writing conferences, younger agents practically genuflected. Then things changed. Seven months into our relationship, she went radio silent. She stopped commenting on my manuscript revisions and failed to inform me about her discussions with publishers. My emails, letters, and calls went unanswered. Frustrated and confused, I terminated our contract.

Now agentless, I contacted my friend Lillian Lincoln Lambert who had recently published a wonderful memoir. She introduced me to her agent. The latter informed me that my book was not suitable for her agency, but she gave me an invaluable piece of advice.

"Several writers with stories similar to yours have gone back to their countries of origin," she told me. "They had their books translated into their native language and published there. You should do that. If the book sells, American publishers will be all over you."

I hung up the phone, inspired by her suggestion—a route I had not considered previously. But, as I contemplated my next step, I ran into a wall. I did not know a soul in the Czech publishing industry, and neither did any of my Czech friends. So, I turned to the last weapon in the arsenal of a salesman—the cold call. I Googled "five largest publishers in Czech Republic," found the list, and sent query emails to the respective acquisition editors. Publishers numbers two through five never responded. But amazingly, I heard back almost immediately from number one. Antonín Kočí, program director of the Book Division of Mladá Fronta, emailed to say that my topic was in his firm's sweet spot and requested the manuscript.

A couple of months later, over breakfast in Prague, we agreed on a book contract. I would use a portion of my advance to pay our good friend and professional translator and interpreter, Irena Zíková, to convert the manuscript to Czech. Together, Irena and I hired a Czech author to edit the translations. Six months later, the project was completed, the publisher's editor contributed a final edit, and Tony and I agreed on the title, *Dlouhá cesta domů* (*Long Journey Home*).

Sue and I arrived in the Czech capital for the book's launch in April 2011. To my astonishment, the launch was something of a national event. The first morning, I appeared on the Czech equivalent of the *Today* show. Following the official launch at the nation's largest bookstore, Luxor, each day was packed with interviews—radio, magazines, newspapers, online news and book sites.

On Friday, April 29, a young lady named Judita Matyášová interviewed me for an article in *Lidové noviny*, a major national daily. She informed me that her piece would run in Monday's paper. Monday would be May 2, 2011, the date of our scheduled departure from Prague.

On that morning at 5:30 a.m., our friend, Vláďa Svoboda, picked us up at our hotel. As we rode through Prague's dark, empty streets, I wondered what weather we might encounter as we flew across Europe. I asked Vláďa to turn on a news-and-weather radio station.

"During the night, in a daring raid, American soldiers killed the world's most notorious terrorist, Osama bin Laden," a solemn voice announced in Czech.

Vláďa and I looked at one another and both raised our fists in triumph.

"Bravo!" he exclaimed.

"Yes!" I shouted and explained the situation to Sue, who was sitting in the back seat and had not understood the announcement. She smiled and patted my hand. But then a selfish thought crossed my mind.

Oh, shit! I thought. *Why couldn't they have waited a day? Now my story in the morning paper will be back on page 64!*

We said goodbye to Vláďa, went through customs, and made our way to the nearest newsstand. However, it was only 6:15 a.m. and the airport stores were still closed. We decided to wait. A half hour later, we spotted a man pushing a cart loaded with stacks of magazines and newspapers through the concourse. I guarded our carry-on bags while Sue walked toward the cart, where she scanned the stacks for *Lidové noviny.* Suddenly, she turned toward me and grinned.

"You're on the front page!"

Finding it difficult to believe that there would be space for me on a day of such historic significance, I waited patiently until the newsstand opened. Finally, I saw it. There was my photo on the front page, and again on the inside, accompanied by Judita's story. There was no mention of the now-dead Islamic terrorist. Obviously, the bin Laden killing had taken place too late to be included in the early edition. But that did not deter me from purchasing a stack of papers, bringing them home, showing them off and informing our American friends that I had bumped Osama bin Laden off the front page.

Once home, the glow of a book launch that had been a national event did not last long. Very quickly, I morphed from celebrity to just another newbie author with a manuscript and no agent, looking for an American publisher. Following several unsuccessful attempts to interest university presses in my book, I had a "come to Jesus" meeting with myself.

You're seventy-five years old. You have at least three more books in you. Do you really want to spend the next year or two sending out query letters and dealing with rejections?

Impatient to bring my memoir to American readers and to get on with other writing projects, I decided to go indie. I compiled a detailed spreadsheet of indie publishers and eventually pared it down to a short-list of four. Of those, I selected Abbott Press in Bloomington, Indiana, then a subsidiary of *Writer's Digest* magazine. We signed a contract in August 2011, and I was informed that the book would be out in time for the Christmas buying season. On December 27—too late for the holiday rush and too early to be considered a 2012 book—copies of *Prague: My Long Journey Home* hit the market.

The timing was horrible. Not only did we miss the period during which the majority of books are sold, but the book became ineligible for a number of 2012 prizes because, only five days after its distribution, it was considered a year old. However, good things did happen. *Writer's Digest* awarded it its "Mark of Excellence"—the first Abbott book to receive this honor. It was a finalist in the National Indie Book Awards competition, and it received honorable mention at the Los Angeles Book Fair.

Nearly every review was favorable, and messages by the hundreds poured in to my website. I was overwhelmed with requests for talks and signings. I addressed groups as small as a six-person book club in Annapolis to an audience of six hundred in Orlando, Florida. I went on a number of book tours, the most memorable of which was one organized by my OSU classmate and friend, Bart Childs, professor emeritus at Texas A&M. We visited Czech and Slovak communities throughout Texas; we began in Dallas and eventually ended up in Houston. In-between, I had speaking and signing gigs in towns where descendants of Czech and Slovak immigrants remarkably maintain the traditions of their ancestors.

I spoke at universities, museums, libraries, and the George H. W. Bush Presidential Library. I was interviewed on National Public Radio, and numerous newspaper articles about the book appeared in various parts of the country. An international magazine with more than a million subscribers ran an article.

People liked the book! Yet, from the moment *Prague* became reality, I was most anxious and concerned about the reaction of the three "critics" whose opinions would be most significant to me. Until then, our three grandchildren—Sam, Sarah, and Caroline—had expressed little interest in the history of the Heller side of their family. Although I hoped that my book might provide both inspiration and a history lesson for a general audience, I worried most about the reaction of our grandkids. Would they care about our—actually, their—history? Would these Christian kids be shocked to discover that a fraction of their blood was Jewish? Would they deny or embrace their Czech identity? My past obsession with gaining the respect of strangers had been replaced by a consuming passion to leave a legacy for my family, along with their appreciation for the courage, suffering, and accomplishments of their ancestors.

I received my answer in the summer of 2014, when Sue and I brought our entire family—our son David, our daughter-in-law Bobbi, and our three grandchildren, Sam, Sarah, and Caroline—to Prague. I had planned an itinerary filled with visits to places about which they had read in my book and meetings with Czech friends whom they had not met. I braced for a pushback after a couple of days of intensive teaching moments. The opposite took place: Eighteen-year-old Sam, fifteen-year-old Sarah, and twelve-year-old Caroline embraced their family's history and fell in love with the Czech Republic. Upon their return home, the children wrote me letters which they presented to me on Christmas Eve. Following are excerpts from those letters:

Sam: "From the day we arrived in Prague to the day we left, I felt astounded by the sights we had seen. It was incredible to get the opportunity to view all the places you and our family have been. Visiting all these places opened my eyes to our past . . . It gave me passion for our family's home country and makes me want to return . . . Thank you for giving me the opportunity to visit such an amazing place."

Sarah: "Knowing that the people I am related to were involved in the Holocaust makes me even more proud of our history, and that is why I was so grateful that you and Nana took us to the Czech Republic . . . When we went to the Jewish cemetery, I felt extremely privileged to be there. I still feel that way and I think I always will. Having that experience impacted me significantly and, if I could, I would bring everyone I know there because it is really just amazing to see what the human race is capable of, if we let it . . . I feel like it is my duty as a person to continue to educate myself and those around me, so that there will not be any more mass graves to look at, or lists that go on for miles of families that have been destroyed . . . I will never forget the trip we took and hope to soon return."

Caroline: "You took us to a wonderful place where we learned about how great somewhere else can be, you took us to a place where you grew up, where you lived and suffered. I am so grateful because something to desire is to know your family tree . . . Now my family, as well as I, knows the town, the country, the continent where our family was created . . . I have fallen in love with this amazing place . . . I appreciated learning about the Holocaust from you and by seeing Terezín. This is something everyone should know about because it was one of the times when society was at its worst . . . Thank you for this overwhelmingly amazing experience. I will always remember it."

How could I be more proud of the children of our son? It has been said that dreams set one up for disappointment. But I have had dreams—of making a mark in my adopted country, of being respected, of earning the love of my family, of leaving a legacy. These letters fulfilled most of them. My father told me years ago that the American Dream means that one has the freedom to do anything he wishes to do. I believe that despite—or perhaps because of—my entrepreneurial terrors and achievements, I may have captured that American Dream. Perhaps even more importantly, I may have helped to create more dreamers.

How did I do, Papa?

Author's Note and Acknowledgments

I earned some notoriety, and even the media-created nickname of "Mr. Entrepreneurship," while running the Michael D. Dingman Center for Entrepreneurship at the University of Maryland in the 1990s. Following nearly twenty years of starting and running companies, I was able to impart my knowledge and experience to students as well as entrepreneurs starting ventures throughout the mid-Atlantic region.

One day, the editor of a major textbook publishing firm approached me about writing a book. I agreed, cobbled together an outline and gave the project the working title of *High-Technology Entrepreneurship*. The publisher sent me a generous advance and gave me a twelve-month deadline to come up with a manuscript. I tried. However, each time I finished a chapter, I tore the papers from the yellow pad and threw them away. A year later, I had nothing. The editor extended the contract another twelve months. At the end of the second year, same story: nothing.

Finally, I realized why I kept on rejecting my own work. There was nothing unique about it. I was addressing the same topics, raising the same issues, and teaching the same solutions as the authors of so many other books on entrepreneurship already on the market. The only difference was that the other authors were dealing with generic businesses, while I was customizing my writing for the technology entrepreneur. In my mind, that was not enough of a differentiator. I explained my reasons and returned the advance to the publisher.

"Why don't you tell your own story?" I was asked by an entrepreneur attending one of my workshops one day in 1999. "Anecdotal accounts by a 'been there, done that' entrepreneur like you would be a hell of a lot more valuable to us than another textbook."

I was not convinced immediately and stored the idea somewhere deep in the recesses of my brain. It was only some ten years later, after a stint as a venture capitalist—a period during which I was able to see and evaluate entrepreneurial ventures from the viewpoint of an outside investor—that I determined I had "the whole picture."

It was at this point that I decided to tell my story, hoping to present it as a riveting adventure, but one with valuable takeaways for present and budding entrepreneurs.

All my adult life, I have regretted the fact that I have a terrible memory. It is not an age-related malady; I had the same trouble recalling names and events in my twenties as I have today. When I began writing *Ready, Fire, Aim! An Immigrant's Tales of Entrepreneurial Terror*, my deficiency proved to be a blessing. Early in my professional career, in order to counteract my memory problem, I began to keep journals.

Using spiral notebooks, I made detailed entries of meetings, phone calls, and private thoughts. Today, I have two stacks of these journals in my office, and they have become invaluable sources for my writing, especially for this book, which spans my life as an engineer, academic, entrepreneur, new venture advisor, venture capitalist, and writer.

When I asked some of my former partners and colleagues to fact-check a particular vignette, a common response was "How can you possibly remember such details?" My journal entries brought memories back to them, too.

I realize that, outside of the precise notes in my journals, memory is not always accurate and that it is occasionally selective. Some of the conversations in the book are many years old. While the words inside quotation marks sometimes may not be the precise words, they represent my recollection of the conversations.

One of the greatest joys of writing *Ready, Fire, Aim!* as well as my previous books, has been the encouragement and assistance I have received from my family, colleagues, and friends. Among those who took the time to give me advice and to provide a different point of view of events in which they were involved, I am particularly indebted to my former business partners, John Gebhardt and Phil Samper.

Susan Moger—my teacher, writing guru, wonderful writer, and friend—is responsible for extracting many of the stories that are the heart of the book from me. She, as well as my other colleagues in our two writers' groups—Karen Cain, Paul Harrell, Penny Henderson, Ren Klein, Hank Parker, and Marilyn Recknor—stood by me as critics and cheerleaders.

The support I have received at WriteLife Publishing has been amazing. Publisher Terri Leidich has overseen the project, guided me through the mysterious labyrinth of social media marketing, and brought *Ready, Fire, Aim!* to press with breakneck speed. It was a joy to work with my editor, Olivia Swenson, who not only kept me on the straight and narrow when it came to following the edicts of the *Chicago Manual of Style*, but who made invaluable suggestions to make my story more readable and interesting.

More than anything, I have always aspired to be a good son, husband, father, and grandfather. I owe everything to my parents, Ilona and Rudolph Heller. They fought against the Nazis, suffered unimaginable losses in the Holocaust, resisted the Communists, and—having started from nothing—became successful, patriotic, and happy Americans. They brought me to this country and taught me that hard work and perseverance would help me reach the proverbial American Dream.

I am very proud of our son, David, and his three children—our grandchildren—Sam, Sarah, and Caroline. I hope all of them realize how much their love and support means to me, and that it is for them that I hope to leave a legacy through my writing.

As for my wife Sue, with whom I have spent more than fifty years of my life, I could not be more grateful for her love and support, and for the freedom she gave me to follow that elusive dream. Without her, none of this would have been possible.

About the Author

Charles Ota Heller was born in Prague, Czechoslovakia, and came to the United States at the age of thirteen, following a boyhood as a "hidden child" during Nazi occupation and, later, a harrowing escape from Czechoslovakia's Communist regime. He has been an engineer, an academic, an entrepreneur founder of two companies, a mentor to hundreds of entrepreneurs, and a venture capitalist.

Today he is a writer, having published the award-winning *Prague: My Long Journey Home* and a lighthearted memoir, *Name-droppings: Close Encounters with the Famous and Near Famous.*

He earned three engineering degrees—a BS and a MS from Oklahoma State University and a PhD from The Catholic University of America. He was recipient of Maryland's "Entrepreneur of the Year" award, OSU's Lohmann Medal, and CUA's Alumni Achievement Award. He was the youngest-ever tenured professor at the Naval Academy and the first Professor of Practice in the history of the University of Maryland. In 2015, he was inducted into the Oklahoma State University Engineering Hall of Fame.

He is married and has one son and three grandchildren. He and his wife Sue live in Annapolis, Maryland.

His website is www.charlesoheller.com.